MARVEL

SPIDER-MAN

Far From Home

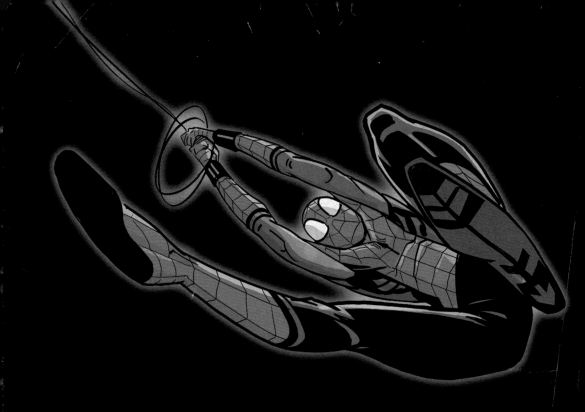

AMAZING SPIDER-MAN (1963) #95
WRITER: **STAN LEE**
PENCILER: **JOHN ROMITA SR.**
INKER: **SAL BUSCEMA**
LETTERER: **ART SIMEK**

AMAZING SPIDER-MAN (1963) #311
WRITER: **DAVID MICHELINIE**
ARTIST: **TODD McFARLANE**
COLORISTS: **BOB SHAREN & EVELYN STEIN**
LETTERER: **RICK PARKER**
EDITOR: **JIM SALICRUP**

AMAZING SPIDER-MAN (2015) #9-10
WRITER: **DAN SLOTT**
PENCILER: **GIUSEPPE CAMUNCOLI**
INKER: **CAM SMITH**
COLORIST: **MARTE GRACIA**
LETTERER: **VC'S JOE CARAMAGNA**
COVER ART: **ALEX ROSS**
ASSISTANT EDITOR: **DEVIN LEWIS**
EDITOR: **NICK LOWE**

SPIDER-MAN: FAR FROM HOME PRELUDE. Contains material originally published in magazine form as SPIDER-MAN: FAR FROM HOME PRELUDE #1-2, AMAZING SPIDER-MAN (1963) #95 and #311, and AMAZ
SPIDER-MAN (2015) #9-10. Second printing 2019. ISBN 978-1-302-91785-2. Published by MARVEL WORLDWIDE, INC., a subsidiary of MARVEL ENTERTAINMENT, LLC. OFFICE OF PUBLICATION: 135 West 50th Str
New York, NY 10020. © 2019 MARVEL No similarity between any of the names, characters, persons, and/or institutions in this magazine with those of any living or dead person or institution is intended, and any s
similarity which may exist is purely coincidental. **Printed in Canada.** DAN BUCKLEY, President, Marvel Entertainment; JOHN NEE, Publisher; JOE QUESADA, Chief Creative Officer; TOM BREVOORT, SVP of Publishing; DA
BOGART, Associate Publisher & SVP of Talent Affairs; Publishing & Partnership; DAVID GABRIEL, SVP of Sales & Marketing, Publishing; JEFF YOUNGQUIST, VP of Production & Special Projects; DAN CARR, Executive Dire
of Publishing Technology; ALEX MORALES, Director of Publishing Operations; DAN EDINGTON, Managing Editor; SUSAN CRESPI, Production Manager; STAN LEE, Chairman Emeritus. For information regarding advertis
in Marvel Comics or on Marvel.com, please contact Vit DeBellis, Custom Solutions & Integrated Advertising Manager, at vdebellis@marvel.com. For Marvel subscription inquiries, please call 888-511-5480. **Manufactu
between 5/8/2019 and 5/28/19 by SOLISCO PRINTERS, SCOTT, QC, CANADA.**

10 9 8 7 6 5 4 3 2

MARVEL

SPIDER-MAN

Far From Home

SCREENPLAY BY **JONATHAN GOLDSTEIN** & **JOHN FRANCIS DALEY** AND
JON WATTS & **CHRISTOPHER FORD** AND **CHRIS MCKENNA** & **ERIK SOMMERS**
SCREEN STORY BY **JONATHAN GOLDSTEIN** & **JOHN FRANCIS DALEY**

WRITERS: **WILL CORONA PILGRIM** (#1) & **PETER DAVID** (#2)
ARTIST: **LUCA MARESCA**

COLOR ARTIST: **LEE LOUGHRIDGE**
LETTERER: **VC'S TRAVIS LANHAM**
ASSISTANT EDITOR: **LAUREN AMARO**
EDITOR: **MARK BASSO**

SPIDER-MAN CREATED BY **STAN LEE** & **STEVE DITKO**

FOR MARVEL STUDIOS
MANAGER, PRODUCTION & DEVELOPMENT: **RICHIE PALMER**
EXECUTIVE, PRODUCTION & DEVELOPMENT: **ERIC CARROLL**
PRESIDENT: **KEVIN FEIGE**

COLLECTION EDITOR: JENNIFER GRÜNWALD
ASSISTANT EDITOR: CAITLIN O'CONNELL
ASSOCIATE MANAGING EDITOR: KATERI WOODY
EDITOR, SPECIAL PROJECTS: MARK D. BEAZLEY
VP PRODUCTION & SPECIAL PROJECTS: JEFF YOUNGQUIST
SVP PRINT, SALES & MARKETING: DAVID GABRIEL

EDITOR IN CHIEF: C.B. CEBULSKI
CHIEF CREATIVE OFFICER: JOE QUESADA
PRESIDENT: DAN BUCKLEY

SPIDER-MAN: FAR FROM HOME

MARVEL

SPIDER-MAN

Far From Home

PRELUDE

Peter Parker was bitten by a genetically altered spider and gained the proportional speed, strength, and agility of a SPIDER, adhesive fingertips and toes, and the precognitive awareness of danger called "SPIDER-SENSE"!

Choosing to use his newfound abilities to protect his neighborhood in Queens as SPIDER-MAN, Peter juggled the weight of power, responsibility, and high school commitments until his secret identity was discovered by Tony Stark, A.K.A. Iron Man, after a viral video surfaced of the web-slinger in action!

Taking the fledgling hero under his wing, Tony gifted him a technologically enhanced spider suit and has taken it upon himself to mentor Peter. With Tony's guidance and a few super hero battles under his belt, Peter Parker believes he's ready to step up and join the Avengers...

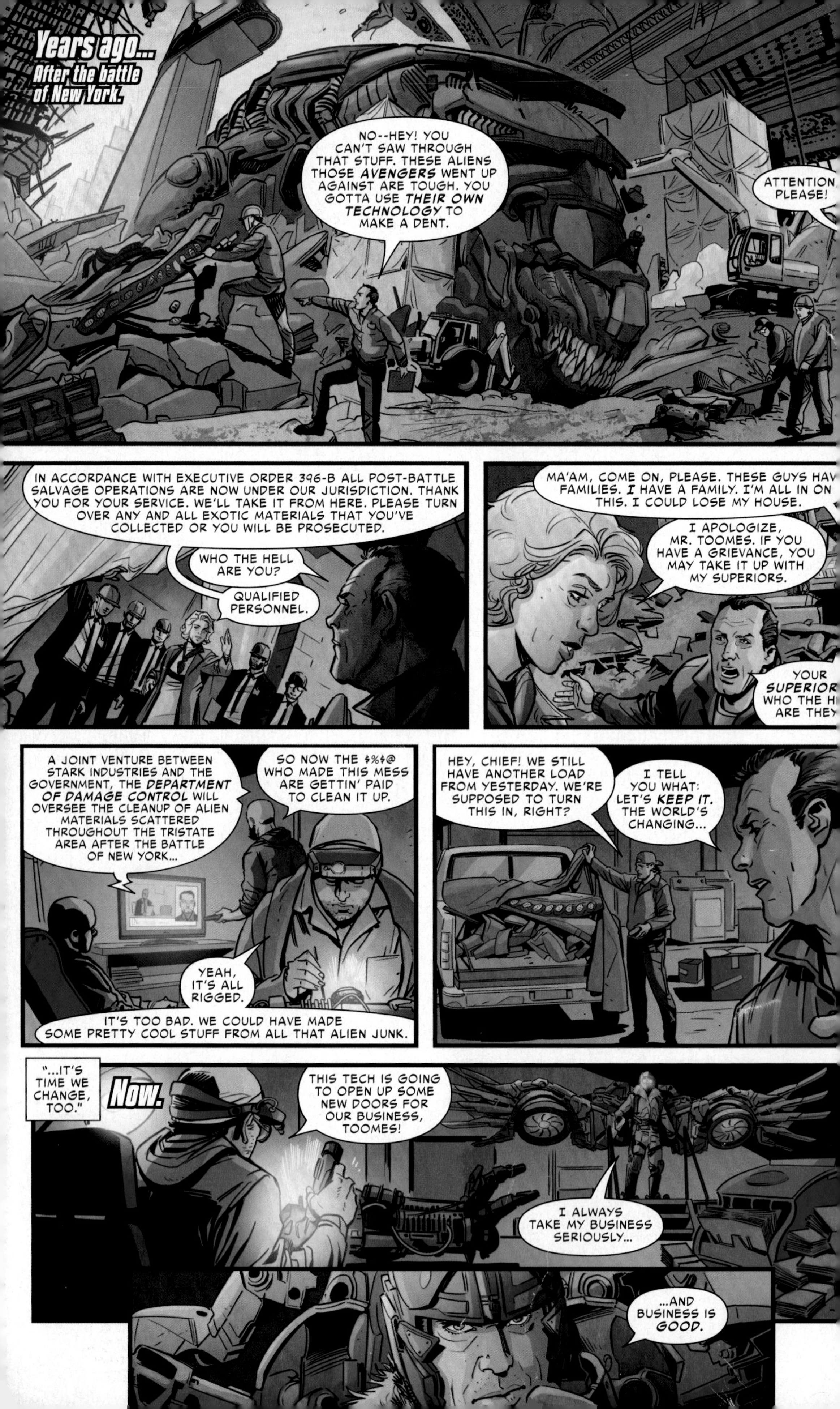

Years ago... After the battle of New York.
NO--HEY! YOU CAN'T SAW THROUGH THAT STUFF. THESE ALIENS THOSE AVENGERS WENT UP AGAINST ARE TOUGH. YOU GOTTA USE THEIR OWN TECHNOLOGY TO MAKE A DENT.
ATTENTION PLEASE!
IN ACCORDANCE WITH EXECUTIVE ORDER 396-B ALL POST-BATTLE SALVAGE OPERATIONS ARE NOW UNDER OUR JURISDICTION. THANK YOU FOR YOUR SERVICE. WE'LL TAKE IT FROM HERE. PLEASE TURN OVER ANY AND ALL EXOTIC MATERIALS THAT YOU'VE COLLECTED OR YOU WILL BE PROSECUTED.
WHO THE HELL ARE YOU?
QUALIFIED PERSONNEL.
MA'AM, COME ON, PLEASE. THESE GUYS HAV FAMILIES. I HAVE A FAMILY. I'M ALL IN ON THIS. I COULD LOSE MY HOUSE.
I APOLOGIZE, MR. TOOMES. IF YOU HAVE A GRIEVANCE, YOU MAY TAKE IT UP WITH MY SUPERIORS.
YOUR SUPERIOR WHO THE H ARE THEY
A JOINT VENTURE BETWEEN STARK INDUSTRIES AND THE GOVERNMENT, THE DEPARTMENT OF DAMAGE CONTROL WILL OVERSEE THE CLEANUP OF ALIEN MATERIALS SCATTERED THROUGHOUT THE TRISTATE AREA AFTER THE BATTLE OF NEW YORK...
SO NOW THE $%$@ WHO MADE THIS MESS ARE GETTIN' PAID TO CLEAN IT UP.
YEAH, IT'S ALL RIGGED.
IT'S TOO BAD. WE COULD HAVE MADE SOME PRETTY COOL STUFF FROM ALL THAT ALIEN JUNK.
HEY, CHIEF! WE STILL HAVE ANOTHER LOAD FROM YESTERDAY. WE'RE SUPPOSED TO TURN THIS IN, RIGHT?
I TELL YOU WHAT: LET'S KEEP IT. THE WORLD'S CHANGING...
"...IT'S TIME WE CHANGE, TOO."
Now.
THIS TECH IS GOING TO OPEN UP SOME NEW DOORS FOR OUR BUSINESS, TOOMES!
I ALWAYS TAKE MY BUSINESS SERIOUSLY...
...AND BUSINESS IS GOOD.

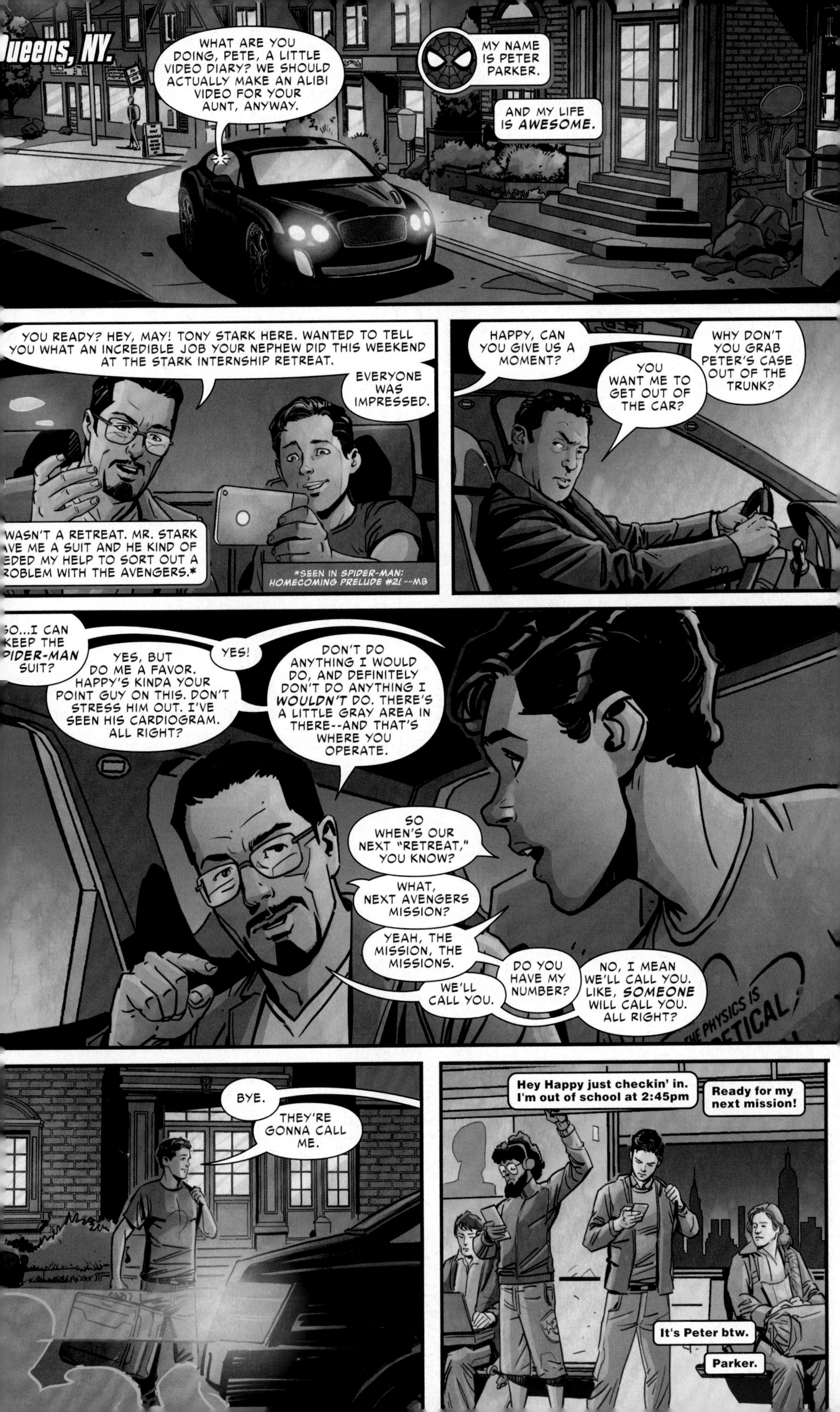

ueens, NY.
WHAT ARE YOU DOING, PETE, A LITTLE VIDEO DIARY? WE SHOULD ACTUALLY MAKE AN ALIBI VIDEO FOR YOUR AUNT, ANYWAY.
MY NAME IS PETER PARKER.
AND MY LIFE IS *AWESOME.*
YOU READY? HEY, MAY! TONY STARK HERE. WANTED TO TELL YOU WHAT AN INCREDIBLE JOB YOUR NEPHEW DID THIS WEEKEND AT THE STARK INTERNSHIP RETREAT.
EVERYONE WAS IMPRESSED.
WASN'T A RETREAT. MR. STARK VE ME A SUIT AND HE KIND OF EDED MY HELP TO SORT OUT A ROBLEM WITH THE AVENGERS.*
*SEEN IN *SPIDER-MAN: HOMECOMING PRELUDE #2!* --MB
HAPPY, CAN YOU GIVE US A MOMENT?
YOU WANT ME TO GET OUT OF THE CAR?
WHY DON'T YOU GRAB PETER'S CASE OUT OF THE TRUNK?
O...I CAN KEEP THE *PIDER-MAN* SUIT?
YES!
YES, BUT DO ME A FAVOR. HAPPY'S KINDA YOUR POINT GUY ON THIS. DON'T STRESS HIM OUT. I'VE SEEN HIS CARDIOGRAM. ALL RIGHT?
DON'T DO ANYTHING I WOULD DO, AND DEFINITELY DON'T DO ANYTHING I *WOULDN'T* DO. THERE'S A LITTLE GRAY AREA IN THERE--AND THAT'S WHERE YOU OPERATE.
SO WHEN'S OUR NEXT "RETREAT," YOU KNOW?
WHAT, NEXT AVENGERS MISSION?
YEAH, THE MISSION, THE MISSIONS.
WE'LL CALL YOU.
DO YOU HAVE MY NUMBER?
NO, I MEAN WE'LL CALL YOU. LIKE, *SOMEONE* WILL CALL YOU. ALL RIGHT?
BYE.
THEY'RE GONNA CALL ME.
Hey Happy just checkin' in. I'm out of school at 2:45pm
Ready for my next mission!
It's Peter btw.
Parker.

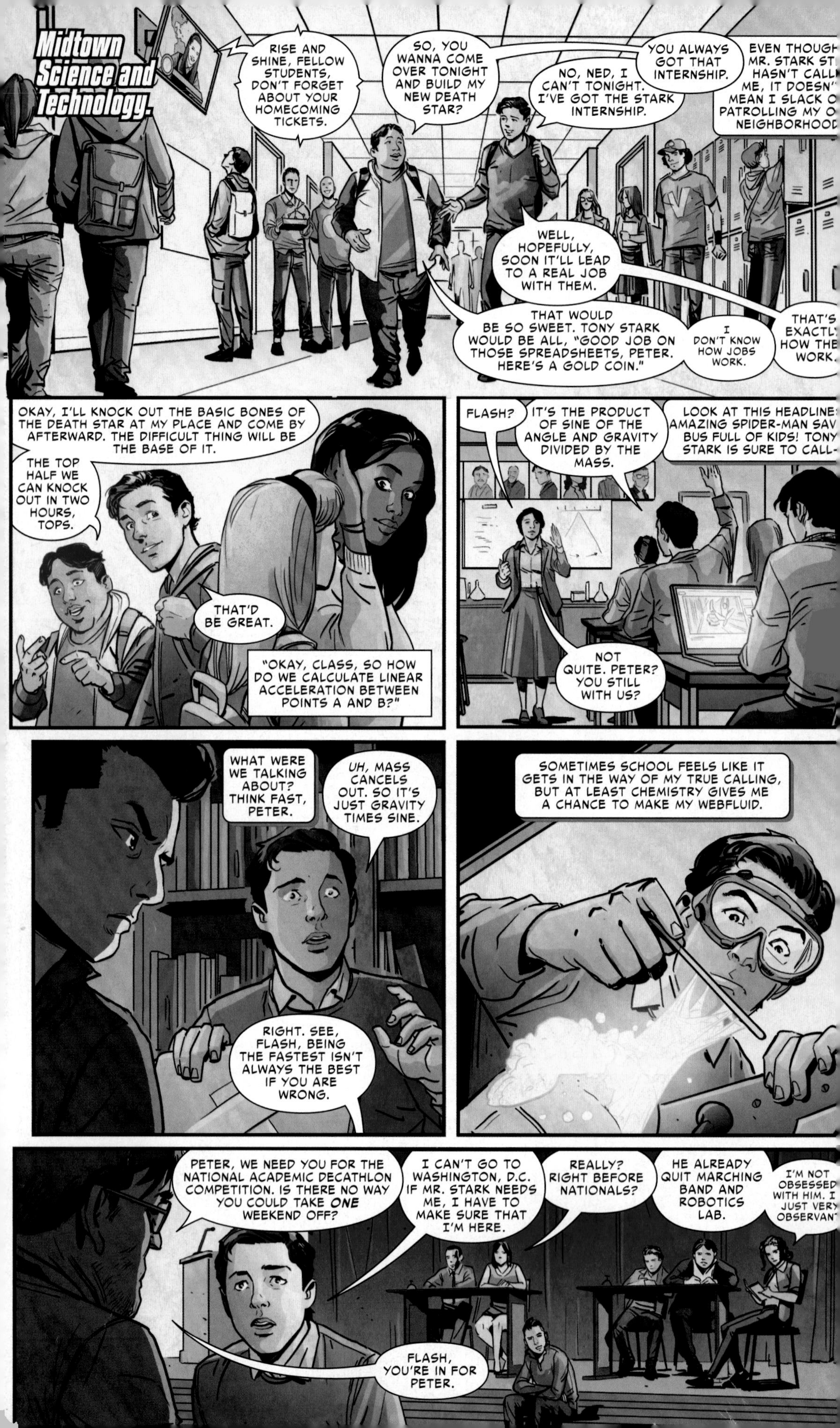
Midtown Science and Technology.
RISE AND SHINE, FELLOW STUDENTS, DON'T FORGET ABOUT YOUR HOMECOMING TICKETS.
SO, YOU WANNA COME OVER TONIGHT AND BUILD MY NEW DEATH STAR?
NO, NED, I CAN'T TONIGHT. I'VE GOT THE STARK INTERNSHIP.
YOU ALWAYS GOT THAT INTERNSHIP.
EVEN THOUG MR. STARK ST HASN'T CALL ME, IT DOESN' MEAN I SLACK O PATROLLING MY O NEIGHBORHOOD
WELL, HOPEFULLY, SOON IT'LL LEAD TO A REAL JOB WITH THEM.
THAT WOULD BE SO SWEET. TONY STARK WOULD BE ALL, "GOOD JOB ON THOSE SPREADSHEETS, PETER. HERE'S A GOLD COIN."
I DON'T KNOW HOW JOBS WORK.
THAT'S EXACTL HOW THE WORK.
OKAY, I'LL KNOCK OUT THE BASIC BONES OF THE DEATH STAR AT MY PLACE AND COME BY AFTERWARD. THE DIFFICULT THING WILL BE THE BASE OF IT.
THE TOP HALF WE CAN KNOCK OUT IN TWO HOURS, TOPS.
THAT'D BE GREAT.
"OKAY, CLASS, SO HOW DO WE CALCULATE LINEAR ACCELERATION BETWEEN POINTS A AND B?"
FLASH?
IT'S THE PRODUCT OF SINE OF THE ANGLE AND GRAVITY DIVIDED BY THE MASS.
LOOK AT THIS HEADLINE AMAZING SPIDER-MAN SAV BUS FULL OF KIDS! TONY STARK IS SURE TO CALL-
NOT QUITE. PETER? YOU STILL WITH US?
WHAT WERE WE TALKING ABOUT? THINK FAST, PETER.
UH, MASS CANCELS OUT. SO IT'S JUST GRAVITY TIMES SINE.
RIGHT. SEE, FLASH, BEING THE FASTEST ISN'T ALWAYS THE BEST IF YOU ARE WRONG.
SOMETIMES SCHOOL FEELS LIKE IT GETS IN THE WAY OF MY TRUE CALLING, BUT AT LEAST CHEMISTRY GIVES ME A CHANCE TO MAKE MY WEBFLUID.
PETER, WE NEED YOU FOR THE NATIONAL ACADEMIC DECATHLON COMPETITION. IS THERE NO WAY YOU COULD TAKE ONE WEEKEND OFF?
I CAN'T GO TO WASHINGTON, D.C. IF MR. STARK NEEDS ME, I HAVE TO MAKE SURE THAT I'M HERE.
REALLY? RIGHT BEFORE NATIONALS?
HE ALREADY QUIT MARCHING BAND AND ROBOTICS LAB.
I'M NOT OBSESSED WITH HIM. I JUST VERY OBSERVAN
FLASH, YOU'RE IN FOR PETER.

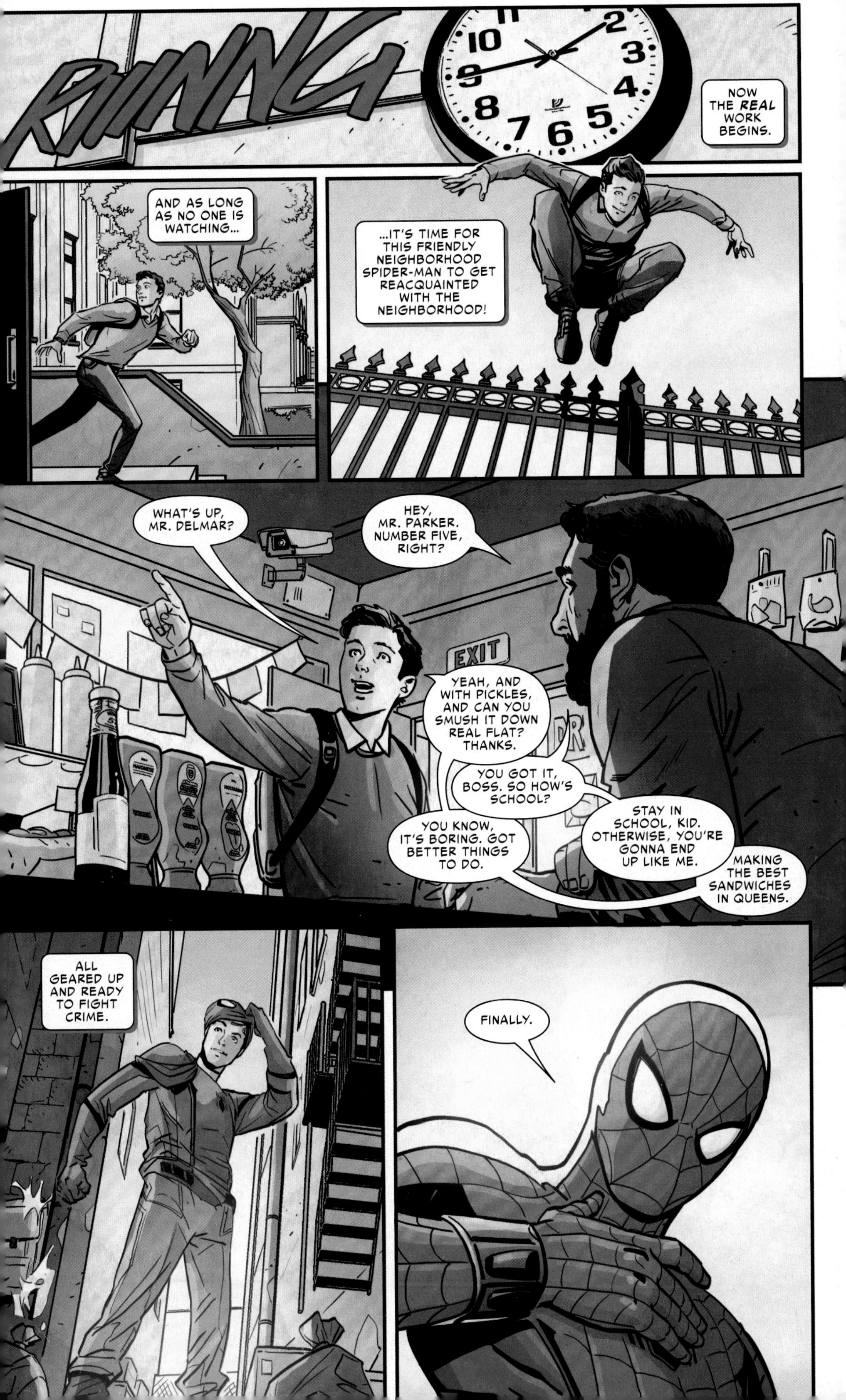
RIIINNG
NOW THE REAL WORK BEGINS.
AND AS LONG AS NO ONE IS WATCHING...
...IT'S TIME FOR THIS FRIENDLY NEIGHBORHOOD SPIDER-MAN TO GET REACQUAINTED WITH THE NEIGHBORHOOD!
WHAT'S UP, MR. DELMAR?
HEY, MR. PARKER. NUMBER FIVE, RIGHT?
EXIT
YEAH, AND WITH PICKLES, AND CAN YOU SMUSH IT DOWN REAL FLAT? THANKS.
YOU GOT IT, BOSS. SO HOW'S SCHOOL?
YOU KNOW, IT'S BORING. GOT BETTER THINGS TO DO.
STAY IN SCHOOL, KID. OTHERWISE, YOU'RE GONNA END UP LIKE ME.
MAKING THE BEST SANDWICHES IN QUEENS.
ALL GEARED UP AND READY TO FIGHT CRIME.
FINALLY.

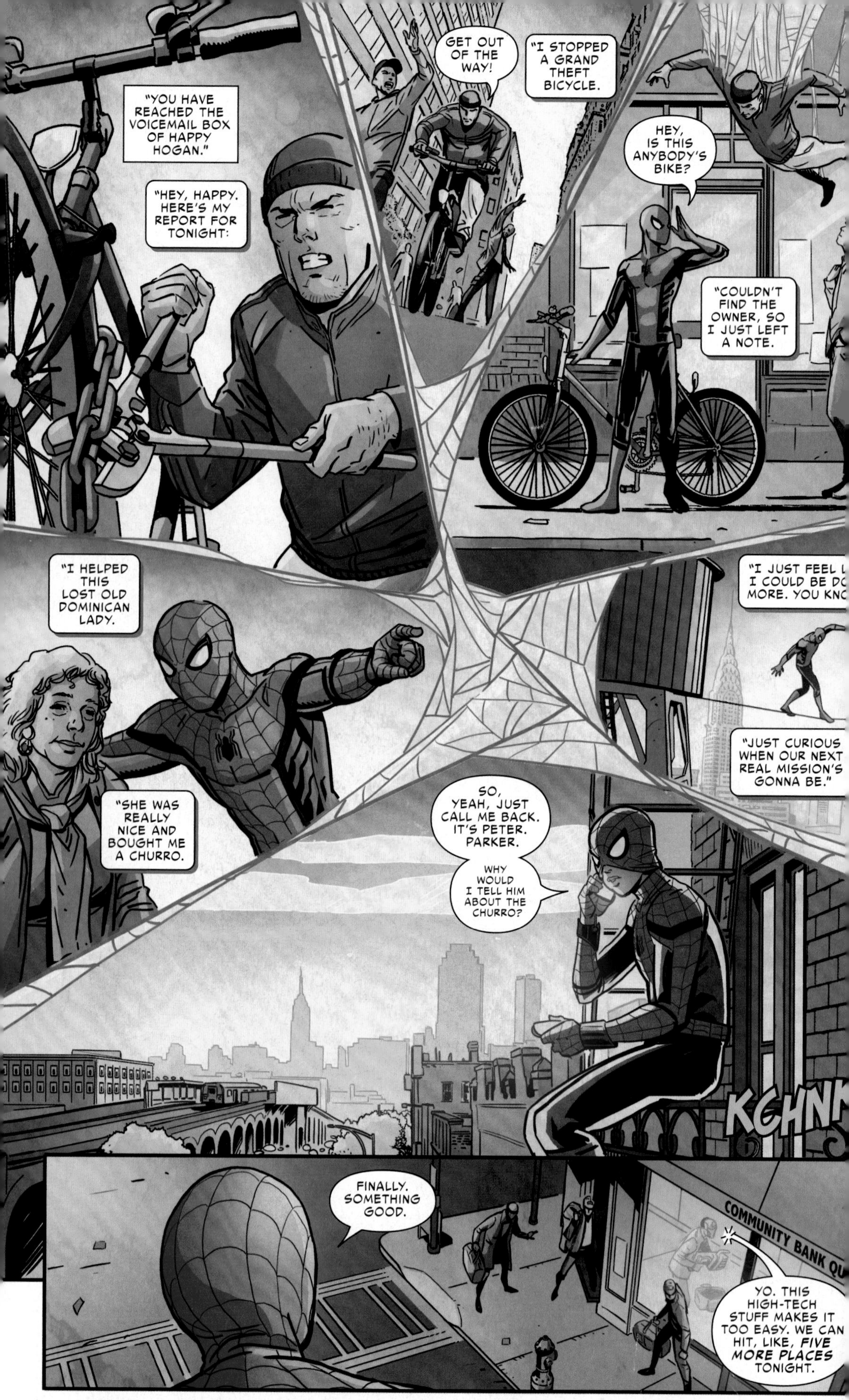
"YOU HAVE REACHED THE VOICEMAIL BOX OF HAPPY HOGAN."
"HEY, HAPPY. HERE'S MY REPORT FOR TONIGHT:
GET OUT OF THE WAY!
"I STOPPED A GRAND THEFT BICYCLE.
HEY, IS THIS ANYBODY'S BIKE?
"COULDN'T FIND THE OWNER, SO I JUST LEFT A NOTE.
"I HELPED THIS LOST OLD DOMINICAN LADY.
"SHE WAS REALLY NICE AND BOUGHT ME A CHURRO.
"JUST CURIOUS WHEN OUR NEXT REAL MISSION'S GONNA BE."
SO, YEAH, JUST CALL ME BACK. IT'S PETER. PARKER.
WHY WOULD I TELL HIM ABOUT THE CHURRO?
FINALLY. SOMETHING GOOD.
COMMUNITY BANK
YO. THIS HIGH-TECH STUFF MAKES IT TOO EASY. WE CAN HIT, LIKE, *FIVE MORE PLACES* TONIGHT.

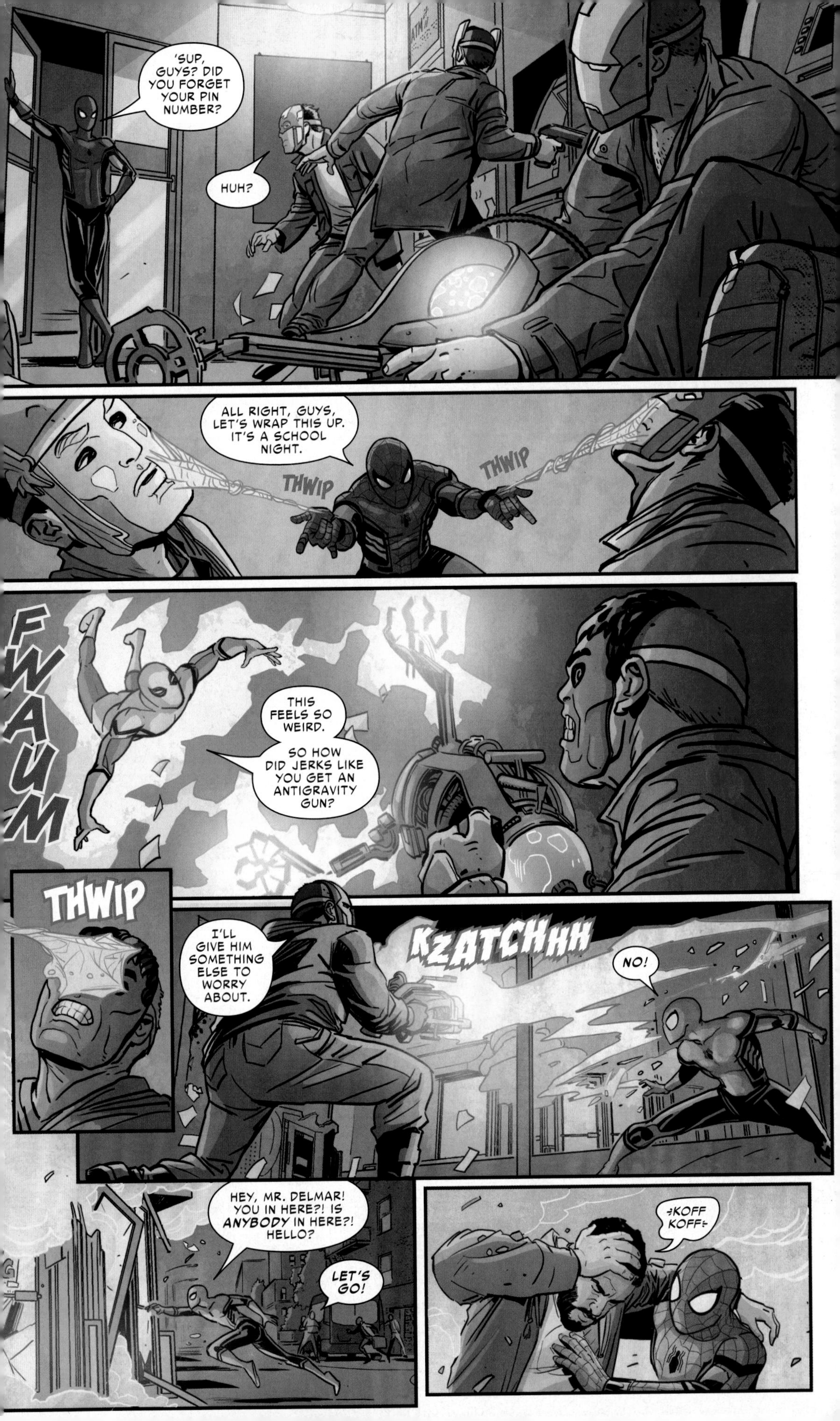
'SUP, GUYS? DID YOU FORGET YOUR PIN NUMBER?
HUH?
ALL RIGHT, GUYS, LET'S WRAP THIS UP. IT'S A SCHOOL NIGHT.
THWIP
THWIP
FWAUM
THIS FEELS SO WEIRD.
SO HOW DID JERKS LIKE YOU GET AN ANTIGRAVITY GUN?
THWIP
I'LL GIVE HIM SOMETHING ELSE TO WORRY ABOUT.
KZATCHHH
NO!
HEY, MR. DELMAR! YOU IN HERE?! IS ANYBODY IN HERE?! HELLO?
LET'S GO!
KOFF KOFF

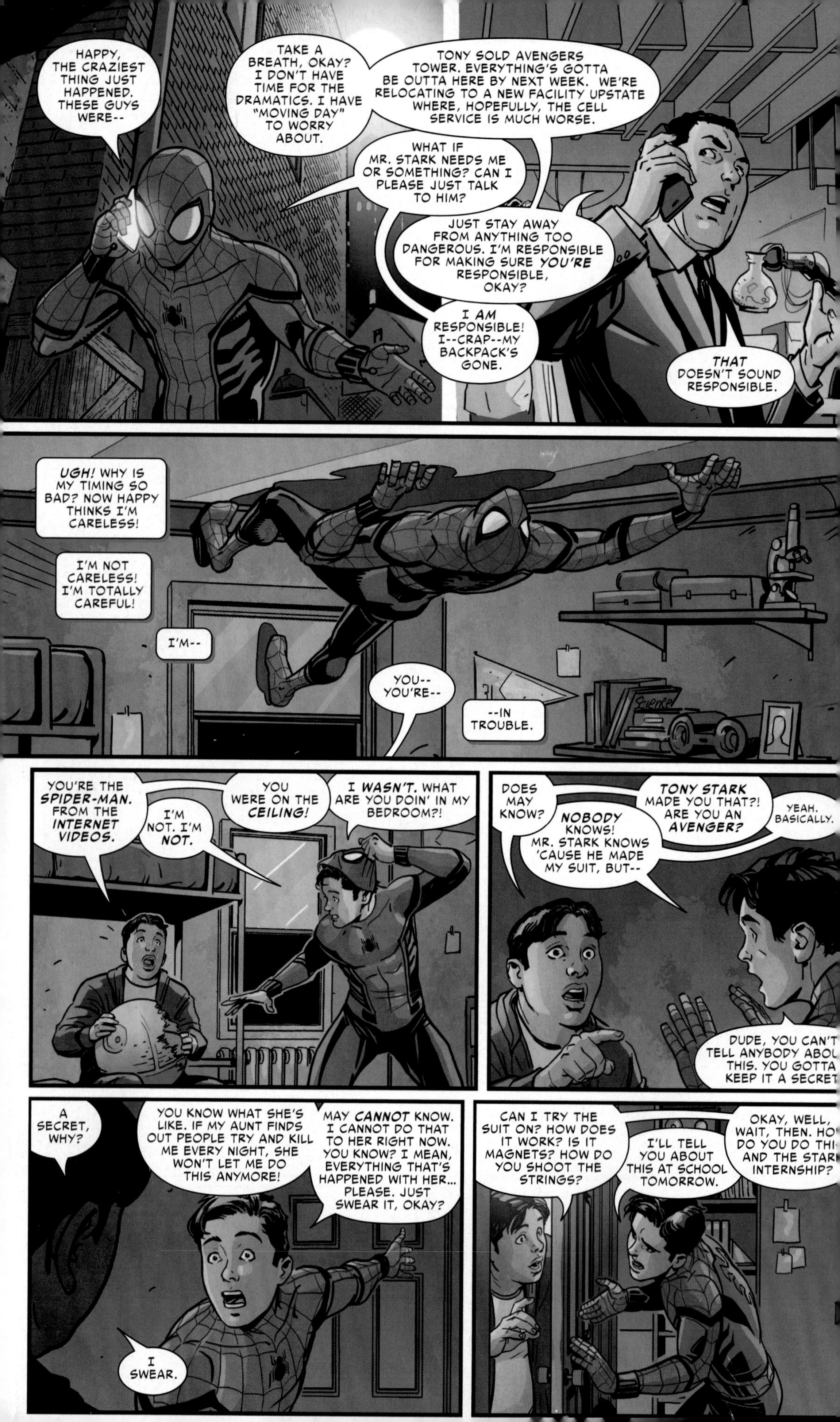
HAPPY, THE CRAZIEST THING JUST HAPPENED. THESE GUYS WERE--
TAKE A BREATH, OKAY? I DON'T HAVE TIME FOR THE DRAMATICS. I HAVE "MOVING DAY" TO WORRY ABOUT.
TONY SOLD AVENGERS TOWER. EVERYTHING'S GOTTA BE OUTTA HERE BY NEXT WEEK. WE'RE RELOCATING TO A NEW FACILITY UPSTATE WHERE, HOPEFULLY, THE CELL SERVICE IS MUCH WORSE.
WHAT IF MR. STARK NEEDS ME OR SOMETHING? CAN I PLEASE JUST TALK TO HIM?
JUST STAY AWAY FROM ANYTHING TOO DANGEROUS. I'M RESPONSIBLE FOR MAKING SURE *YOU'RE* RESPONSIBLE, OKAY?
I AM RESPONSIBLE! I--CRAP--MY BACKPACK'S GONE.
THAT DOESN'T SOUND RESPONSIBLE.
UGH! WHY IS MY TIMING SO BAD? NOW HAPPY THINKS I'M CARELESS!
I'M NOT CARELESS! I'M TOTALLY CAREFUL!
I'M--
YOU-- YOU'RE--
--IN TROUBLE.
YOU'RE THE *SPIDER-MAN.* FROM THE *INTERNET VIDEOS.*
I'M NOT. I'M *NOT.*
YOU WERE ON THE *CEILING!*
I *WASN'T.* WHAT ARE YOU DOIN' IN MY BEDROOM?!
DOES MAY KNOW?
NOBODY KNOWS! MR. STARK KNOWS 'CAUSE HE MADE MY SUIT, BUT--
TONY STARK MADE YOU THAT?! ARE YOU AN *AVENGER?*
YEAH. BASICALLY.
DUDE, YOU CAN'T TELL ANYBODY ABOU THIS. YOU GOTTA KEEP IT A SECRET
A SECRET, WHY?
YOU KNOW WHAT SHE'S LIKE. IF MY AUNT FINDS OUT PEOPLE TRY AND KILL ME EVERY NIGHT, SHE WON'T LET ME DO THIS ANYMORE!
MAY *CANNOT* KNOW. I CANNOT DO THAT TO HER RIGHT NOW. YOU KNOW? I MEAN, EVERYTHING THAT'S HAPPENED WITH HER... PLEASE. JUST SWEAR IT, OKAY?
I SWEAR.
CAN I TRY THE SUIT ON? HOW DOES IT WORK? IS IT MAGNETS? HOW DO YOU SHOOT THE STRINGS?
I'LL TELL YOU ABOUT THIS AT SCHOOL TOMORROW.
OKAY, WELL, WAIT, THEN. HO DO YOU DO THI AND THE STAR INTERNSHIP?

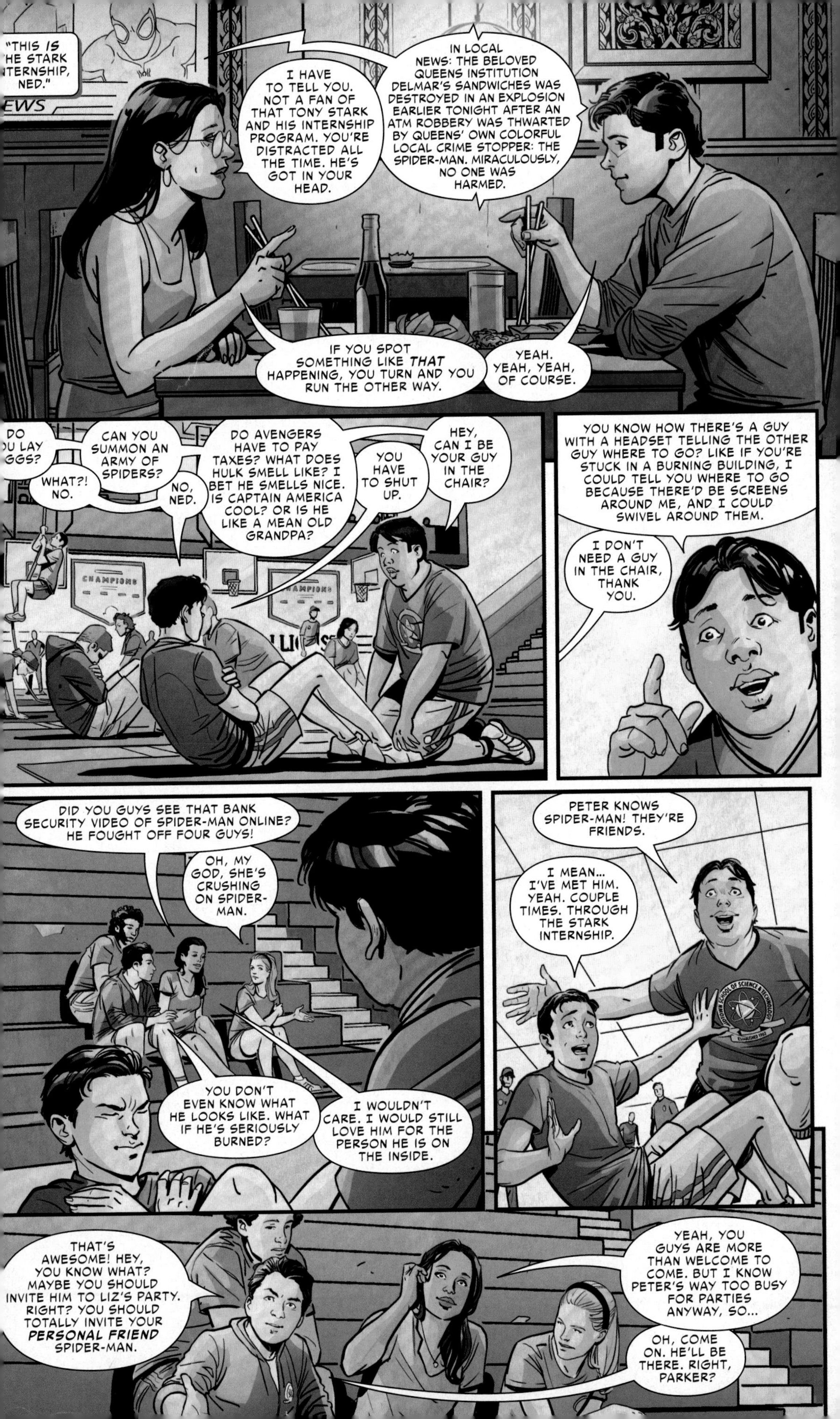
"THIS IS
HE STARK
NTERNSHIP,
NED."
EWS
I HAVE TO TELL YOU. NOT A FAN OF THAT TONY STARK AND HIS INTERNSHIP PROGRAM. YOU'RE DISTRACTED ALL THE TIME. HE'S GOT IN YOUR HEAD.
IN LOCAL NEWS: THE BELOVED QUEENS INSTITUTION DELMAR'S SANDWICHES WAS DESTROYED IN AN EXPLOSION EARLIER TONIGHT AFTER AN ATM ROBBERY WAS THWARTED BY QUEENS' OWN COLORFUL LOCAL CRIME STOPPER: THE SPIDER-MAN. MIRACULOUSLY, NO ONE WAS HARMED.
IF YOU SPOT SOMETHING LIKE THAT HAPPENING, YOU TURN AND YOU RUN THE OTHER WAY.
YEAH. YEAH, YEAH, OF COURSE.
DO
U LAY
GGS?
WHAT?! NO.
CAN YOU SUMMON AN ARMY OF SPIDERS?
NO, NED.
DO AVENGERS HAVE TO PAY TAXES? WHAT DOES HULK SMELL LIKE? I BET HE SMELLS NICE. IS CAPTAIN AMERICA COOL? OR IS HE LIKE A MEAN OLD GRANDPA?
YOU HAVE TO SHUT UP.
HEY, CAN I BE YOUR GUY IN THE CHAIR?
CHAMPIONS
CHAMPIONS
YOU KNOW HOW THERE'S A GUY WITH A HEADSET TELLING THE OTHER GUY WHERE TO GO? LIKE IF YOU'RE STUCK IN A BURNING BUILDING, I COULD TELL YOU WHERE TO GO BECAUSE THERE'D BE SCREENS AROUND ME, AND I COULD SWIVEL AROUND THEM.
I DON'T NEED A GUY IN THE CHAIR, THANK YOU.
DID YOU GUYS SEE THAT BANK SECURITY VIDEO OF SPIDER-MAN ONLINE? HE FOUGHT OFF FOUR GUYS!
OH, MY GOD, SHE'S CRUSHING ON SPIDER-MAN.
YOU DON'T EVEN KNOW WHAT HE LOOKS LIKE. WHAT IF HE'S SERIOUSLY BURNED?
I WOULDN'T CARE. I WOULD STILL LOVE HIM FOR THE PERSON HE IS ON THE INSIDE.
PETER KNOWS SPIDER-MAN! THEY'RE FRIENDS.
I MEAN... I'VE MET HIM. YEAH. COUPLE TIMES. THROUGH THE STARK INTERNSHIP.
THAT'S AWESOME! HEY, YOU KNOW WHAT? MAYBE YOU SHOULD INVITE HIM TO LIZ'S PARTY. RIGHT? YOU SHOULD TOTALLY INVITE YOUR PERSONAL FRIEND SPIDER-MAN.
YEAH, YOU GUYS ARE MORE THAN WELCOME TO COME. BUT I KNOW PETER'S WAY TOO BUSY FOR PARTIES ANYWAY, SO...
OH, COME ON. HE'LL BE THERE. RIGHT, PARKER?

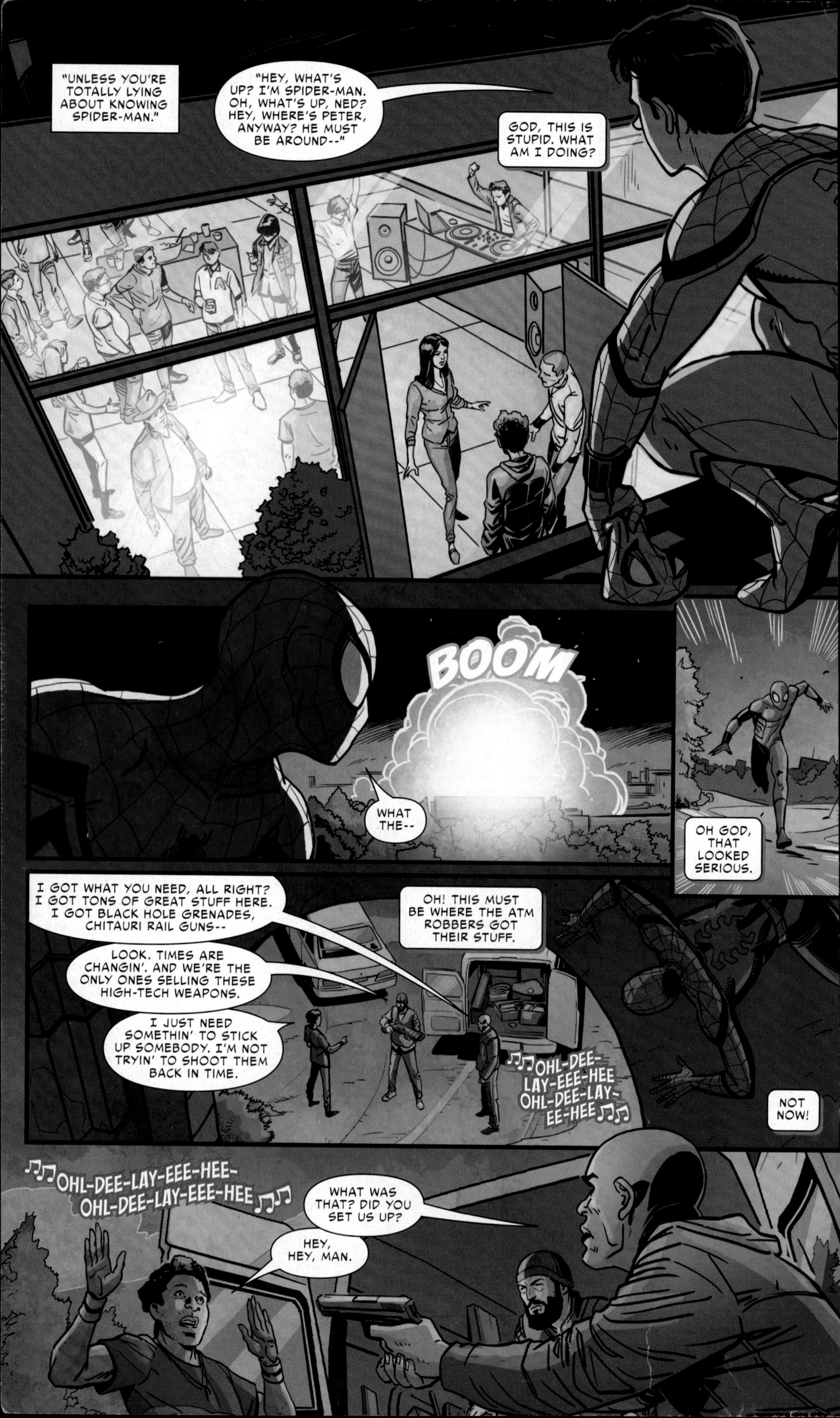
"UNLESS YOU'RE TOTALLY LYING ABOUT KNOWING SPIDER-MAN."
"HEY, WHAT'S UP? I'M SPIDER-MAN. OH, WHAT'S UP, NED? HEY, WHERE'S PETER, ANYWAY? HE MUST BE AROUND--"
GOD, THIS IS STUPID. WHAT AM I DOING?
BOOM
WHAT THE--
OH GOD, THAT LOOKED SERIOUS.
I GOT WHAT YOU NEED, ALL RIGHT? I GOT TONS OF GREAT STUFF HERE. I GOT BLACK HOLE GRENADES, CHITAURI RAIL GUNS--
OH! THIS MUST BE WHERE THE ATM ROBBERS GOT THEIR STUFF.
LOOK. TIMES ARE CHANGIN'. AND WE'RE THE ONLY ONES SELLING THESE HIGH-TECH WEAPONS.
I JUST NEED SOMETHIN' TO STICK UP SOMEBODY. I'M NOT TRYIN' TO SHOOT THEM BACK IN TIME.
OHL-DEE-LAY-EEE-HEE OHL-DEE-LAY-EE-HEE
NOT NOW!
OHL-DEE-LAY-EEE-HEE-OHL-DEE-LAY-EEE-HEE
WHAT WAS THAT? DID YOU SET US UP?
HEY, HEY, MAN.

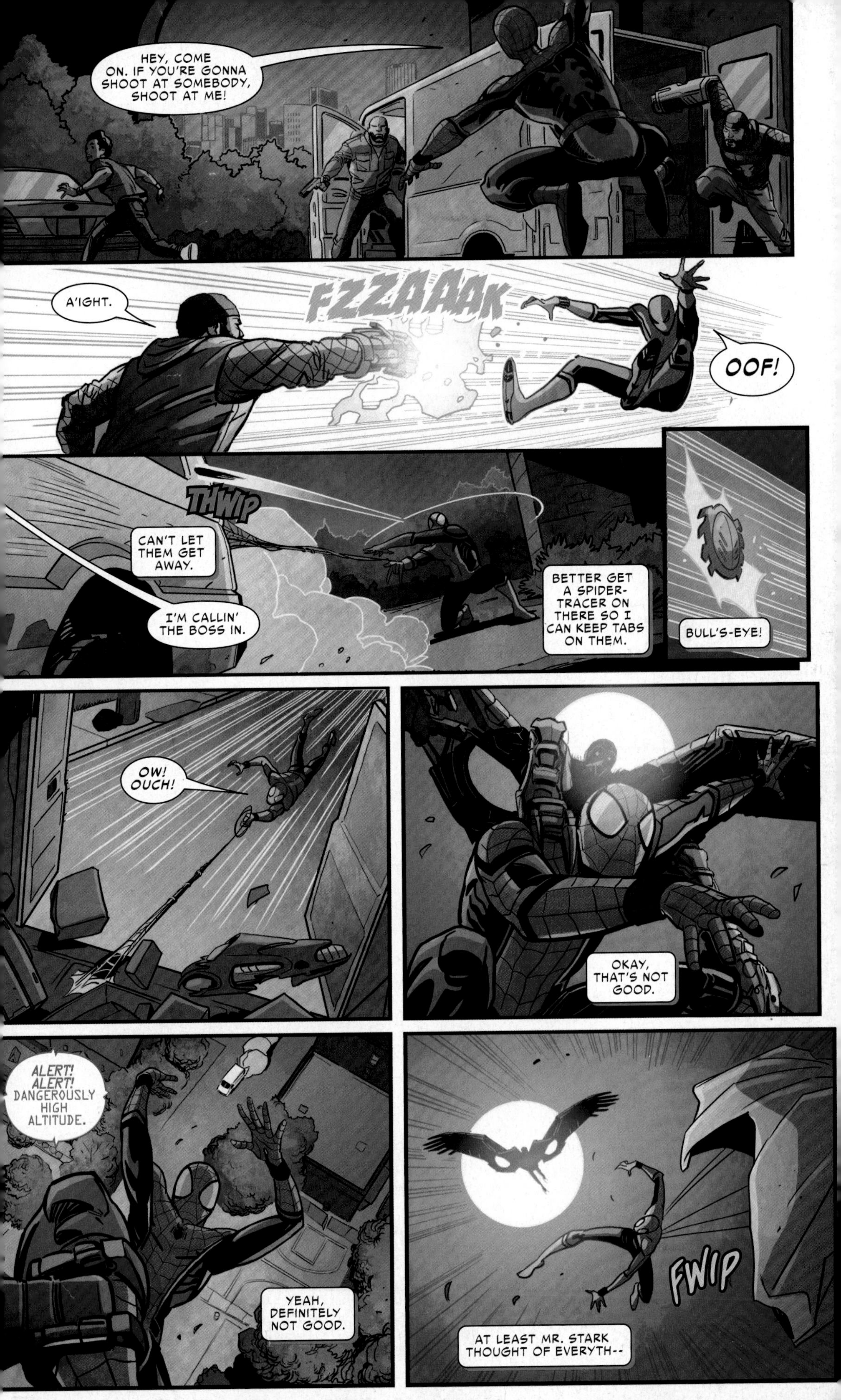
HEY, COME ON. IF YOU'RE GONNA SHOOT AT SOMEBODY, SHOOT AT ME!
A'IGHT.
FZZAAAK
OOF!
THWIP
CAN'T LET THEM GET AWAY.
I'M CALLIN' THE BOSS IN.
BETTER GET A SPIDER-TRACER ON THERE SO I CAN KEEP TABS ON THEM.
BULL'S-EYE!
OW! OUCH!
OKAY, THAT'S NOT GOOD.
ALERT! ALERT! DANGEROUSLY HIGH ALTITUDE.
YEAH, DEFINITELY NOT GOOD.
FWIP
AT LEAST MR. STARK THOUGHT OF EVERYTH--

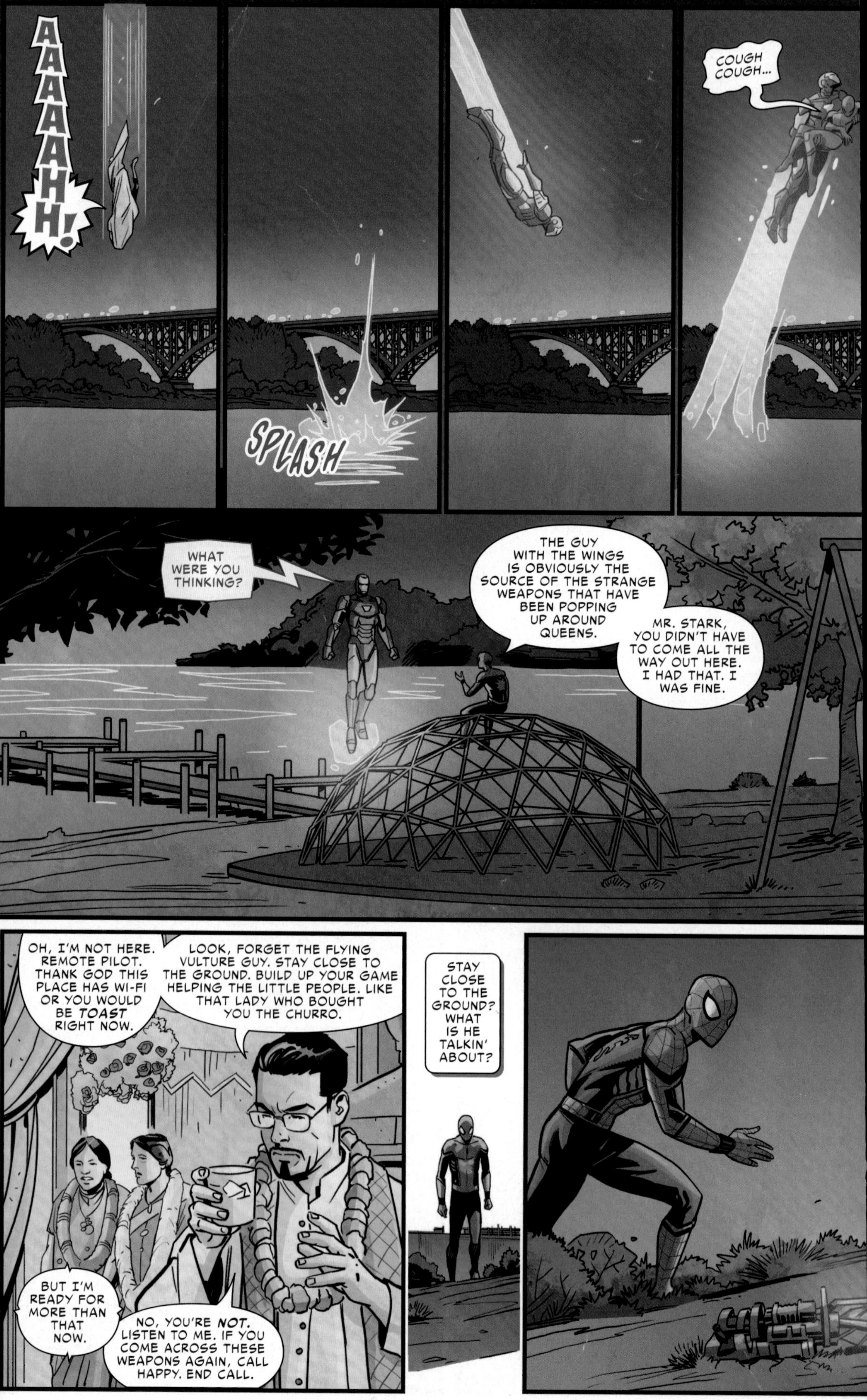
AAAAAAHH!
SPLASH
COUGH COUGH...
WHAT WERE YOU THINKING?
THE GUY WITH THE WINGS IS OBVIOUSLY THE SOURCE OF THE STRANGE WEAPONS THAT HAVE BEEN POPPING UP AROUND QUEENS.
MR. STARK, YOU DIDN'T HAVE TO COME ALL THE WAY OUT HERE. I HAD THAT. I WAS FINE.
OH, I'M NOT HERE. REMOTE PILOT. THANK GOD THIS PLACE HAS WI-FI OR YOU WOULD BE *TOAST* RIGHT NOW.
LOOK, FORGET THE FLYING VULTURE GUY. STAY CLOSE TO THE GROUND. BUILD UP YOUR GAME HELPING THE LITTLE PEOPLE. LIKE THAT LADY WHO BOUGHT YOU THE CHURRO.
BUT I'M READY FOR MORE THAN THAT NOW.
NO, YOU'RE ***NOT.*** LISTEN TO ME. IF YOU COME ACROSS THESE WEAPONS AGAIN, CALL HAPPY. END CALL.
STAY CLOSE TO THE GROUND? WHAT IS HE TALKIN' ABOUT?

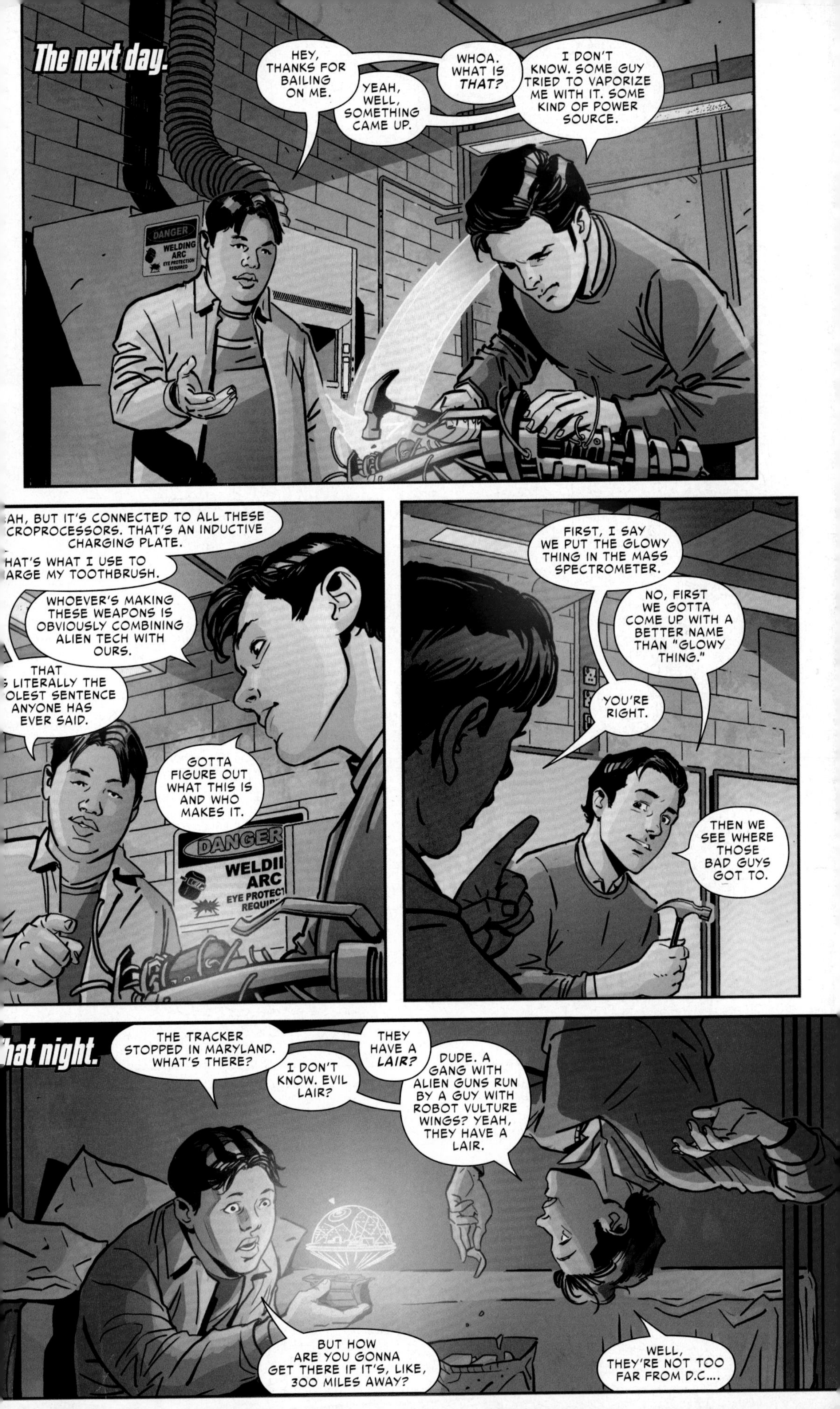
The next day.
HEY, THANKS FOR BAILING ON ME.
YEAH, WELL, SOMETHING CAME UP.
WHOA. WHAT IS *THAT?*
I DON'T KNOW. SOME GUY TRIED TO VAPORIZE ME WITH IT. SOME KIND OF POWER SOURCE.
DANGER
WELDING ARC
EYE PROTECTION REQUIRED
AH, BUT IT'S CONNECTED TO ALL THESE CROPROCESSORS. THAT'S AN INDUCTIVE CHARGING PLATE.
HAT'S WHAT I USE TO ARGE MY TOOTHBRUSH.
WHOEVER'S MAKING THESE WEAPONS IS OBVIOUSLY COMBINING ALIEN TECH WITH OURS.
THAT S LITERALLY THE OLEST SENTENCE ANYONE HAS EVER SAID.
GOTTA FIGURE OUT WHAT THIS IS AND WHO MAKES IT.
DANGER
WELDII ARC
EYE PROTECT REQUIR
FIRST, I SAY WE PUT THE GLOWY THING IN THE MASS SPECTROMETER.
NO, FIRST WE GOTTA COME UP WITH A BETTER NAME THAN "GLOWY THING."
YOU'RE RIGHT.
THEN WE SEE WHERE THOSE BAD GUYS GOT TO.
hat night.
THE TRACKER STOPPED IN MARYLAND. WHAT'S THERE?
I DON'T KNOW. EVIL LAIR?
THEY HAVE A *LAIR?*
DUDE. A GANG WITH ALIEN GUNS RUN BY A GUY WITH ROBOT VULTURE WINGS? YEAH, THEY HAVE A LAIR.
BUT HOW ARE YOU GONNA GET THERE IF IT'S, LIKE, 300 MILES AWAY?
WELL, THEY'RE NOT TOO FAR FROM D.C....

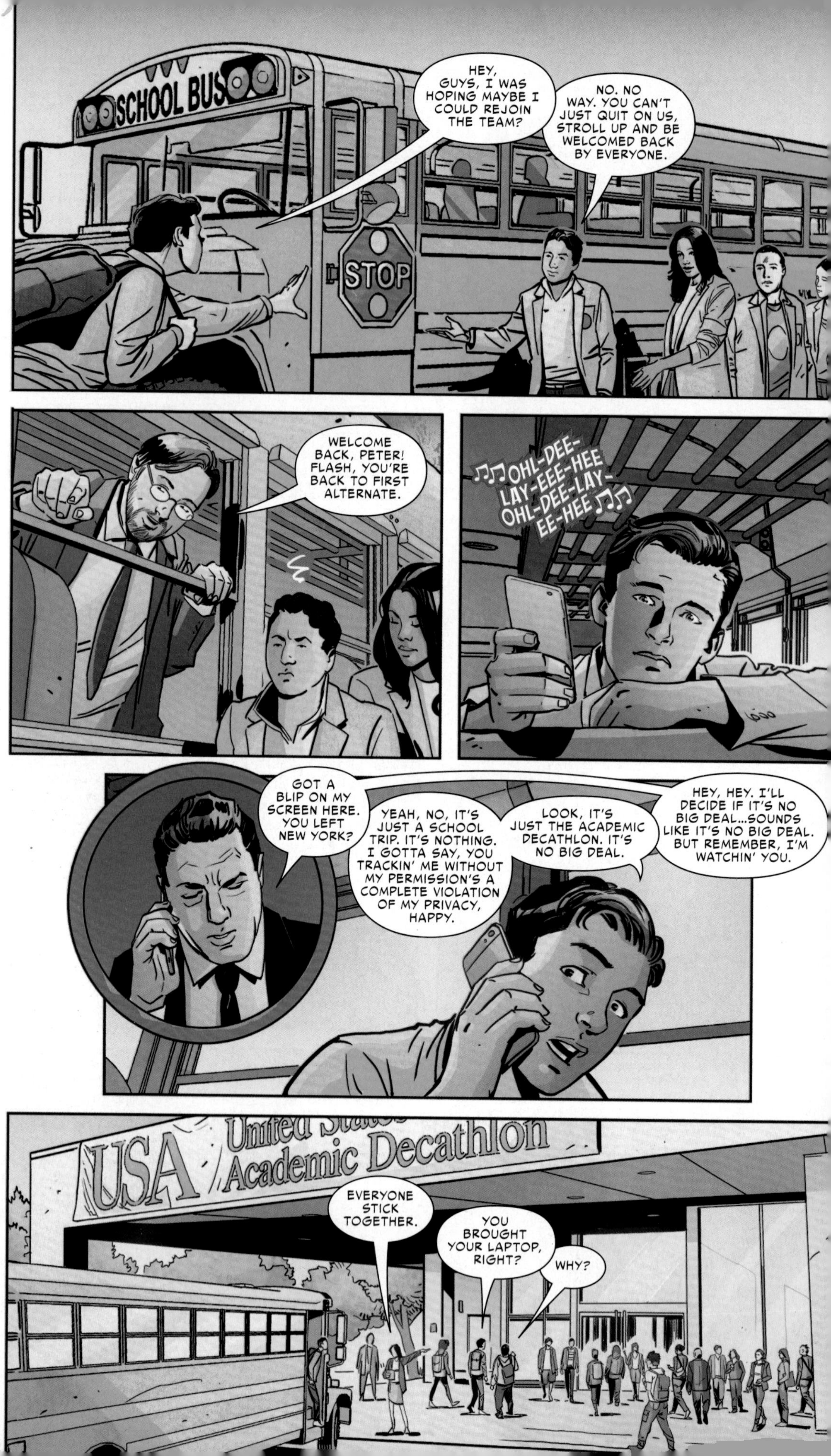
SCHOOL BUS
STOP
HEY, GUYS, I WAS HOPING MAYBE I COULD REJOIN THE TEAM?
NO. NO WAY. YOU CAN'T JUST QUIT ON US, STROLL UP AND BE WELCOMED BACK BY EVERYONE.
WELCOME BACK, PETER! FLASH, YOU'RE BACK TO FIRST ALTERNATE.
♫♫OHL-DEE-LAY-EEE-HEE OHL-DEE-LAY-EE-HEE♫♫
GOT A BLIP ON MY SCREEN HERE. YOU LEFT NEW YORK?
YEAH, NO, IT'S JUST A SCHOOL TRIP. IT'S NOTHING. I GOTTA SAY, YOU TRACKIN' ME WITHOUT MY PERMISSION'S A COMPLETE VIOLATION OF MY PRIVACY, HAPPY.
LOOK, IT'S JUST THE ACADEMIC DECATHLON. IT'S NO BIG DEAL.
HEY, HEY. I'LL DECIDE IF IT'S NO BIG DEAL...SOUNDS LIKE IT'S NO BIG DEAL. BUT REMEMBER, I'M WATCHIN' YOU.
USA United States Academic Decathlon
EVERYONE STICK TOGETHER.
YOU BROUGHT YOUR LAPTOP, RIGHT?
WHY?

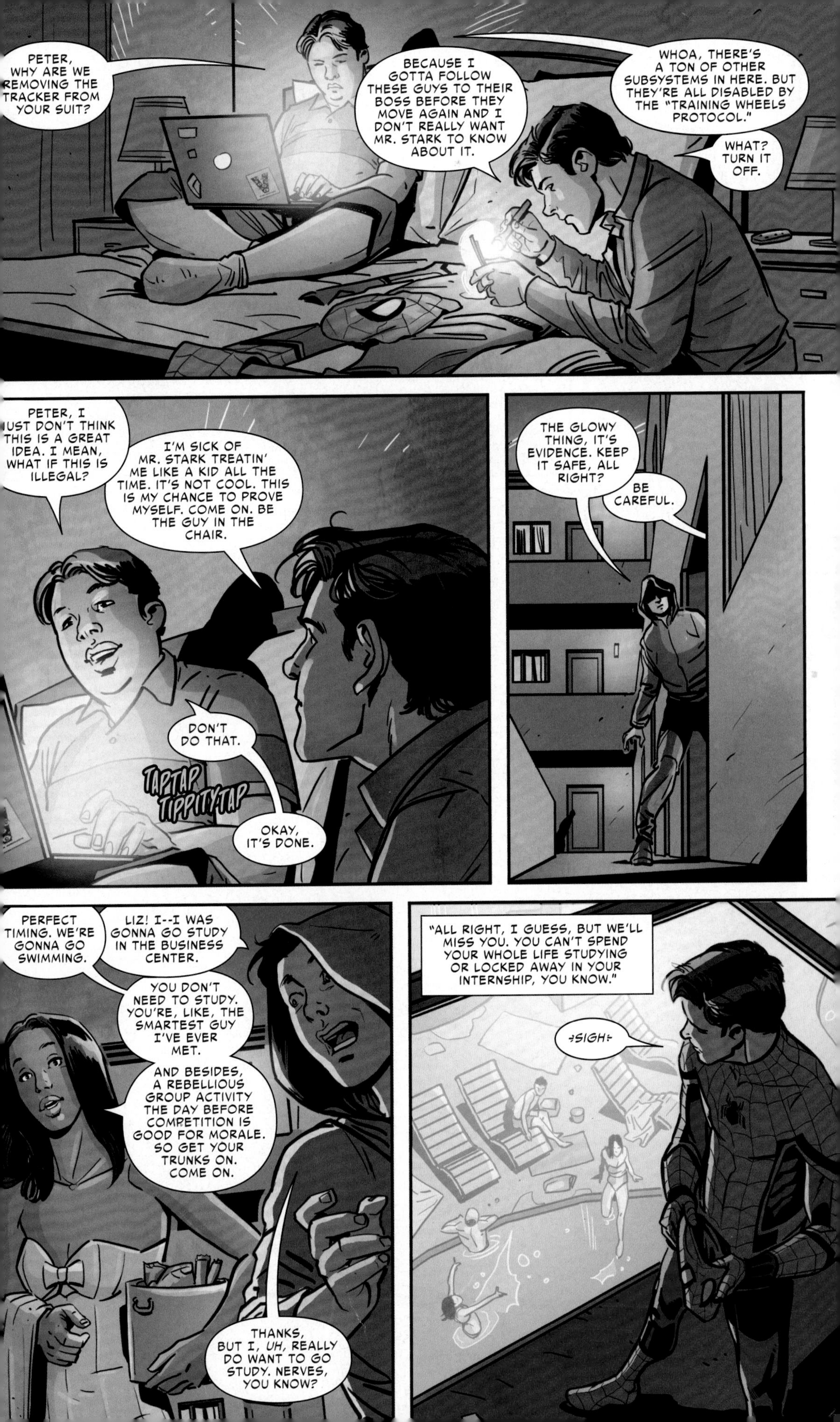
PETER, WHY ARE WE REMOVING THE TRACKER FROM YOUR SUIT?
BECAUSE I GOTTA FOLLOW THESE GUYS TO THEIR BOSS BEFORE THEY MOVE AGAIN AND I DON'T REALLY WANT MR. STARK TO KNOW ABOUT IT.
WHOA, THERE'S A TON OF OTHER SUBSYSTEMS IN HERE. BUT THEY'RE ALL DISABLED BY THE "TRAINING WHEELS PROTOCOL."
WHAT? TURN IT OFF.
PETER, I JUST DON'T THINK THIS IS A GREAT IDEA. I MEAN, WHAT IF THIS IS ILLEGAL?
I'M SICK OF MR. STARK TREATIN' ME LIKE A KID ALL THE TIME. IT'S NOT COOL. THIS IS MY CHANCE TO PROVE MYSELF. COME ON. BE THE GUY IN THE CHAIR.
DON'T DO THAT.
TAPTAP TIPPITYTAP
OKAY, IT'S DONE.
THE GLOWY THING, IT'S EVIDENCE. KEEP IT SAFE, ALL RIGHT?
BE CAREFUL.
PERFECT TIMING. WE'RE GONNA GO SWIMMING.
LIZ! I--I WAS GONNA GO STUDY IN THE BUSINESS CENTER.
YOU DON'T NEED TO STUDY. YOU'RE, LIKE, THE SMARTEST GUY I'VE EVER MET.
AND BESIDES, A REBELLIOUS GROUP ACTIVITY THE DAY BEFORE COMPETITION IS GOOD FOR MORALE. SO GET YOUR TRUNKS ON. COME ON.
THANKS, BUT I, *UH*, REALLY DO WANT TO GO STUDY. NERVES, YOU KNOW?
"ALL RIGHT, I GUESS, BUT WE'LL MISS YOU. YOU CAN'T SPEND YOUR WHOLE LIFE STUDYING OR LOCKED AWAY IN YOUR INTERNSHIP, YOU KNOW."
SIGH

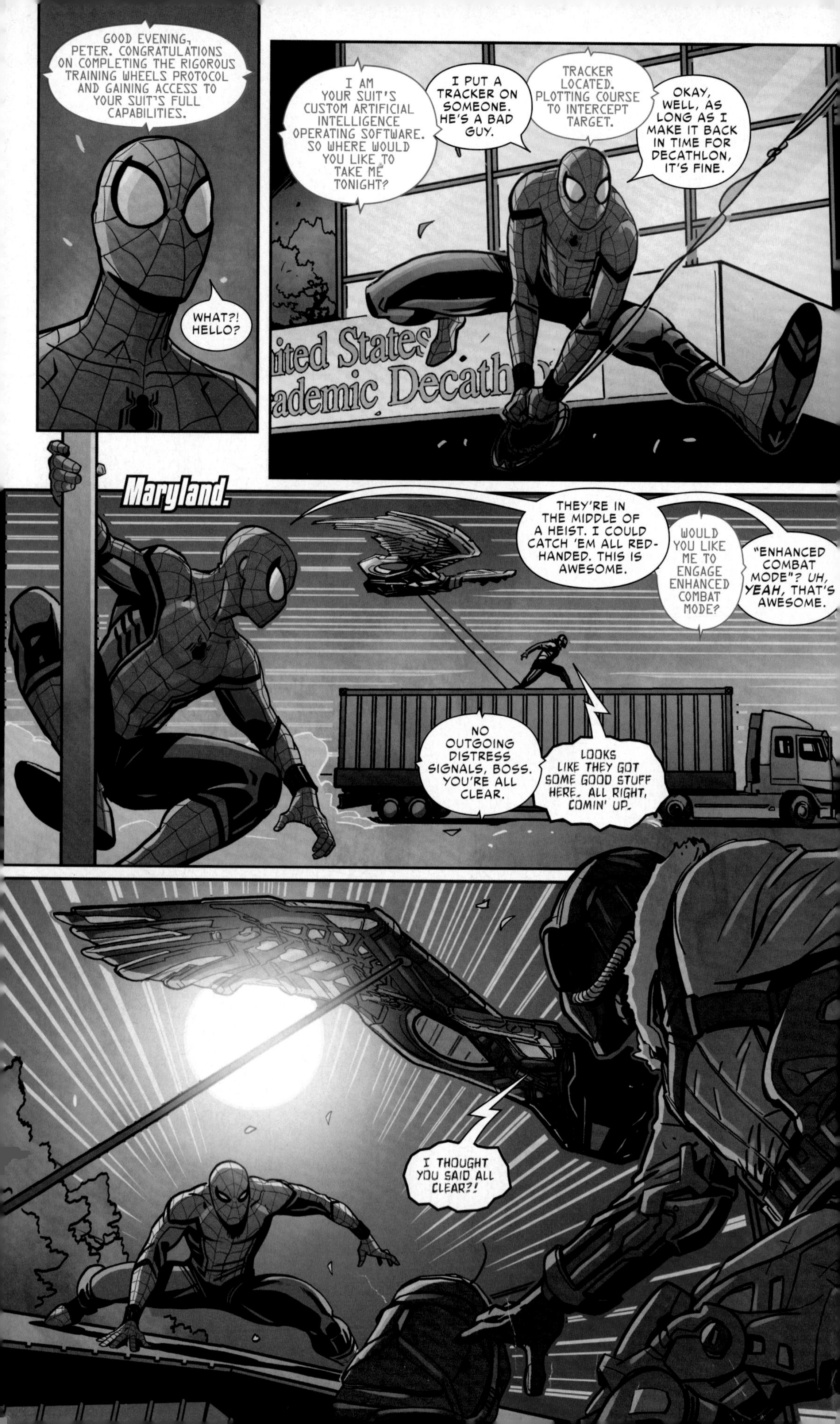
GOOD EVENING, PETER. CONGRATULATIONS ON COMPLETING THE RIGOROUS TRAINING WHEELS PROTOCOL AND GAINING ACCESS TO YOUR SUIT'S FULL CAPABILITIES.
WHAT?! HELLO?
I AM YOUR SUIT'S CUSTOM ARTIFICIAL INTELLIGENCE OPERATING SOFTWARE. SO WHERE WOULD YOU LIKE TO TAKE ME TONIGHT?
I PUT A TRACKER ON SOMEONE. HE'S A BAD GUY.
TRACKER LOCATED. PLOTTING COURSE TO INTERCEPT TARGET.
OKAY, WELL, AS LONG AS I MAKE IT BACK IN TIME FOR DECATHLON, IT'S FINE.
ited States
ademic Decath
Maryland.
THEY'RE IN THE MIDDLE OF A HEIST. I COULD CATCH 'EM ALL RED-HANDED. THIS IS AWESOME.
WOULD YOU LIKE ME TO ENGAGE ENHANCED COMBAT MODE?
"ENHANCED COMBAT MODE"? UH, YEAH, THAT'S AWESOME.
NO OUTGOING DISTRESS SIGNALS, BOSS. YOU'RE ALL CLEAR.
LOOKS LIKE THEY GOT SOME GOOD STUFF HERE. ALL RIGHT, COMIN' UP.
I THOUGHT YOU SAID ALL CLEAR?!

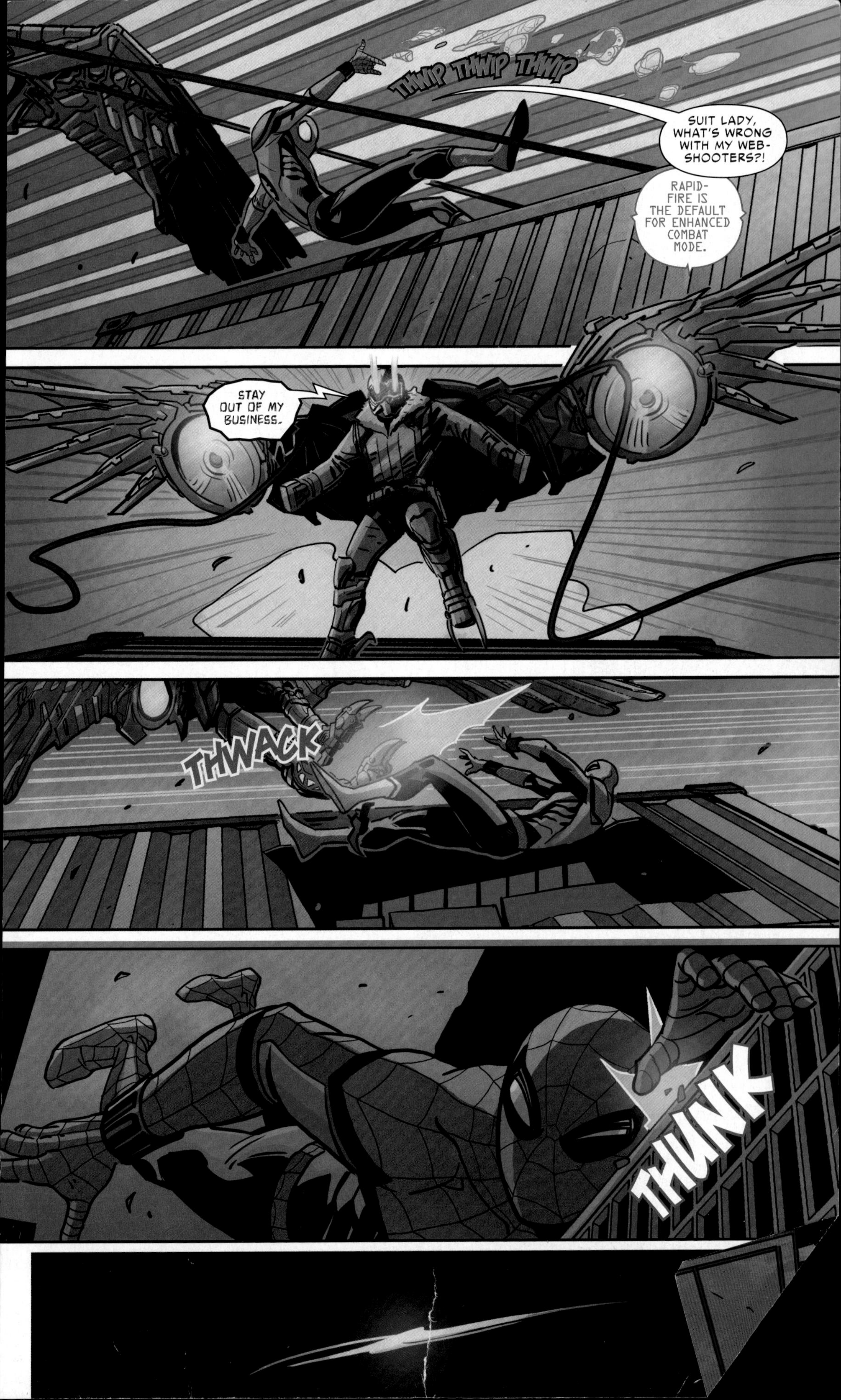
THWIP THWIP THWIP
SUIT LADY, WHAT'S WRONG WITH MY WEB-SHOOTERS?!
RAPID-FIRE IS THE DEFAULT FOR ENHANCED COMBAT MODE.
STAY OUT OF MY BUSINESS.
THWACK
THUNK

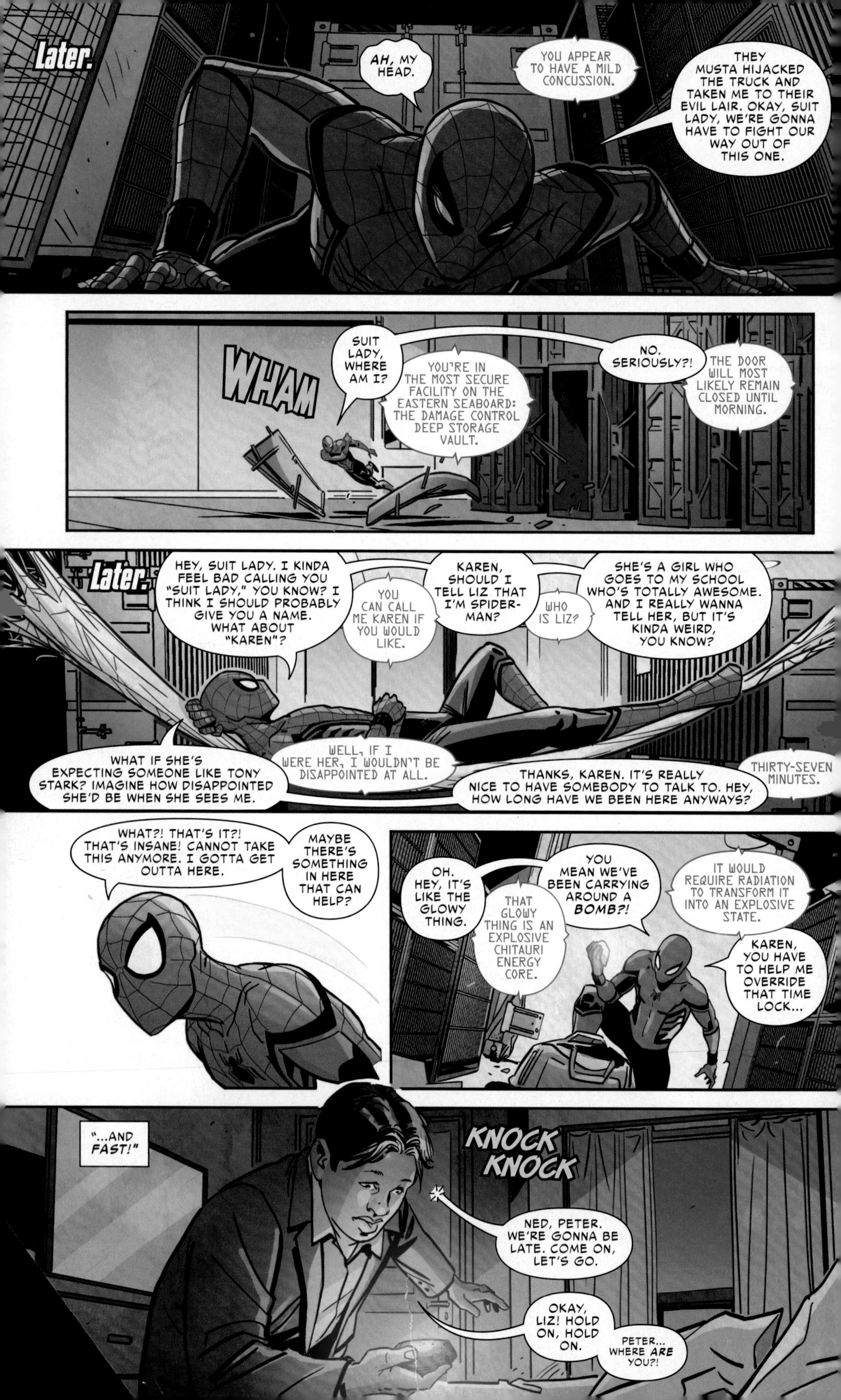
Later.
AH, MY HEAD.
YOU APPEAR TO HAVE A MILD CONCUSSION.
THEY MUSTA HIJACKED THE TRUCK AND TAKEN ME TO THEIR EVIL LAIR. OKAY, SUIT LADY, WE'RE GONNA HAVE TO FIGHT OUR WAY OUT OF THIS ONE.
WHAM
SUIT LADY, WHERE AM I?
YOU'RE IN THE MOST SECURE FACILITY ON THE EASTERN SEABOARD: THE DAMAGE CONTROL DEEP STORAGE VAULT.
NO. SERIOUSLY?!
THE DOOR WILL MOST LIKELY REMAIN CLOSED UNTIL MORNING.
Later.
HEY, SUIT LADY. I KINDA FEEL BAD CALLING YOU "SUIT LADY," YOU KNOW? I THINK I SHOULD PROBABLY GIVE YOU A NAME. WHAT ABOUT "KAREN"?
YOU CAN CALL ME KAREN IF YOU WOULD LIKE.
KAREN, SHOULD I TELL LIZ THAT I'M SPIDER-MAN?
WHO IS LIZ?
SHE'S A GIRL WHO GOES TO MY SCHOOL WHO'S TOTALLY AWESOME. AND I REALLY WANNA TELL HER, BUT IT'S KINDA WEIRD, YOU KNOW?
WHAT IF SHE'S EXPECTING SOMEONE LIKE TONY STARK? IMAGINE HOW DISAPPOINTED SHE'D BE WHEN SHE SEES ME.
WELL, IF I WERE HER, I WOULDN'T BE DISAPPOINTED AT ALL.
THANKS, KAREN. IT'S REALLY NICE TO HAVE SOMEBODY TO TALK TO. HEY, HOW LONG HAVE WE BEEN HERE ANYWAYS?
THIRTY-SEVEN MINUTES.
WHAT?! THAT'S IT?! THAT'S INSANE! CANNOT TAKE THIS ANYMORE. I GOTTA GET OUTTA HERE.
MAYBE THERE'S SOMETHING IN HERE THAT CAN HELP?
OH. HEY, IT'S LIKE THE GLOWY THING.
THAT GLOWY THING IS AN EXPLOSIVE CHITAURI ENERGY CORE.
YOU MEAN WE'VE BEEN CARRYING AROUND A BOMB?!
IT WOULD REQUIRE RADIATION TO TRANSFORM IT INTO AN EXPLOSIVE STATE.
KAREN, YOU HAVE TO HELP ME OVERRIDE THAT TIME LOCK...
"...AND FAST!"
KNOCK KNOCK
NED, PETER. WE'RE GONNA BE LATE. COME ON, LET'S GO.
OKAY, LIZ! HOLD ON, HOLD ON.
PETER... WHERE ARE YOU?!

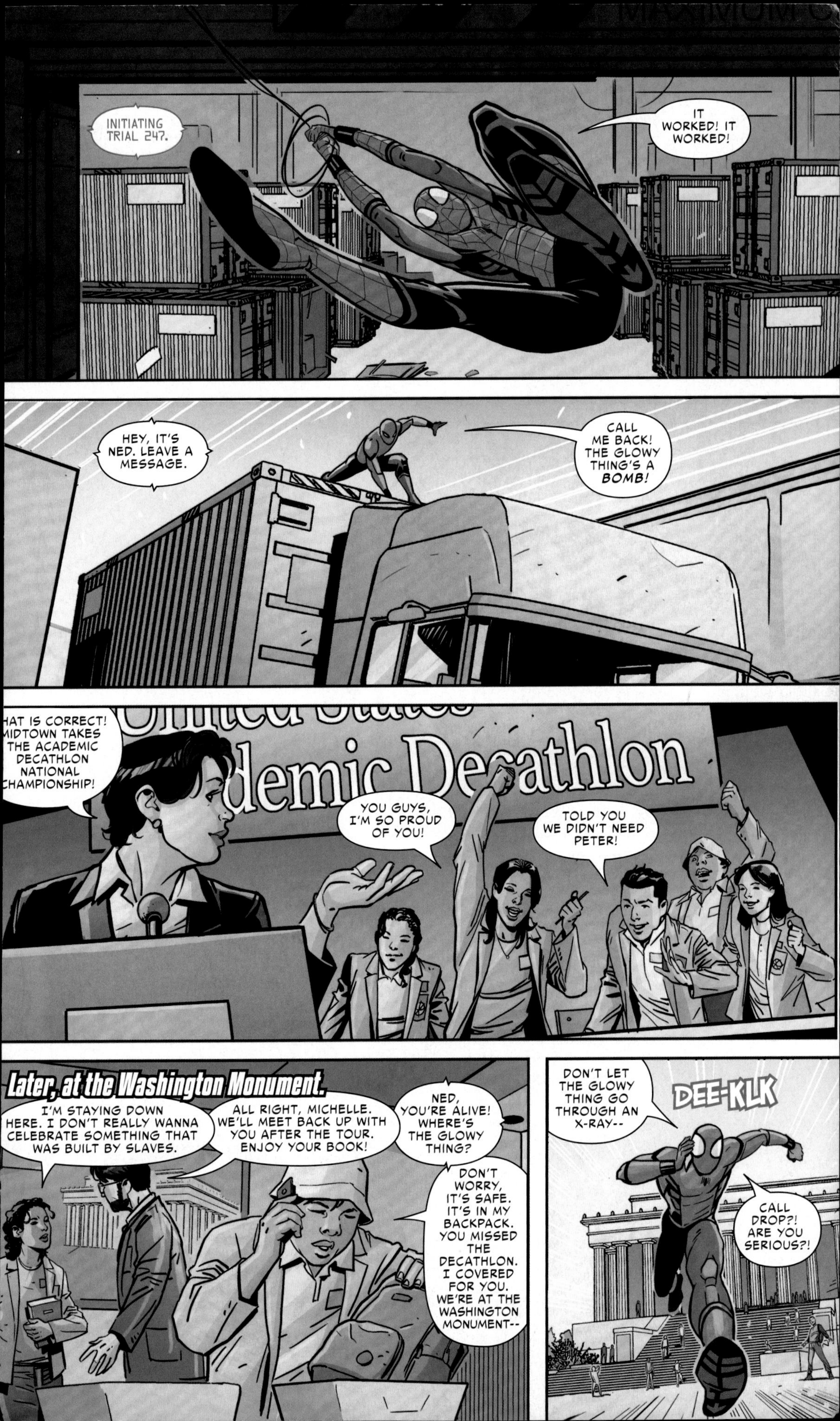

INITIATING TRIAL 247.
IT WORKED! IT WORKED!
HEY, IT'S NED. LEAVE A MESSAGE.
CALL ME BACK! THE GLOWY THING'S A *BOMB!*
HAT IS CORRECT! MIDTOWN TAKES THE ACADEMIC DECATHLON NATIONAL CHAMPIONSHIP!
YOU GUYS, I'M SO PROUD OF YOU!
TOLD YOU WE DIDN'T NEED PETER!
Later, at the Washington Monument.
I'M STAYING DOWN HERE. I DON'T REALLY WANNA CELEBRATE SOMETHING THAT WAS BUILT BY SLAVES.
ALL RIGHT, MICHELLE. WE'LL MEET BACK UP WITH YOU AFTER THE TOUR. ENJOY YOUR BOOK!
NED, YOU'RE ALIVE! WHERE'S THE GLOWY THING?
DON'T WORRY, IT'S SAFE. IT'S IN MY BACKPACK. YOU MISSED THE DECATHLON. I COVERED FOR YOU. WE'RE AT THE WASHINGTON MONUMENT--
DON'T LET THE GLOWY THING GO THROUGH AN X-RAY--
DEE-KLK
CALL DROP?! ARE YOU SERIOUS?!

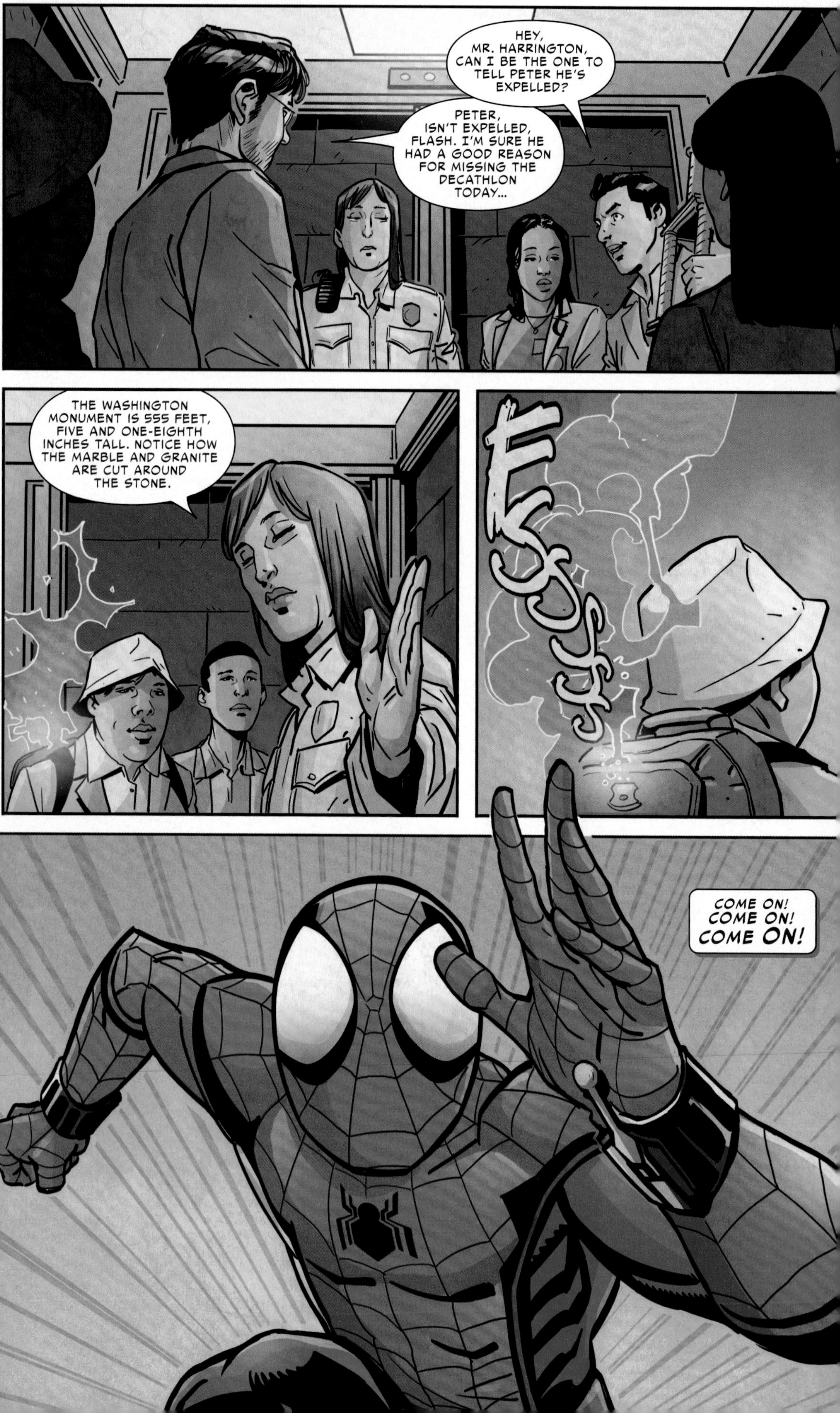
HEY, MR. HARRINGTON, CAN I BE THE ONE TO TELL PETER HE'S EXPELLED?
PETER, ISN'T EXPELLED, FLASH. I'M SURE HE HAD A GOOD REASON FOR MISSING THE DECATHLON TODAY...
THE WASHINGTON MONUMENT IS 555 FEET, FIVE AND ONE-EIGHTH INCHES TALL. NOTICE HOW THE MARBLE AND GRANITE ARE CUT AROUND THE STONE.
TSSSSS
COME ON! COME ON! COME ON!

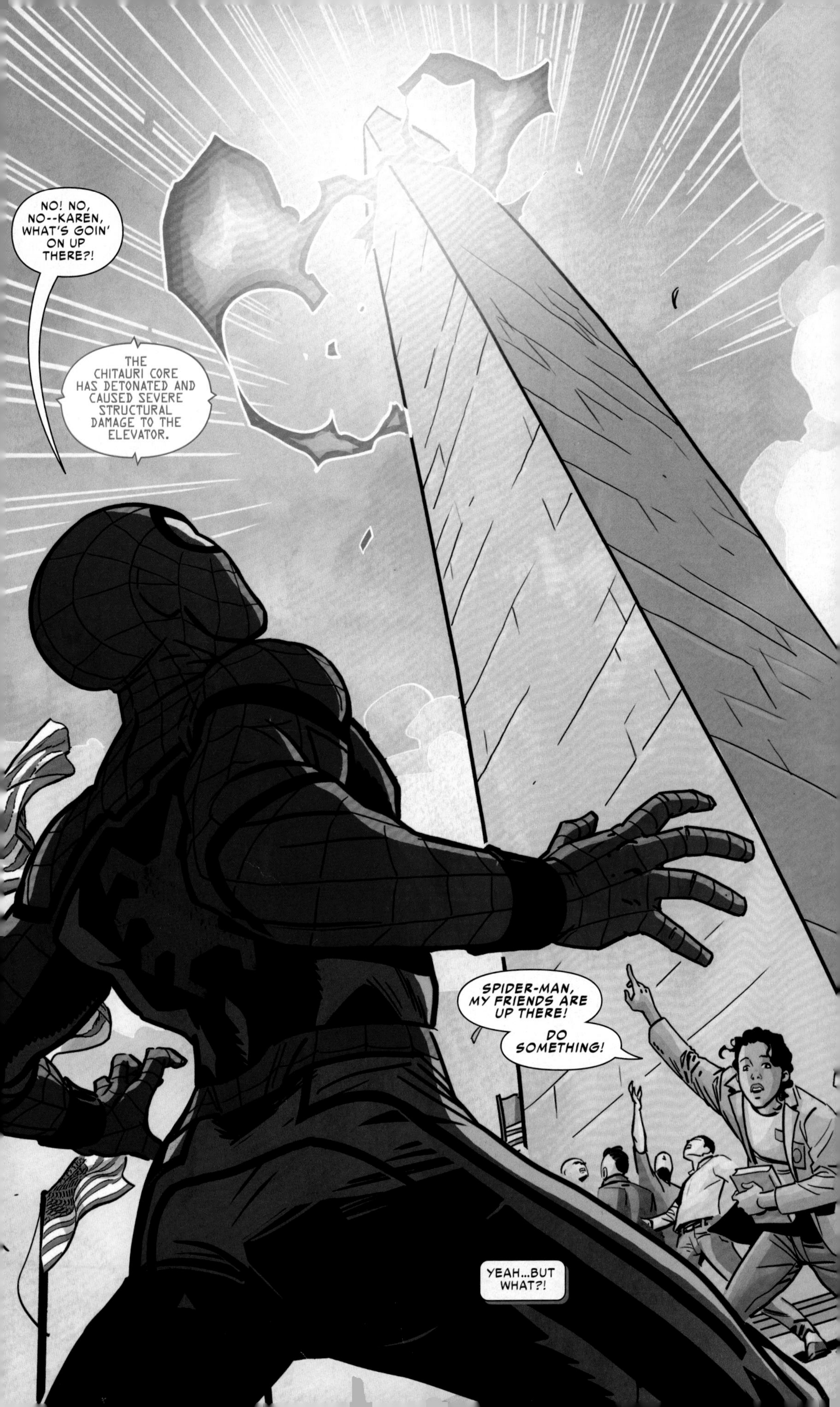

NO! NO, NO--KAREN, WHAT'S GOIN' ON UP THERE?!
THE CHITAURI CORE HAS DETONATED AND CAUSED SEVERE STRUCTURAL DAMAGE TO THE ELEVATOR.
SPIDER-MAN, MY FRIENDS ARE UP THERE!
DO SOMETHING!
YEAH...BUT WHAT?!

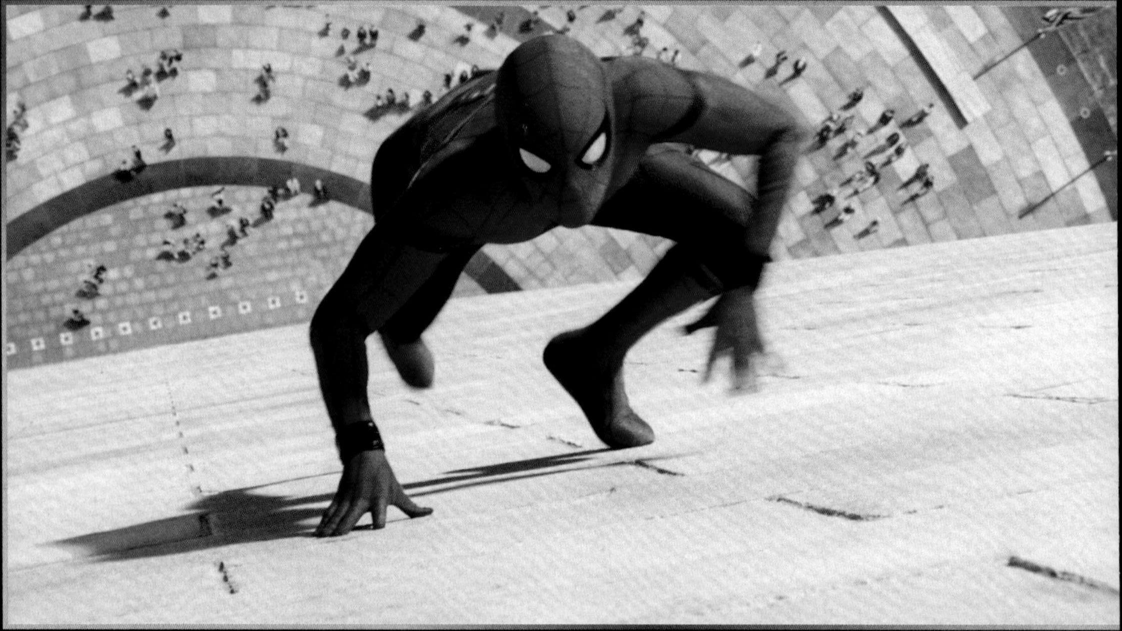

SPIDER-MAN: FAR FROM HOME PRELUDE #2

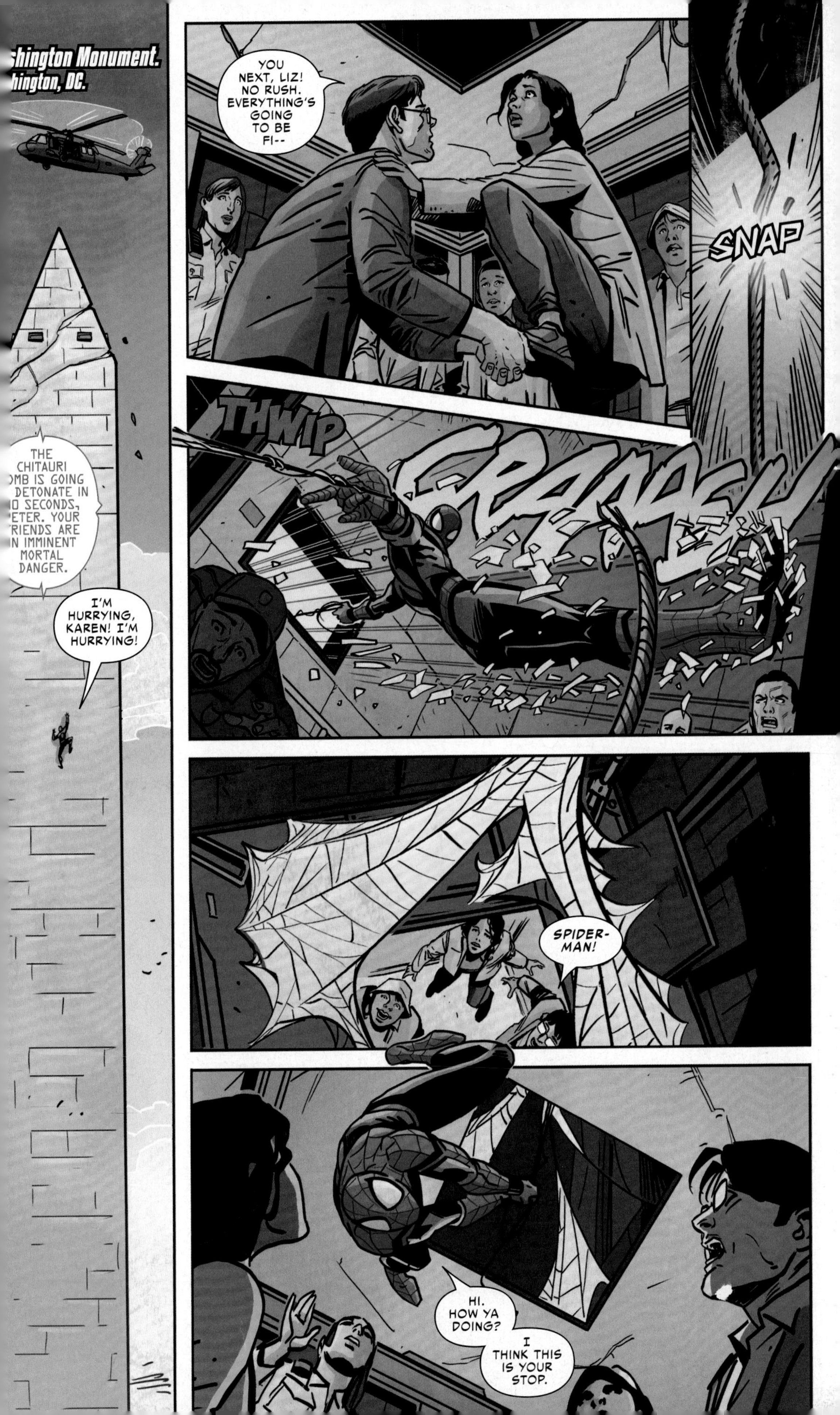
shington Monument.
shington, DC.
THE CHITAURI OMB IS GOING DETONATE IN 0 SECONDS, ETER. YOUR RIENDS ARE N IMMINENT MORTAL DANGER.
I'M HURRYING, KAREN! I'M HURRYING!
YOU NEXT, LIZ! NO RUSH. EVERYTHING'S GOING TO BE FI--
SNAP
THWIP
SPIDER-MAN!
HI. HOW YA DOING?
I THINK THIS IS YOUR STOP.

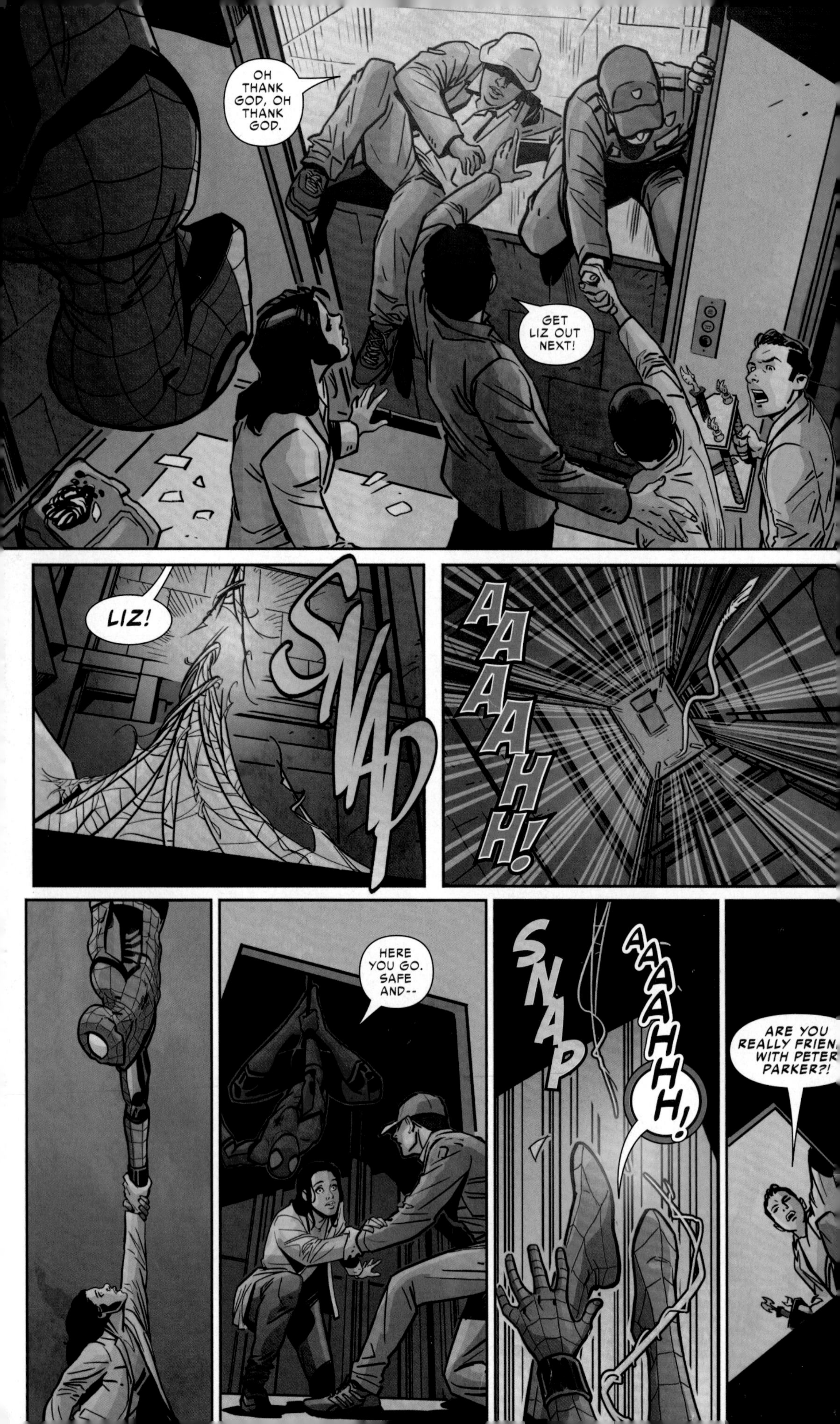
OH THANK GOD, OH THANK GOD.
GET LIZ OUT NEXT!
LIZ!
SNAP
AAAAAHH!
HERE YOU GO. SAFE AND--
SNAP
AAAAHHH!
ARE YOU REALLY FRIEN WITH PETER PARKER?!

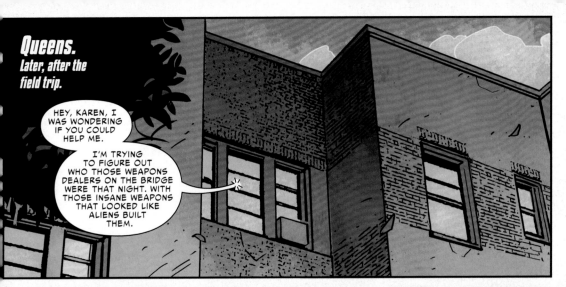

Queens.
Later, after the field trip.

HEY, KAREN, I WAS WONDERING IF YOU COULD HELP ME.

I'M TRYING TO FIGURE OUT WHO THOSE WEAPONS DEALERS ON THE BRIDGE WERE THAT NIGHT. WITH THOSE INSANE WEAPONS THAT LOOKED LIKE ALIENS BUILT THEM.

I CAN RUN FACIAL RECOGNITION ON THE FOOTAGE OF THAT ENCOUNTER.

FOOTAGE?

I RECORD EVERYTHING YOU SEE. IT'S CALLED THE BABY MONITOR PROTOCOL.

YEAH, OF COURSE MR. STARK WOULD CALL IT THAT. JUST ROLL IT BACK TO LAST FRIDAY.

OKAY, THE TWO ON THE RIGHT. WHO ARE THEY?

SEARCHING LAW ENFORCEMENT DATABASE. NO RECORDS FOUND FOR TWO OF THE INDIVIDUALS.

NOTHING?

WHAT ABOUT THE OTHER GUY?

AARON DAVIS, AGE 33. HE HAS A CRIMINAL RECORD. AND AN ADDRESS HERE IN QUEENS.

LET'S PAY HIM A VISIT AND SEE IF HE CAN TELL US WHERE THE WINGED GUY IS...

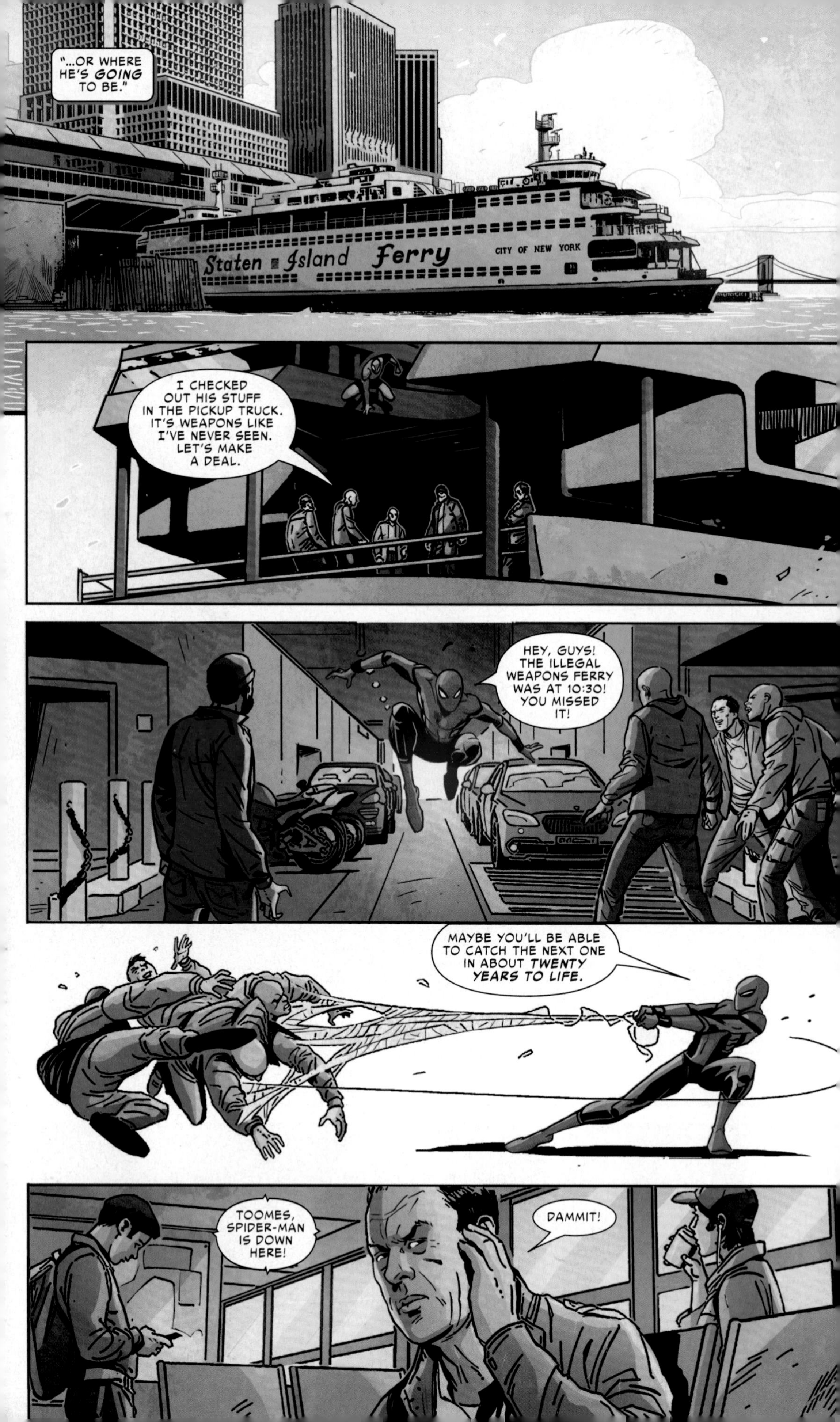
"...OR WHERE HE'S *GOING* TO BE."
Staten Island Ferry
CITY OF NEW YORK
I CHECKED OUT HIS STUFF IN THE PICKUP TRUCK. IT'S WEAPONS LIKE I'VE NEVER SEEN. LET'S MAKE A DEAL.
HEY, GUYS! THE ILLEGAL WEAPONS FERRY WAS AT 10:30! YOU MISSED IT!
MAYBE YOU'LL BE ABLE TO CATCH THE NEXT ONE IN ABOUT *TWENTY YEARS TO LIFE.*
TOOMES, SPIDER-MAN IS DOWN HERE!
DAMMIT!

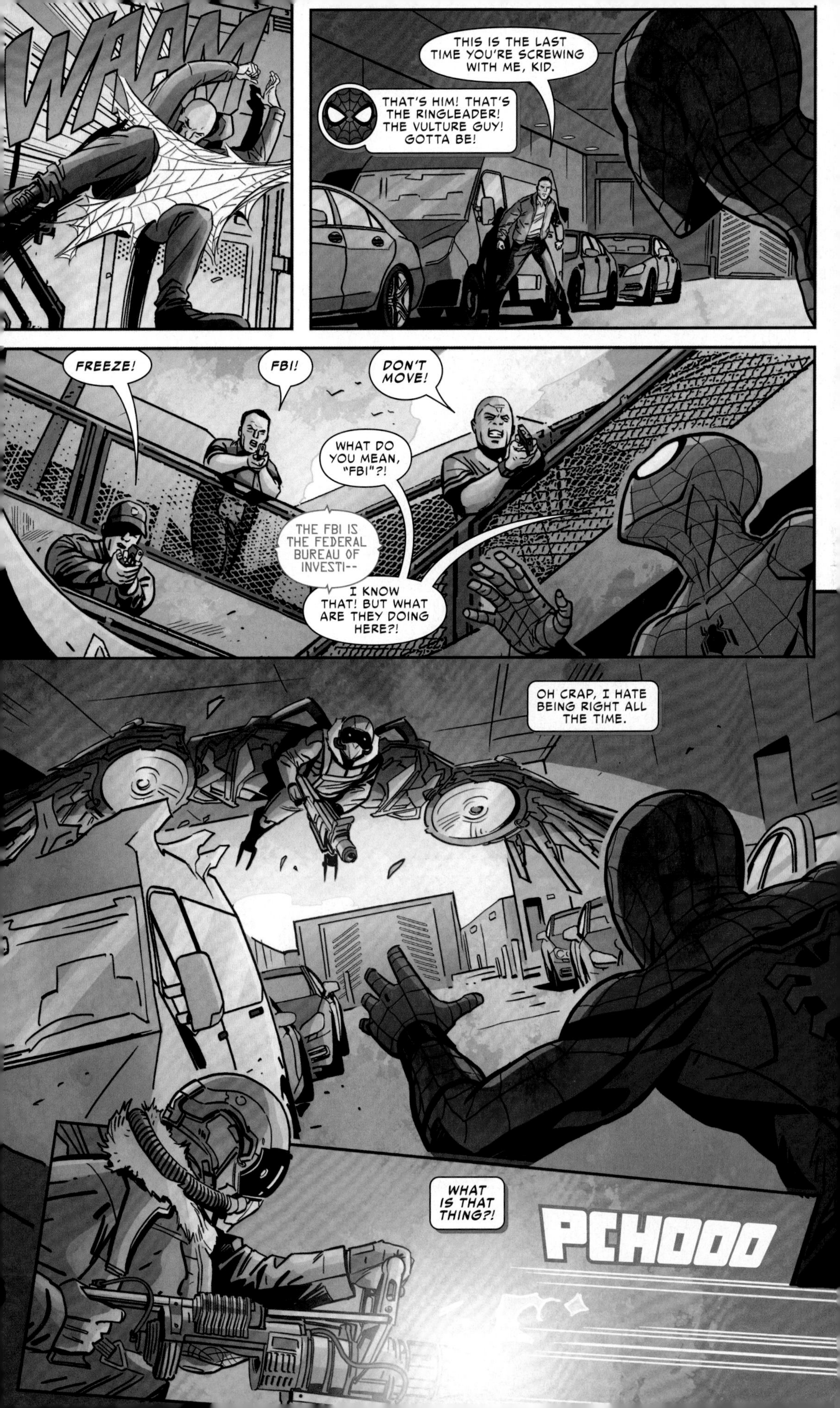

WAAM
THIS IS THE LAST TIME YOU'RE SCREWING WITH ME, KID.
THAT'S HIM! THAT'S THE RINGLEADER! THE VULTURE GUY! GOTTA BE!
FREEZE!
FBI!
DON'T MOVE!
WHAT DO YOU MEAN, "FBI"?!
THE FBI IS THE FEDERAL BUREAU OF INVESTI--
I KNOW THAT! BUT WHAT ARE THEY DOING HERE?!
OH CRAP, I HATE BEING RIGHT ALL THE TIME.
WHAT IS THAT THING?!
PCHOOO

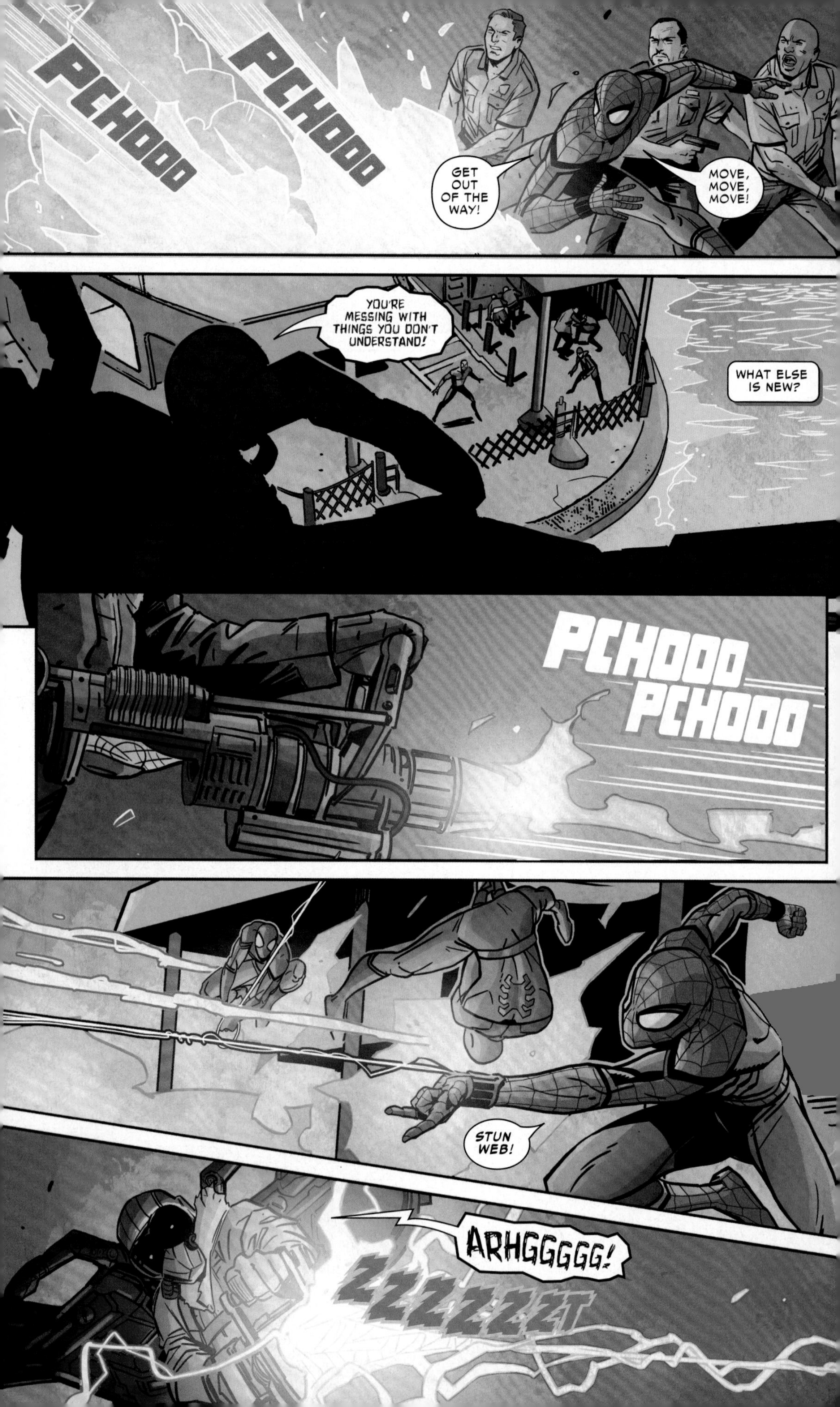
PCHOOO
PCHOOO
GET OUT OF THE WAY!
MOVE, MOVE, MOVE!
YOU'RE MESSING WITH THINGS YOU DON'T UNDERSTAND!
WHAT ELSE IS NEW?
PCHOOO
PCHOOO
STUN WEB!
ARHGGGGG!
ZZZZZZT

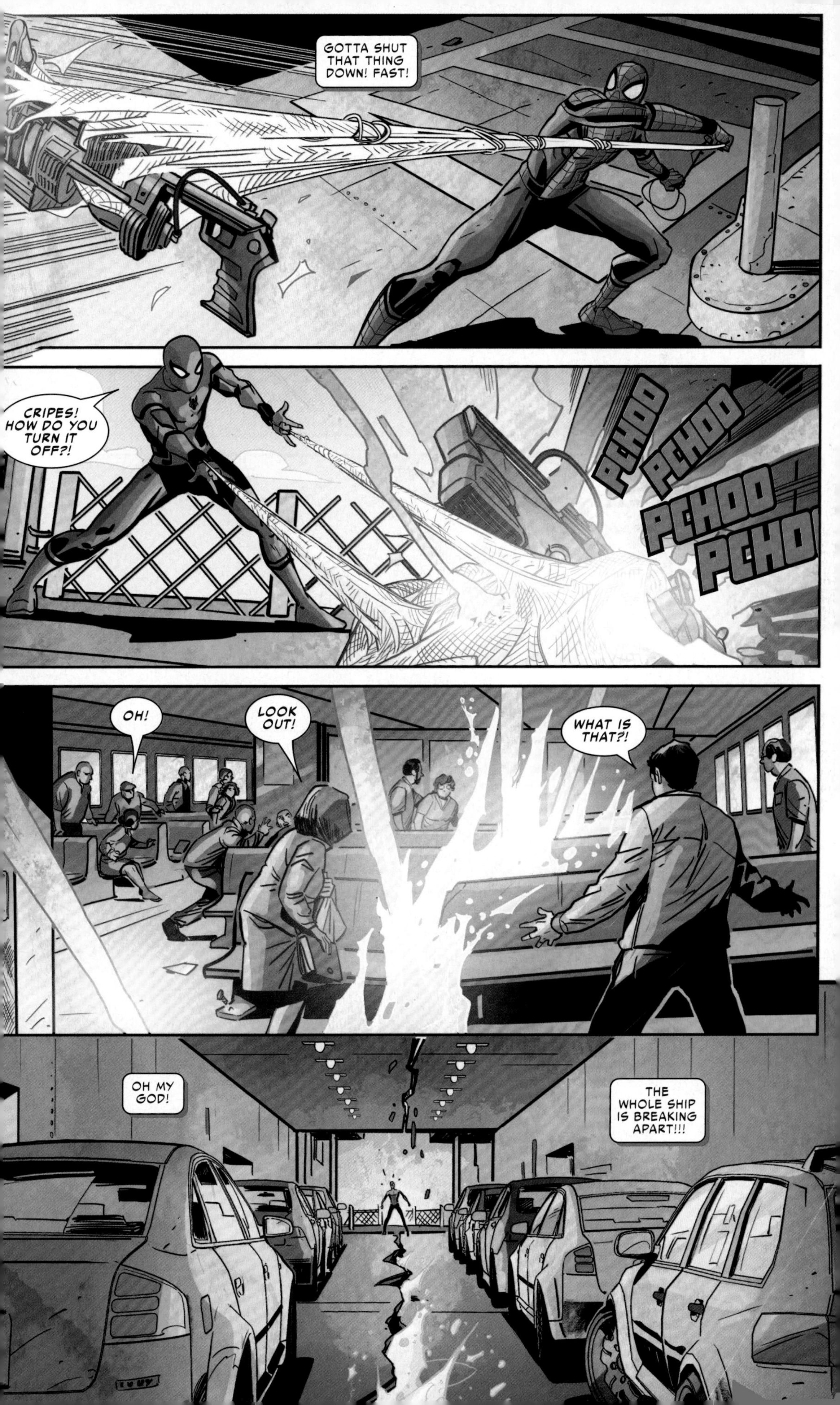
GOTTA SHUT THAT THING DOWN! FAST!
CRIPES! HOW DO YOU TURN IT OFF?!
PCHOO
PCHOO
PCHOO
PCHOO
OH!
LOOK OUT!
WHAT IS THAT?!
OH MY GOD!
THE WHOLE SHIP IS BREAKING APART!!!

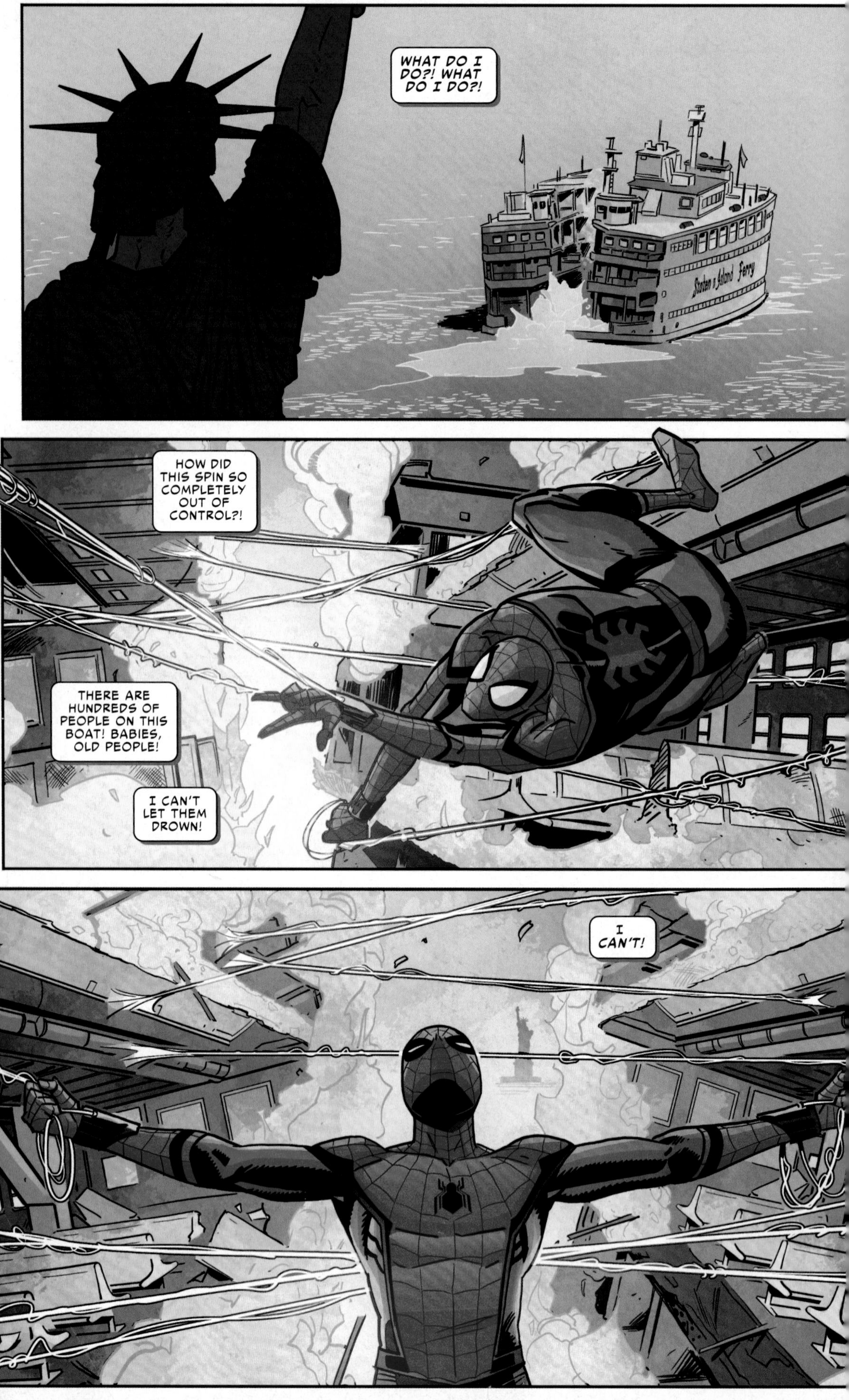
WHAT DO I DO?! WHAT DO I DO?!
Staten Island Ferry
HOW DID THIS SPIN SO COMPLETELY OUT OF CONTROL?!
THERE ARE HUNDREDS OF PEOPLE ON THIS BOAT! BABIES, OLD PEOPLE!
I CAN'T LET THEM DROWN!
I CAN'T!

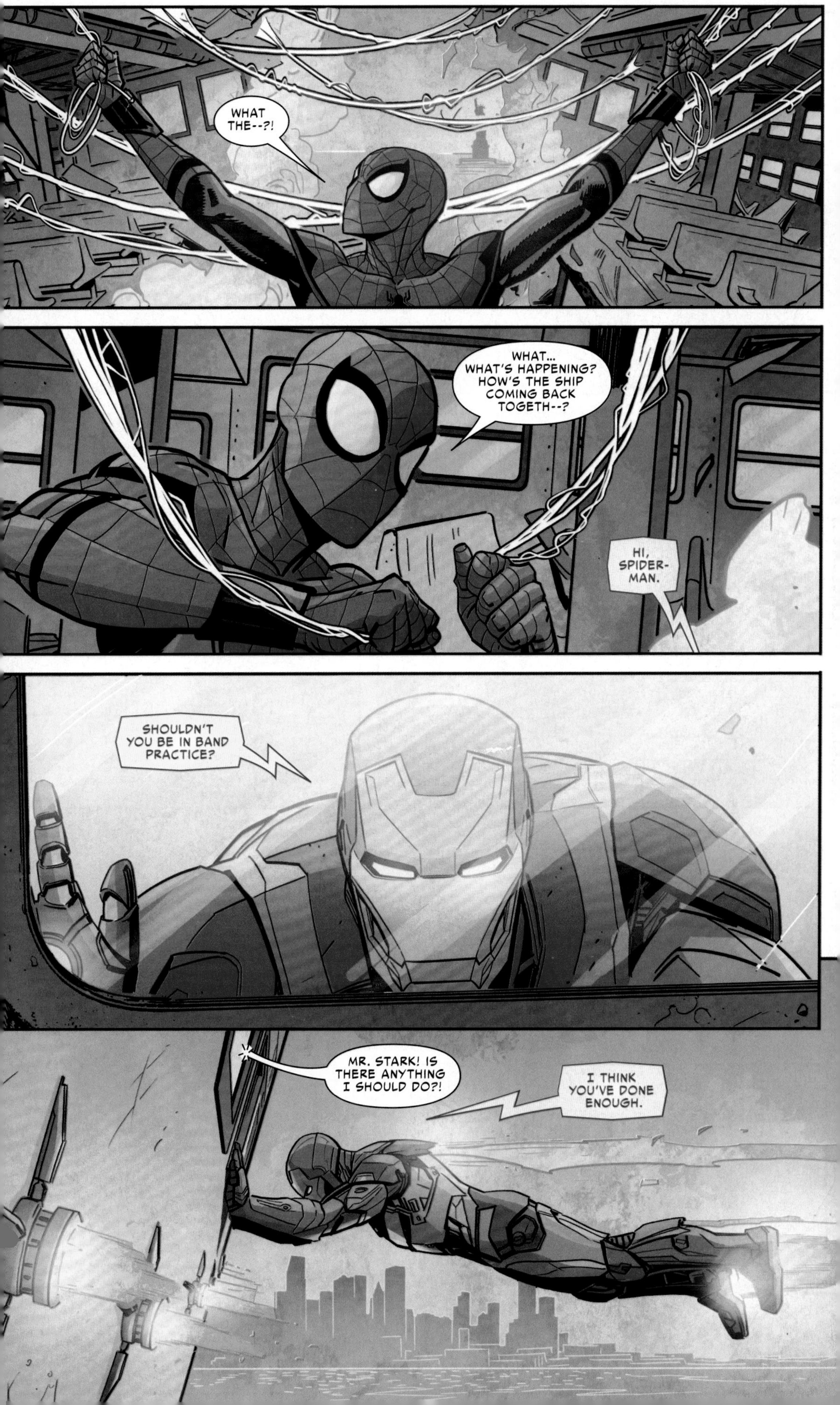
WHAT THE--?!
WHAT... WHAT'S HAPPENING? HOW'S THE SHIP COMING BACK TOGETH--?
HI, SPIDER-MAN.
SHOULDN'T YOU BE IN BAND PRACTICE?
MR. STARK! IS THERE ANYTHING I SHOULD DO?!
I THINK YOU'VE DONE ENOUGH.

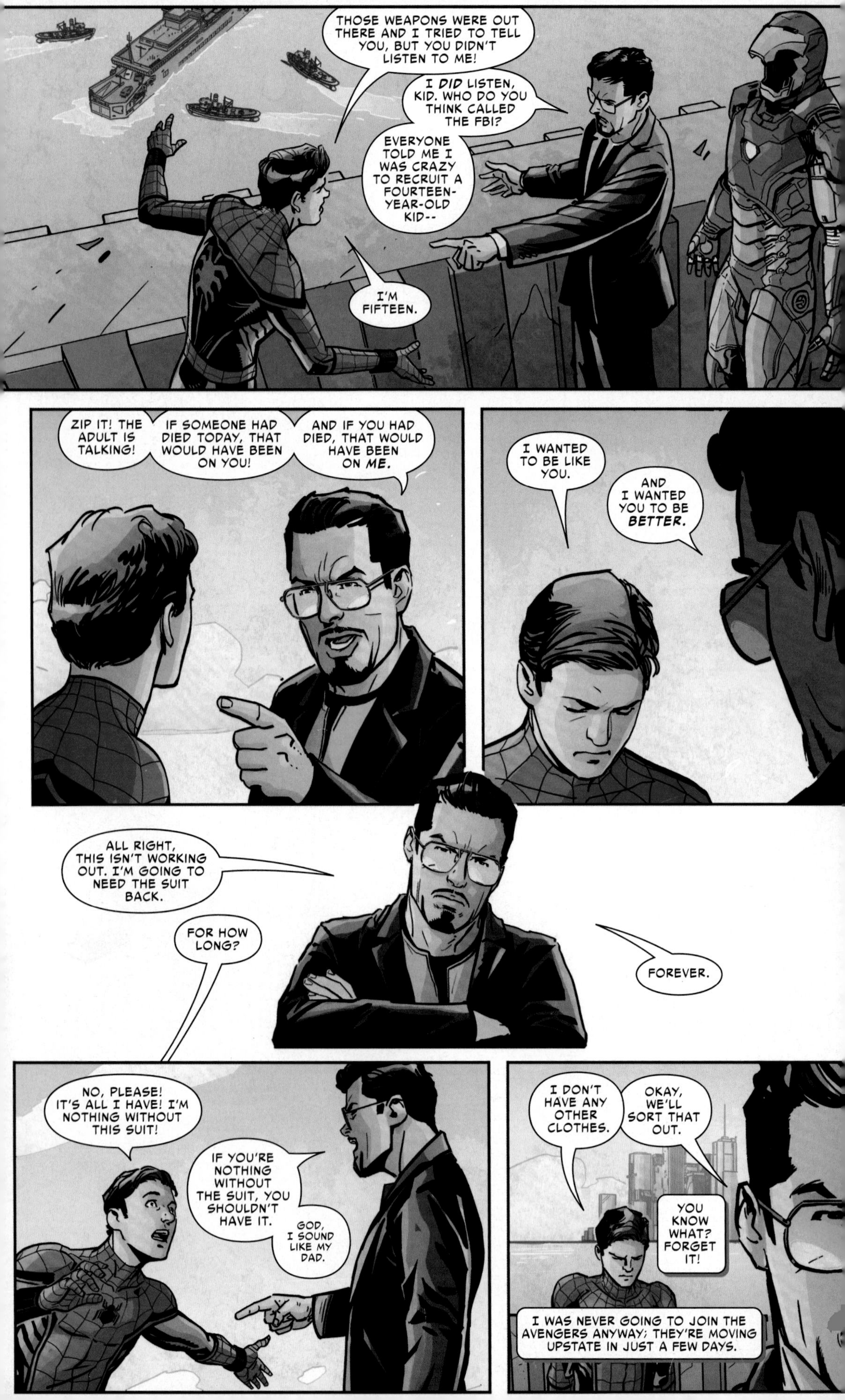
THOSE WEAPONS WERE OUT THERE AND I TRIED TO TELL YOU, BUT YOU DIDN'T LISTEN TO ME!
I *DID* LISTEN, KID. WHO DO YOU THINK CALLED THE FBI?
EVERYONE TOLD ME I WAS CRAZY TO RECRUIT A FOURTEEN-YEAR-OLD KID--
I'M FIFTEEN.
ZIP IT! THE ADULT IS TALKING!
IF SOMEONE HAD DIED TODAY, THAT WOULD HAVE BEEN ON YOU!
AND IF YOU HAD DIED, THAT WOULD HAVE BEEN ON *ME.*
I WANTED TO BE LIKE YOU.
AND I WANTED YOU TO BE *BETTER.*
ALL RIGHT, THIS ISN'T WORKING OUT. I'M GOING TO NEED THE SUIT BACK.
FOR HOW LONG?
FOREVER.
NO, PLEASE! IT'S ALL I HAVE! I'M NOTHING WITHOUT THIS SUIT!
IF YOU'RE NOTHING WITHOUT THE SUIT, YOU SHOULDN'T HAVE IT.
GOD, I SOUND LIKE MY DAD.
I DON'T HAVE ANY OTHER CLOTHES.
OKAY, WE'LL SORT THAT OUT.
YOU KNOW WHAT? FORGET IT!
I WAS NEVER GOING TO JOIN THE AVENGERS ANYWAY; THEY'RE MOVING UPSTATE IN JUST A FEW DAYS.

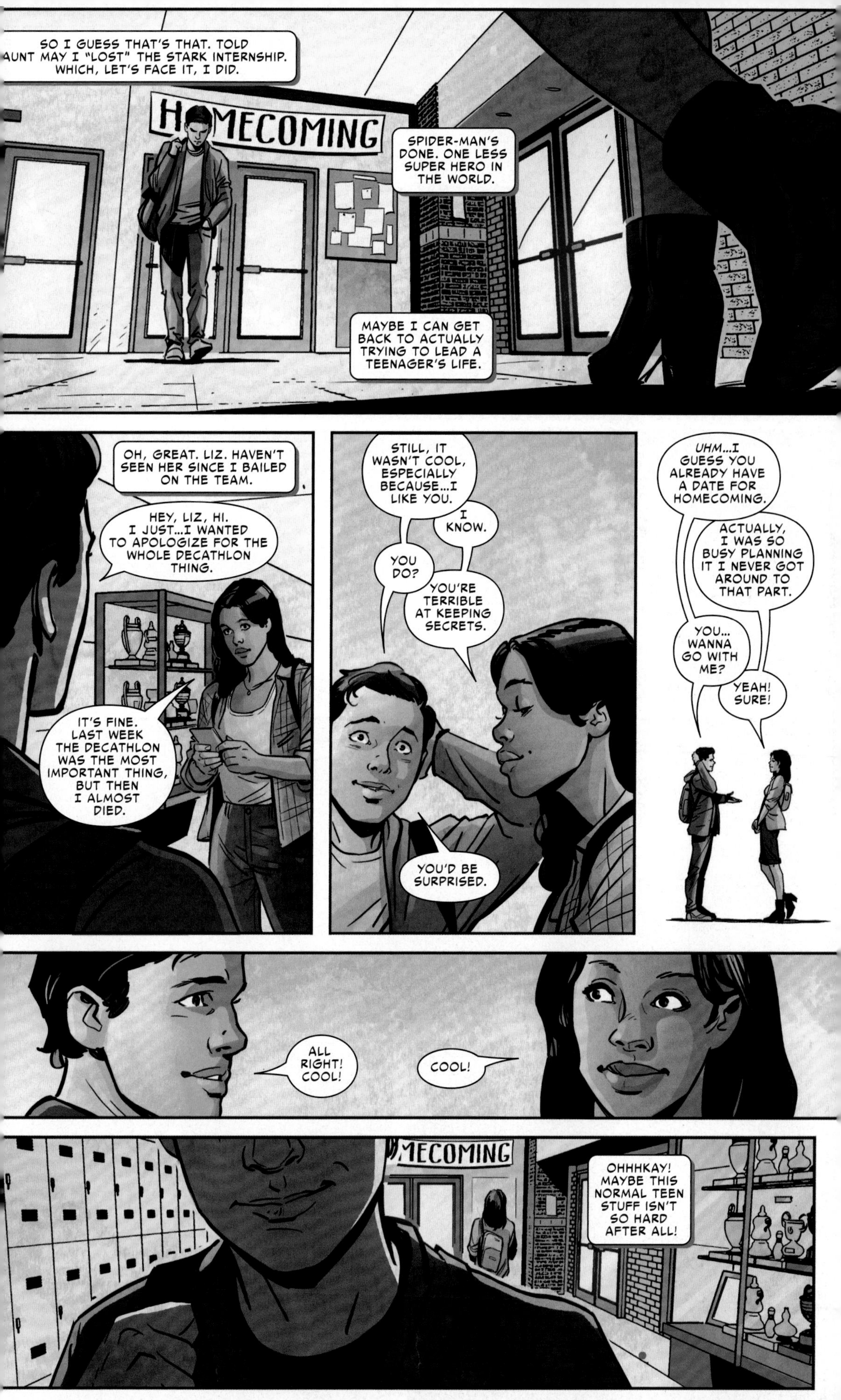
SO I GUESS THAT'S THAT. TOLD AUNT MAY I "LOST" THE STARK INTERNSHIP. WHICH, LET'S FACE IT, I DID.
HOMECOMING
SPIDER-MAN'S DONE. ONE LESS SUPER HERO IN THE WORLD.
MAYBE I CAN GET BACK TO ACTUALLY TRYING TO LEAD A TEENAGER'S LIFE.
OH, GREAT. LIZ. HAVEN'T SEEN HER SINCE I BAILED ON THE TEAM.
HEY, LIZ, HI. I JUST...I WANTED TO APOLOGIZE FOR THE WHOLE DECATHLON THING.
IT'S FINE. LAST WEEK THE DECATHLON WAS THE MOST IMPORTANT THING, BUT THEN I ALMOST DIED.
STILL, IT WASN'T COOL, ESPECIALLY BECAUSE...I LIKE YOU.
I KNOW.
YOU DO?
YOU'RE TERRIBLE AT KEEPING SECRETS.
YOU'D BE SURPRISED.
UHM...I GUESS YOU ALREADY HAVE A DATE FOR HOMECOMING.
ACTUALLY, I WAS SO BUSY PLANNING IT I NEVER GOT AROUND TO THAT PART.
YOU... WANNA GO WITH ME?
YEAH! SURE!
ALL RIGHT! COOL!
COOL!
MECOMING
OHHHKAY! MAYBE THIS NORMAL TEEN STUFF ISN'T SO HARD AFTER ALL!

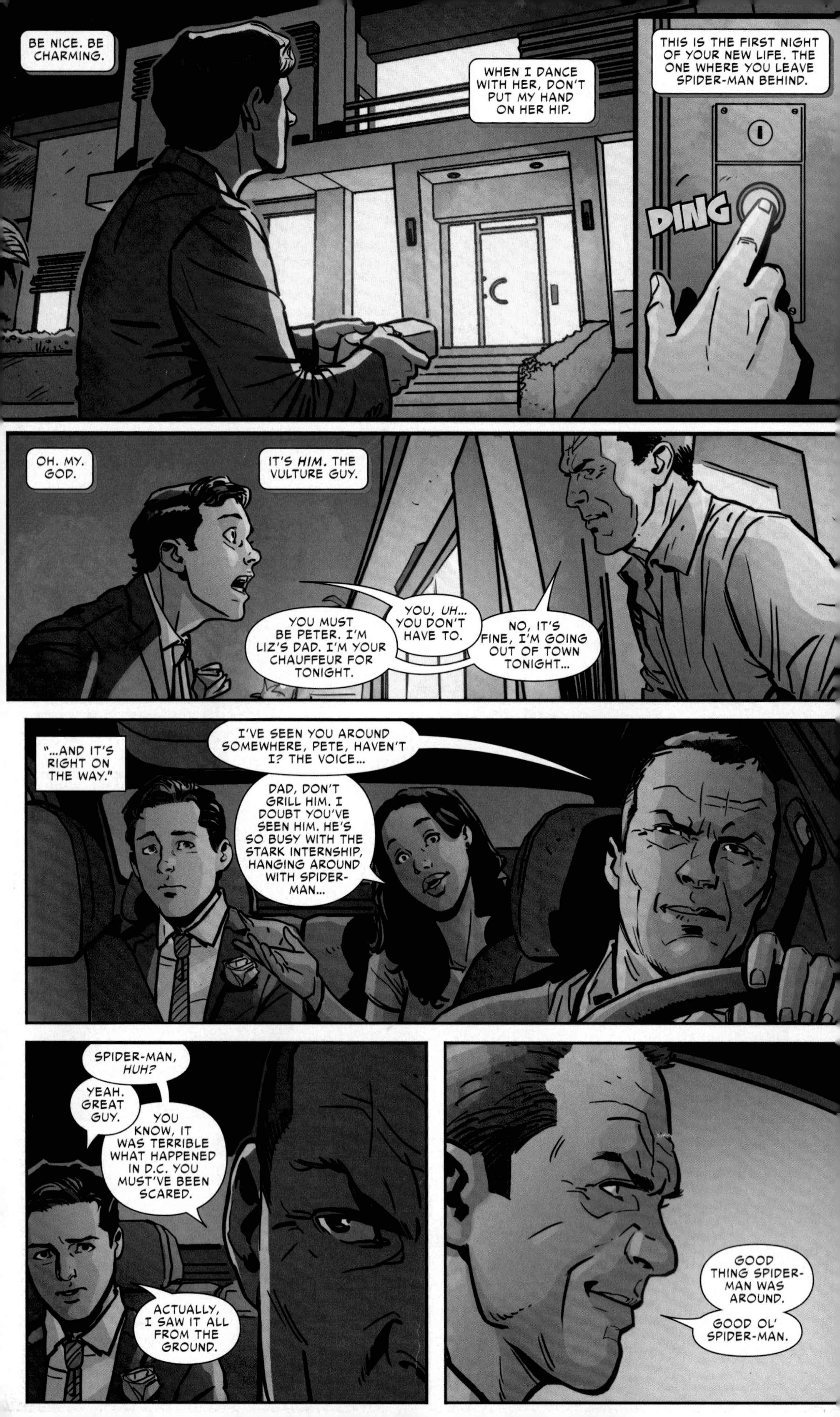
BE NICE. BE CHARMING.
WHEN I DANCE WITH HER, DON'T PUT MY HAND ON HER HIP.
THIS IS THE FIRST NIGHT OF YOUR NEW LIFE. THE ONE WHERE YOU LEAVE SPIDER-MAN BEHIND.
DING
OH. MY. GOD.
IT'S *HIM*. THE VULTURE GUY.
YOU MUST BE PETER. I'M LIZ'S DAD. I'M YOUR CHAUFFEUR FOR TONIGHT.
YOU, *UH*... YOU DON'T HAVE TO.
NO, IT'S FINE, I'M GOING OUT OF TOWN TONIGHT...
"...AND IT'S RIGHT ON THE WAY."
I'VE SEEN YOU AROUND SOMEWHERE, PETE, HAVEN'T I? THE VOICE...
DAD, DON'T GRILL HIM. I DOUBT YOU'VE SEEN HIM. HE'S SO BUSY WITH THE STARK INTERNSHIP, HANGING AROUND WITH SPIDER-MAN...
SPIDER-MAN, *HUH?*
YEAH. GREAT GUY.
YOU KNOW, IT WAS TERRIBLE WHAT HAPPENED IN D.C. YOU MUST'VE BEEN SCARED.
ACTUALLY, I SAW IT ALL FROM THE GROUND.
GOOD THING SPIDER-MAN WAS AROUND.
GOOD OL' SPIDER-MAN.

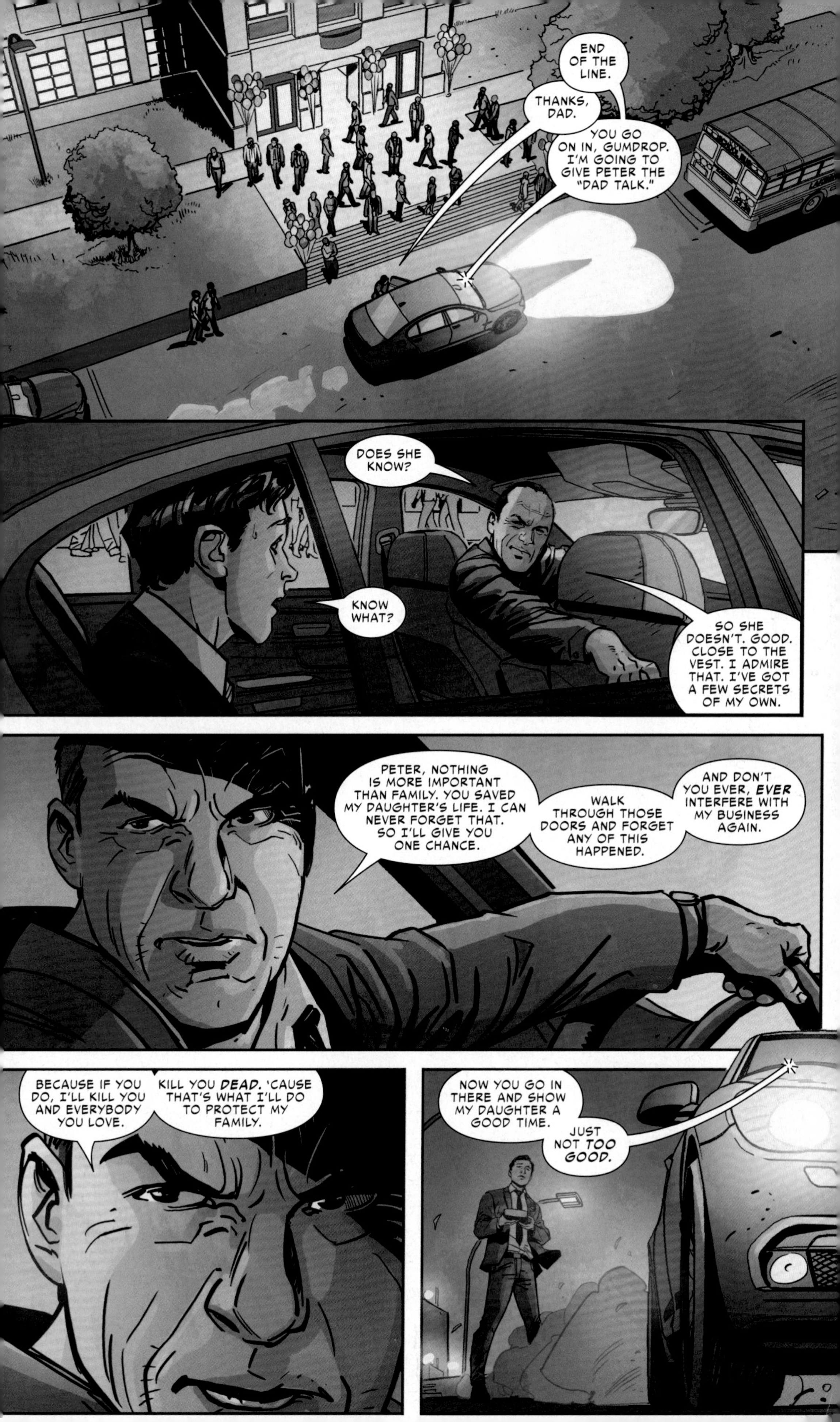
END OF THE LINE.
THANKS, DAD.
YOU GO ON IN, GUMDROP. I'M GOING TO GIVE PETER THE "DAD TALK."
DOES SHE KNOW?
KNOW WHAT?
SO SHE DOESN'T. GOOD. CLOSE TO THE VEST. I ADMIRE THAT. I'VE GOT A FEW SECRETS OF MY OWN.
PETER, NOTHING IS MORE IMPORTANT THAN FAMILY. YOU SAVED MY DAUGHTER'S LIFE. I CAN NEVER FORGET THAT. SO I'LL GIVE YOU ONE CHANCE.
WALK THROUGH THOSE DOORS AND FORGET ANY OF THIS HAPPENED.
AND DON'T YOU EVER, EVER INTERFERE WITH MY BUSINESS AGAIN.
BECAUSE IF YOU DO, I'LL KILL YOU AND EVERYBODY YOU LOVE.
KILL YOU DEAD. 'CAUSE THAT'S WHAT I'LL DO TO PROTECT MY FAMILY.
NOW YOU GO IN THERE AND SHOW MY DAUGHTER A GOOD TIME.
JUST NOT TOO GOOD.

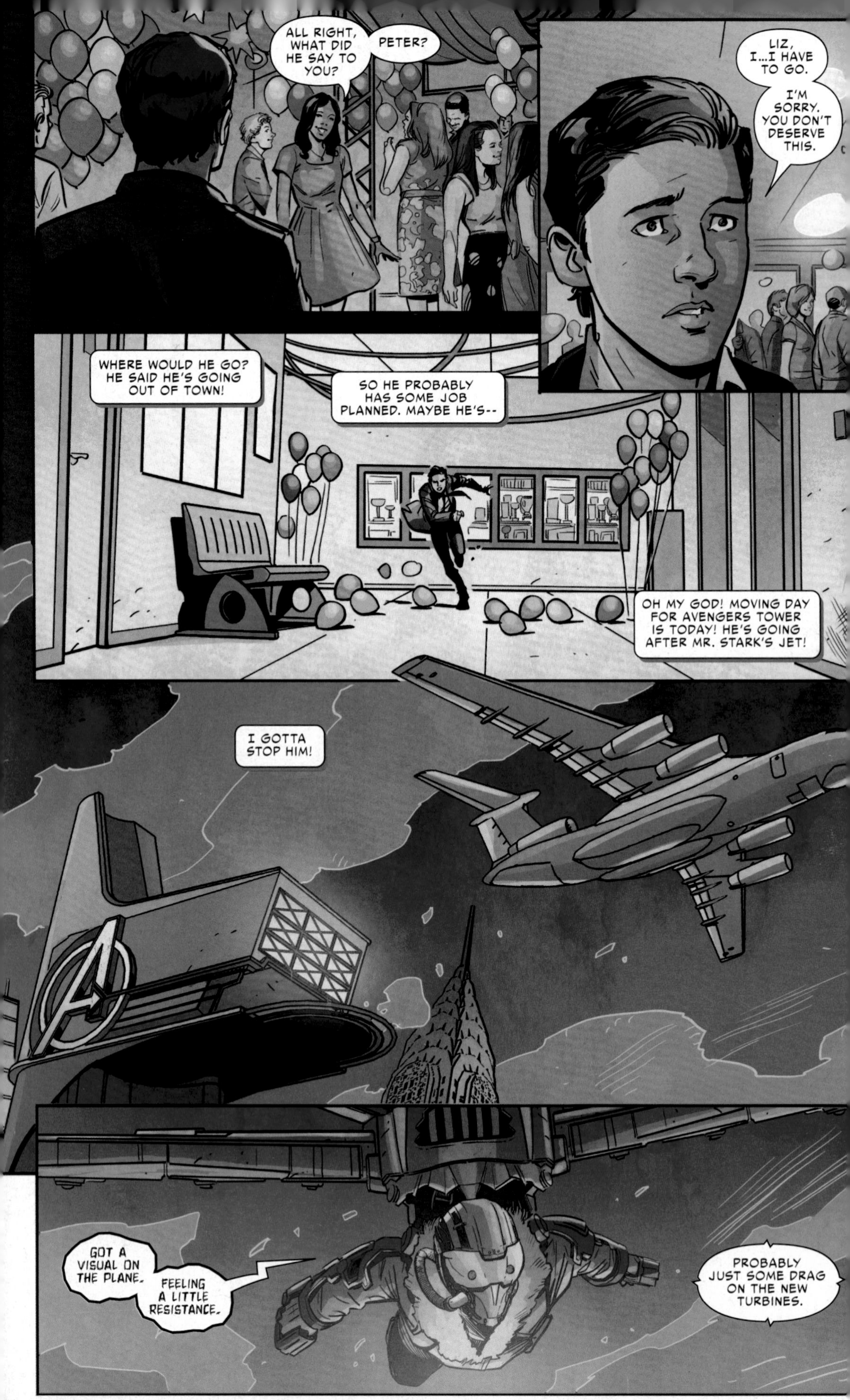
ALL RIGHT, WHAT DID HE SAY TO YOU?
PETER?
LIZ, I...I HAVE TO GO.
I'M SORRY. YOU DON'T DESERVE THIS.
WHERE WOULD HE GO? HE SAID HE'S GOING OUT OF TOWN!
SO HE PROBABLY HAS SOME JOB PLANNED. MAYBE HE'S--
OH MY GOD! MOVING DAY FOR AVENGERS TOWER IS TODAY! HE'S GOING AFTER MR. STARK'S JET!
I GOTTA STOP HIM!
GOT A VISUAL ON THE PLANE.
FEELING A LITTLE RESISTANCE.
PROBABLY JUST SOME DRAG ON THE NEW TURBINES.

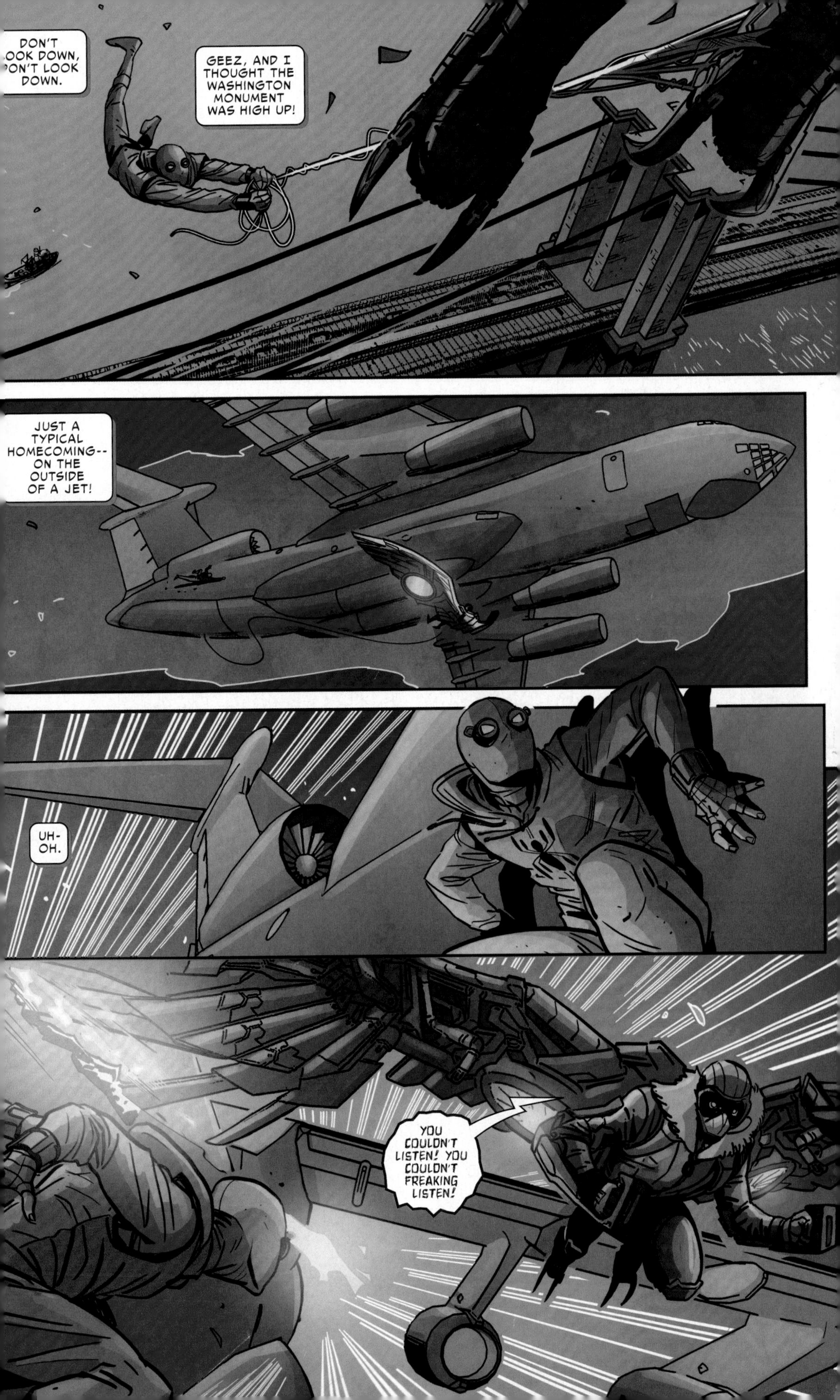
DON'T LOOK DOWN, DON'T LOOK DOWN.
GEEZ, AND I THOUGHT THE WASHINGTON MONUMENT WAS HIGH UP!
JUST A TYPICAL HOMECOMING-- ON THE OUTSIDE OF A JET!
UH- OH.
YOU COULDN'T LISTEN! YOU COULDN'T FREAKING LISTEN!

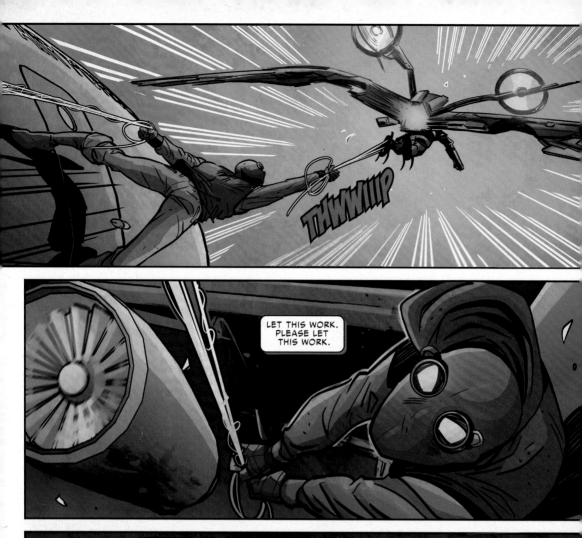

THWWIIIP

LET THIS WORK. PLEASE LET THIS WORK.

BAKOOOOM

OH MY GOD!

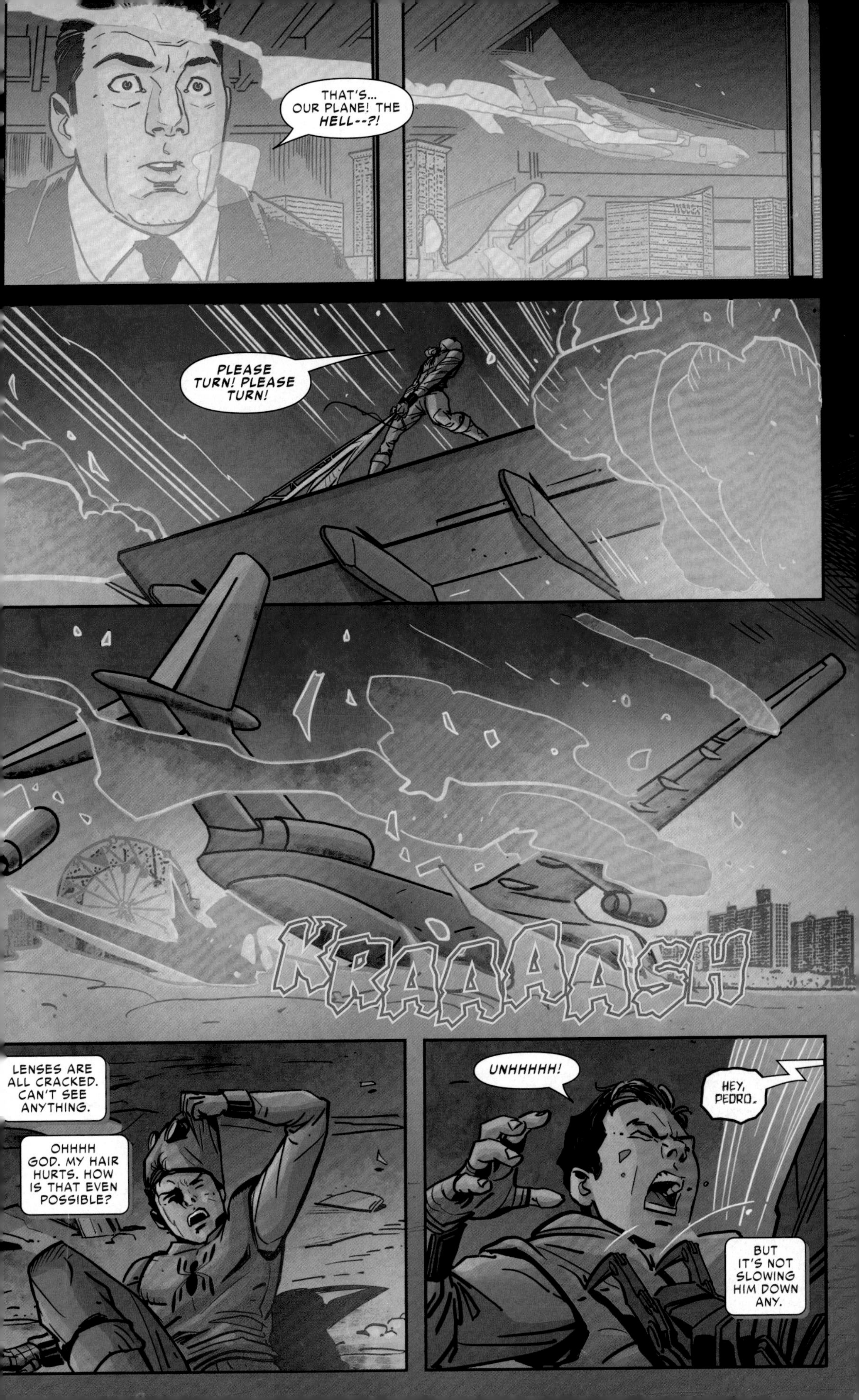
THAT'S... OUR PLANE! THE HELL--?!
PLEASE TURN! PLEASE TURN!
KRAAAASH
LENSES ARE ALL CRACKED. CAN'T SEE ANYTHING.
OHHHH GOD. MY HAIR HURTS. HOW IS THAT EVEN POSSIBLE?
UNHHHHH!
HEY, PEDRO.
BUT IT'S NOT SLOWING HIM DOWN ANY.

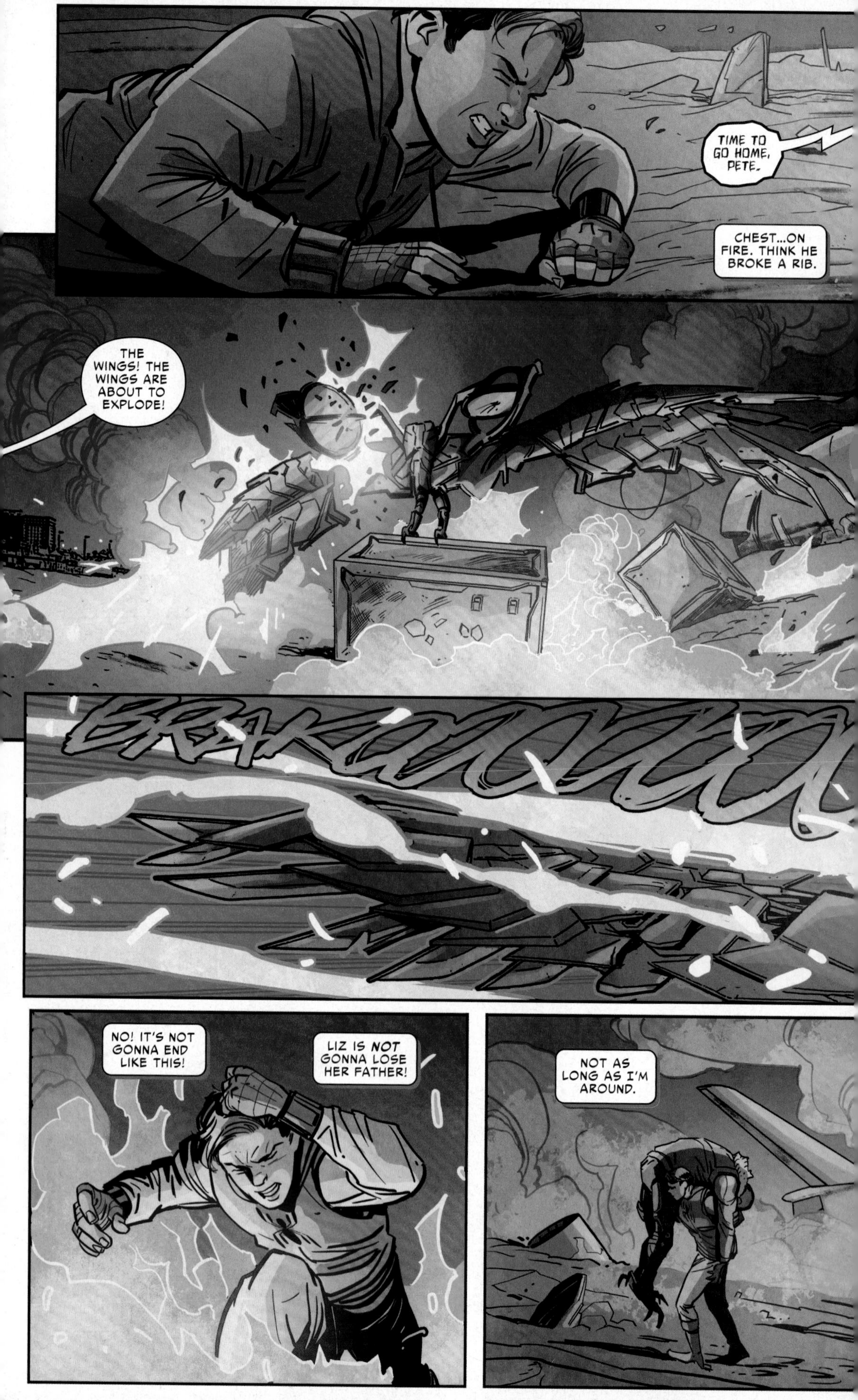
TIME TO GO HOME, PETE.
CHEST...ON FIRE. THINK HE BROKE A RIB.
THE WINGS! THE WINGS ARE ABOUT TO EXPLODE!
BRAKOOOOOM
NO! IT'S NOT GONNA END LIKE THIS!
LIZ IS NOT GONNA LOSE HER FATHER!
NOT AS LONG AS I'M AROUND.

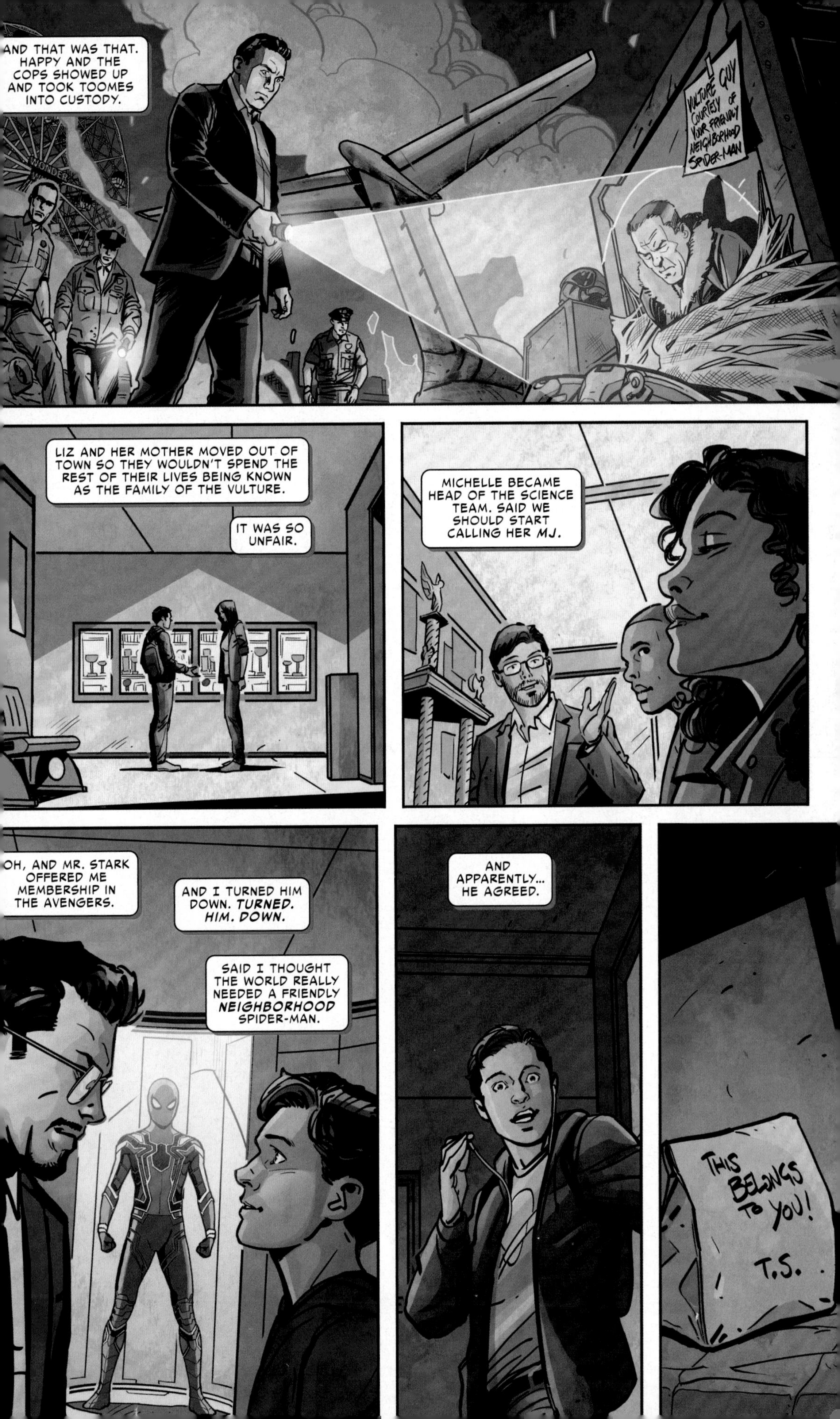
AND THAT WAS THAT. HAPPY AND THE COPS SHOWED UP AND TOOK TOOMES INTO CUSTODY.
WONDER
VULTURE GUY COURTESY OF YOUR FRIENDLY NEIGHBORHOOD SPIDER-MAN
LIZ AND HER MOTHER MOVED OUT OF TOWN SO THEY WOULDN'T SPEND THE REST OF THEIR LIVES BEING KNOWN AS THE FAMILY OF THE VULTURE.
IT WAS SO UNFAIR.
MICHELLE BECAME HEAD OF THE SCIENCE TEAM. SAID WE SHOULD START CALLING HER *MJ*.
OH, AND MR. STARK OFFERED ME MEMBERSHIP IN THE AVENGERS.
AND I TURNED HIM DOWN. *TURNED. HIM. DOWN.*
SAID I THOUGHT THE WORLD REALLY NEEDED A FRIENDLY ***NEIGHBORHOOD*** SPIDER-MAN.
AND APPARENTLY... HE AGREED.
THIS BELONGS TO YOU! T.S.

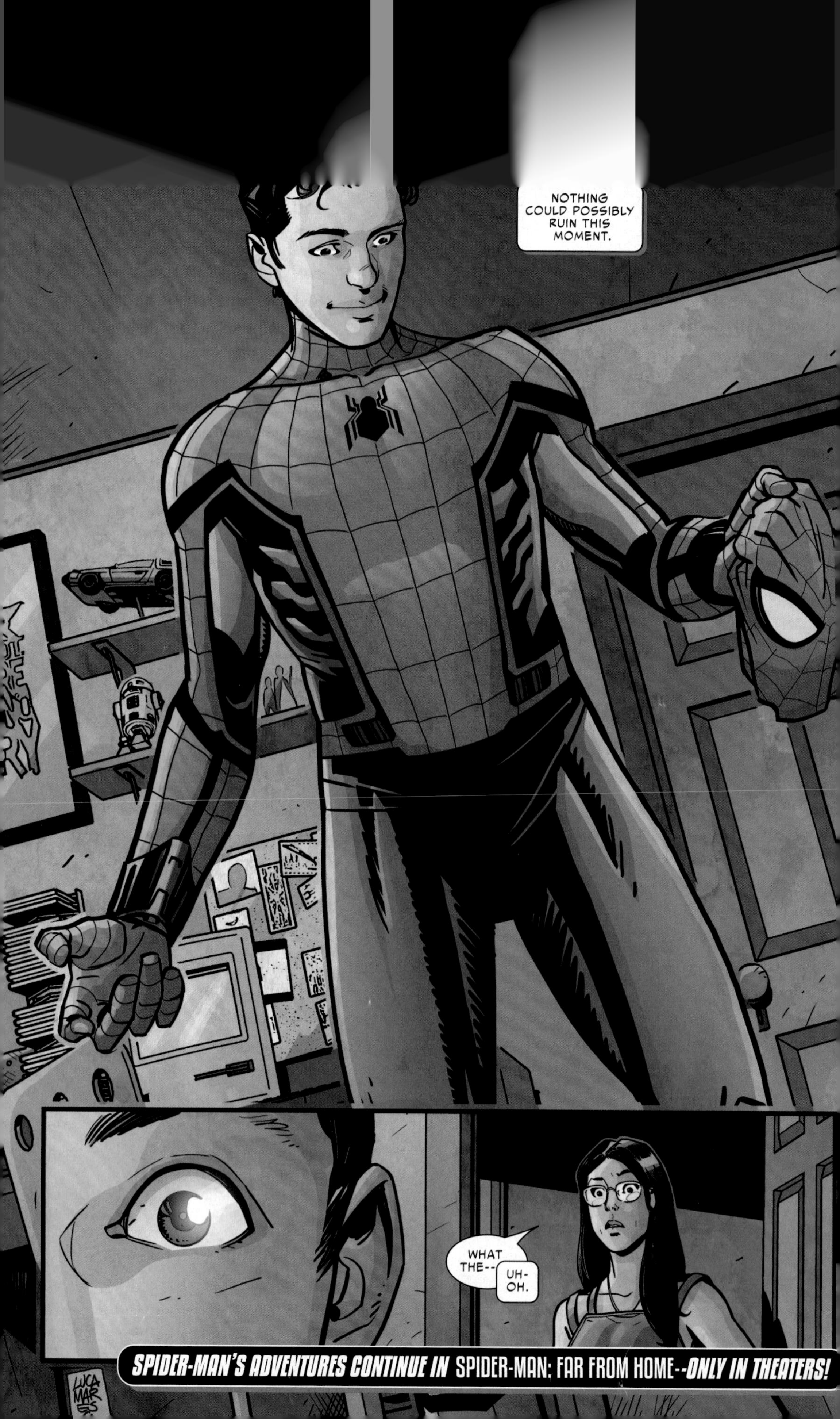
NOTHING COULD POSSIBLY RUIN THIS MOMENT.
WHAT THE--
UH-OH.
SPIDER-MAN'S ADVENTURES CONTINUE IN SPIDER-MAN: FAR FROM HOME--ONLY IN THEATERS!

PETER PARKER GOES INTERNATIONAL AS HE TRAVELS TO LONDON TO VISIT GWEN STACY, ONLY TO GET INVOLVED IN A TERRORIST PLOT!

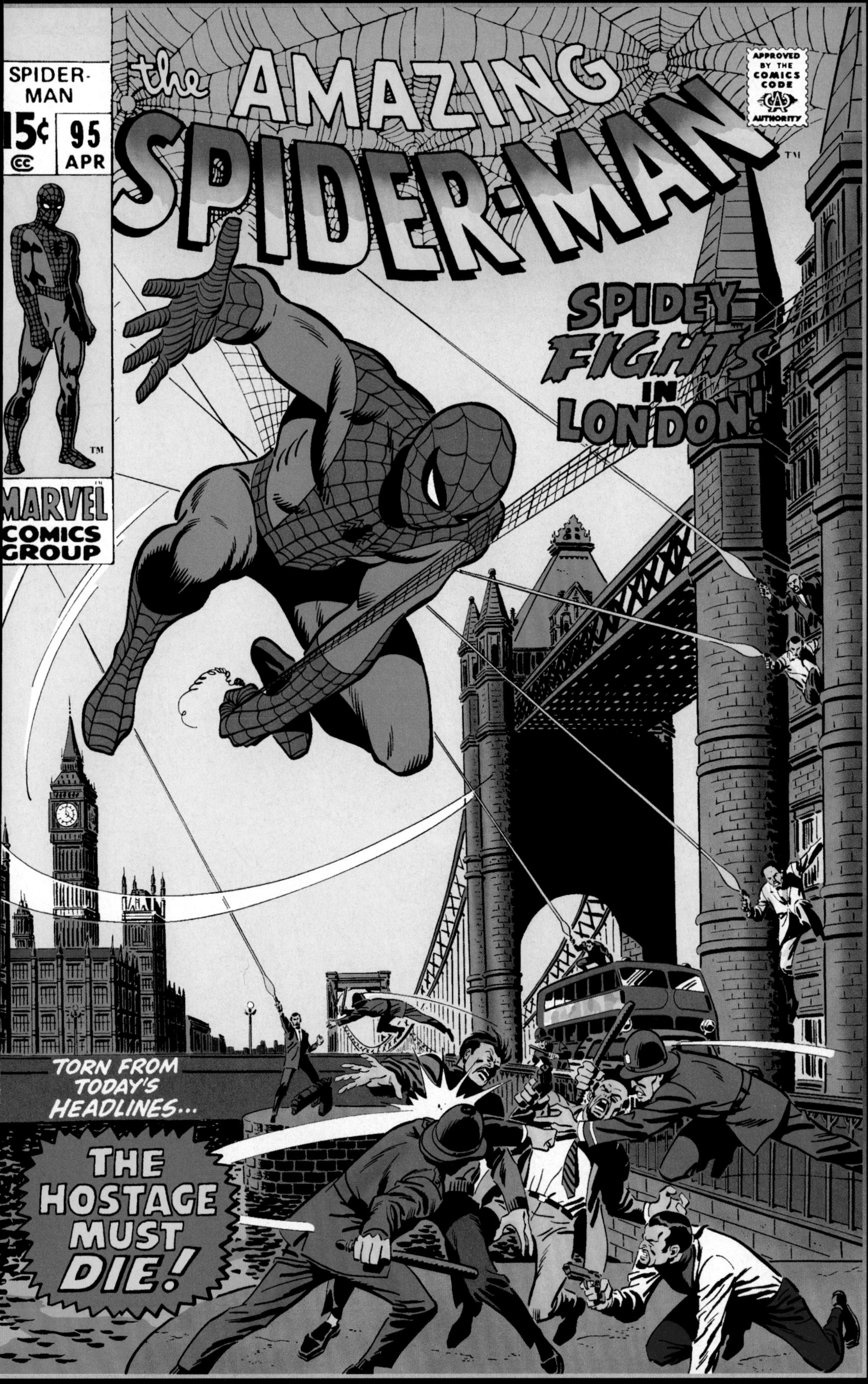

the AMAZING SPIDER-MAN
SPIDER-MAN
15¢
95
APR
APPROVED BY THE COMICS CODE AUTHORITY
MARVEL COMICS GROUP
SPIDEY FIGHTS IN LONDON!
TORN FROM TODAY'S HEADLINES...
THE HOSTAGE MUST DIE!

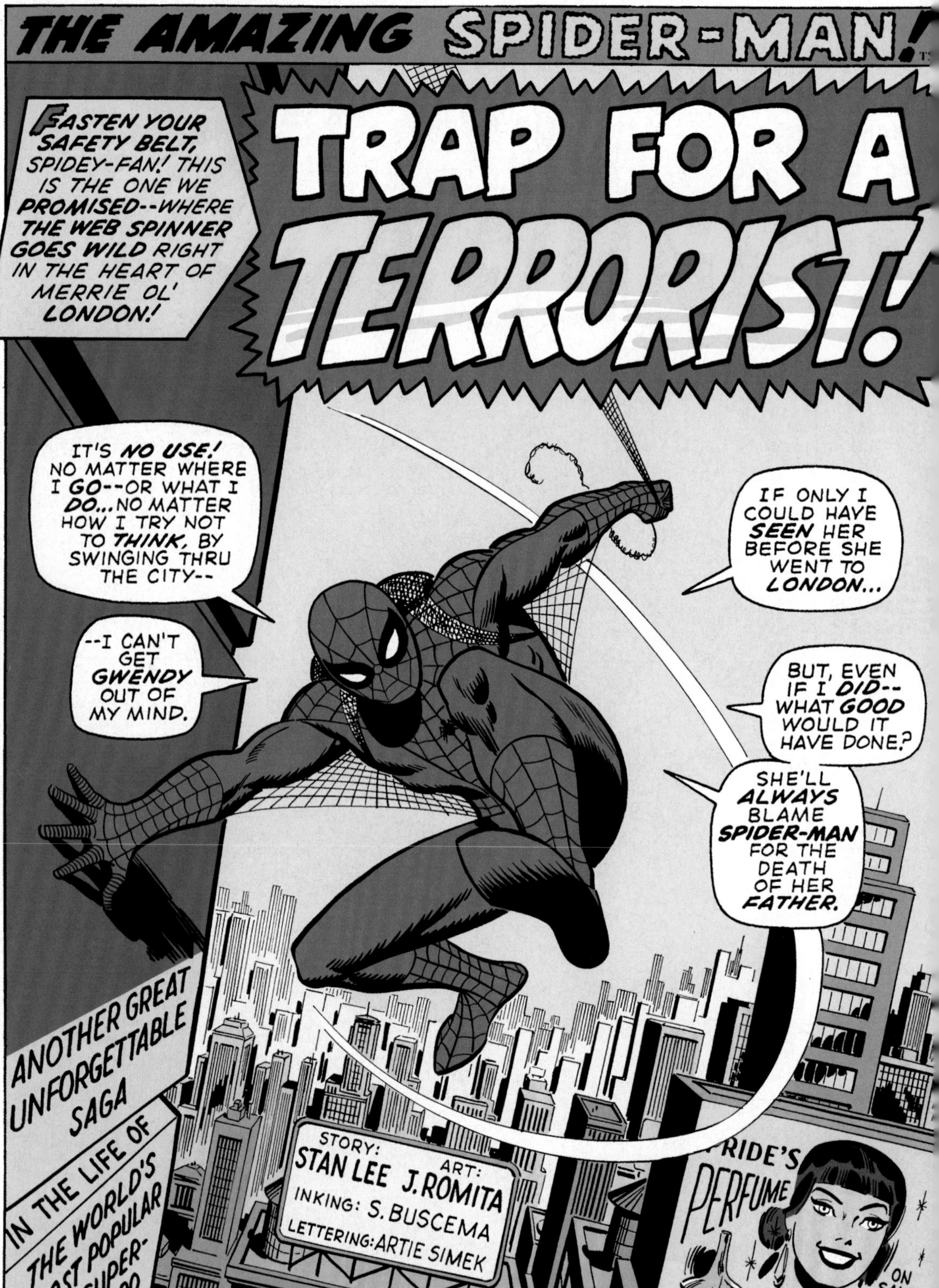
THE AMAZING SPIDER-MAN!
FASTEN YOUR SAFETY BELT, SPIDEY-FAN! THIS IS THE ONE WE PROMISED--WHERE THE WEB SPINNER GOES WILD RIGHT IN THE HEART OF MERRIE OL' LONDON!
TRAP FOR A TERRORIST!
IT'S NO USE! NO MATTER WHERE I GO--OR WHAT I DO...NO MATTER HOW I TRY NOT TO THINK, BY SWINGING THRU THE CITY--
--I CAN'T GET GWENDY OUT OF MY MIND.
IF ONLY I COULD HAVE SEEN HER BEFORE SHE WENT TO LONDON...
BUT, EVEN IF I DID--WHAT GOOD WOULD IT HAVE DONE?
SHE'LL ALWAYS BLAME SPIDER-MAN FOR THE DEATH OF HER FATHER.
ANOTHER GREAT UNFORGETTABLE SAGA
IN THE LIFE OF THE WORLD'S MOST POPULAR SUPER-HERO
STORY: STAN LEE
ART: J. ROMITA
INKING: S. BUSCEMA
LETTERING: ARTIE SIMEK
RIDE'S PERFUME
ON SALE EVERYWHER

BUT WHAT AM I GONNA *DO?*

I SEE HER *FACE* WHEREVER I *LOOK.*

EVERY PLEASANT *SOUND* REMINDS ME OF HER *VOICE.*

I CAN ALMOST *FEEL* HER IN THE *AIR* I BREATHE.

PRIDE'S PERF'

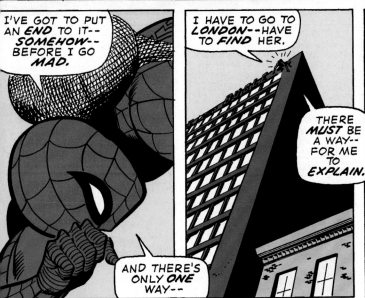

I'VE GOT TO PUT AN *END* TO IT-- SOMEHOW-- BEFORE I GO *MAD.*

I HAVE TO GO TO *LONDON*--HAVE TO *FIND* HER.

THERE *MUST* BE A WAY-- FOR ME TO *EXPLAIN.*

AND THERE'S ONLY *ONE* WAY--

LUCKILY, I'VE NO *CLASSES* THIS WEEK.

BUT, WHAT DO I DO FOR *MONEY?*

IT'S BEEN *WEEKS* SINCE I SOLD ANY *PHOTOS.*

AND I CAN'T ASK POOR *AUNT MAY* FOR A LOAN.

MY ONLY *HOPE* IS TO GET AN *ADVANCE* FROM *JAMESON.*

BUT WHO AM I *KIDDING?* THAT'S LIKE *NO* CHANCE AT ALL.

J.J. JAM
PUBL

ALL THESE *YEARS*--YEARS OF FIGHTING, RISKING MY *LIFE,* TRYING TO *HELP* PEOPLE--AND FOR *WHAT?*

GOD MUST HAVE *LOVED* POOR SLOBS--HE MADE SO *MANY* OF US.

PETER! HOLD IT, SON!

2

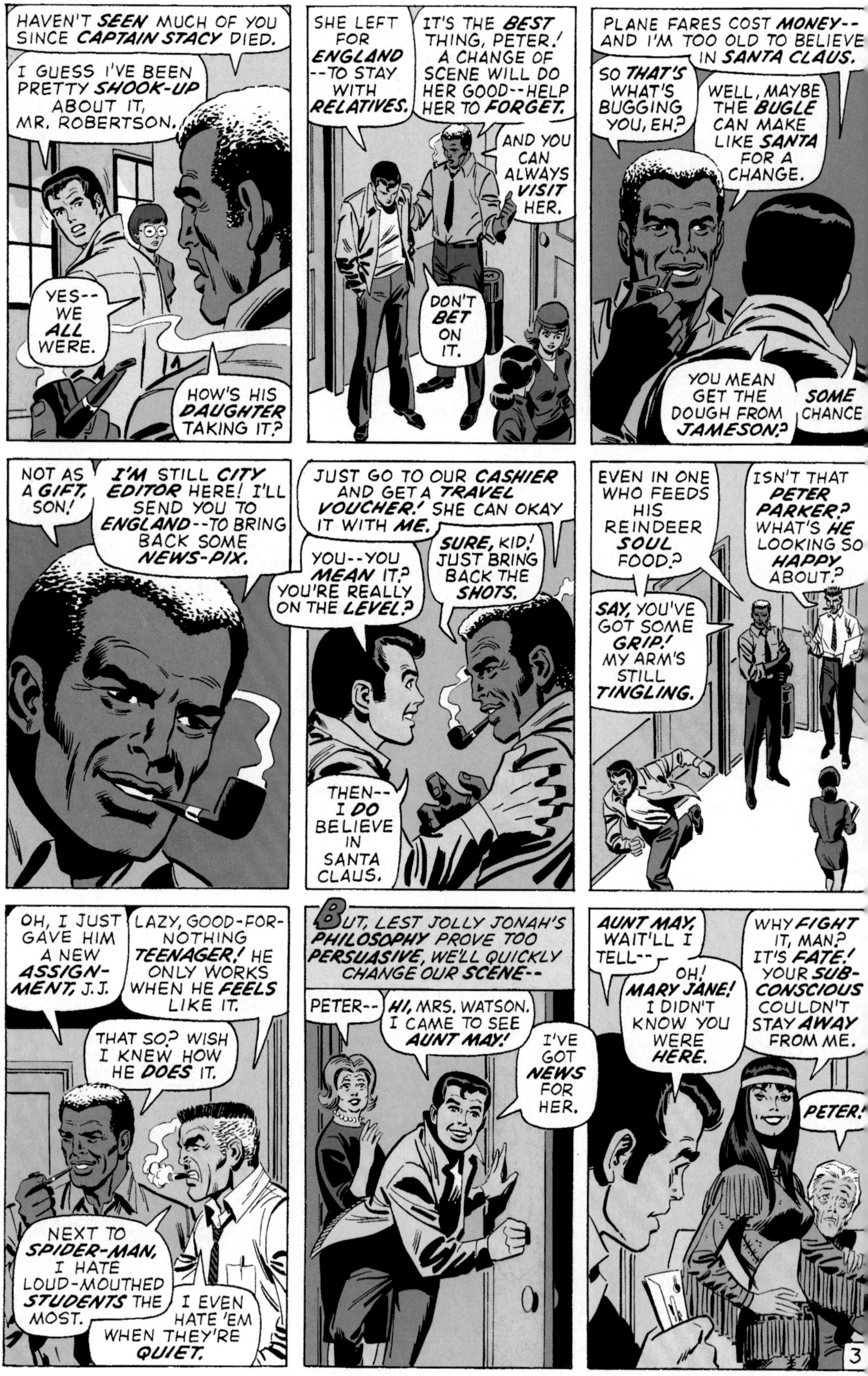
HAVEN'T SEEN MUCH OF YOU SINCE CAPTAIN STACY DIED.
I GUESS I'VE BEEN PRETTY SHOOK-UP ABOUT IT, MR. ROBERTSON.
YES--WE ALL WERE.
HOW'S HIS DAUGHTER TAKING IT?
SHE LEFT FOR ENGLAND--TO STAY WITH RELATIVES.
IT'S THE BEST THING, PETER! A CHANGE OF SCENE WILL DO HER GOOD--HELP HER TO FORGET.
AND YOU CAN ALWAYS VISIT HER.
DON'T BET ON IT.
PLANE FARES COST MONEY--AND I'M TOO OLD TO BELIEVE IN SANTA CLAUS.
SO THAT'S WHAT'S BUGGING YOU, EH?
WELL, MAYBE THE BUGLE CAN MAKE LIKE SANTA FOR A CHANGE.
YOU MEAN GET THE DOUGH FROM JAMESON?
SOME CHANCE
NOT AS A GIFT, SON!
I'M STILL CITY EDITOR HERE! I'LL SEND YOU TO ENGLAND--TO BRING BACK SOME NEWS-PIX.
JUST GO TO OUR CASHIER AND GET A TRAVEL VOUCHER! SHE CAN OKAY IT WITH ME.
YOU--YOU MEAN IT? YOU'RE REALLY ON THE LEVEL?
SURE, KID! JUST BRING BACK THE SHOTS.
THEN--I DO BELIEVE IN SANTA CLAUS.
EVEN IN ONE WHO FEEDS HIS REINDEER SOUL FOOD?
SAY, YOU'VE GOT SOME GRIP! MY ARM'S STILL TINGLING.
ISN'T THAT PETER PARKER? WHAT'S HE LOOKING SO HAPPY ABOUT?
OH, I JUST GAVE HIM A NEW ASSIGNMENT, J.J.
LAZY, GOOD-FOR-NOTHING TEENAGER! HE ONLY WORKS WHEN HE FEELS LIKE IT.
THAT SO? WISH I KNEW HOW HE DOES IT.
NEXT TO SPIDER-MAN, I HATE LOUD-MOUTHED STUDENTS THE MOST.
I EVEN HATE 'EM WHEN THEY'RE QUIET.
BUT, LEST JOLLY JONAH'S PHILOSOPHY PROVE TOO PERSUASIVE, WE'LL QUICKLY CHANGE OUR SCENE--
PETER--
HI, MRS. WATSON. I CAME TO SEE AUNT MAY!
I'VE GOT NEWS FOR HER.
AUNT MAY, WAIT'LL I TELL--
OH! MARY JANE! I DIDN'T KNOW YOU WERE HERE.
WHY FIGHT IT, MAN? IT'S FATE! YOUR SUB-CONSCIOUS COULDN'T STAY AWAY FROM ME.
PETER!

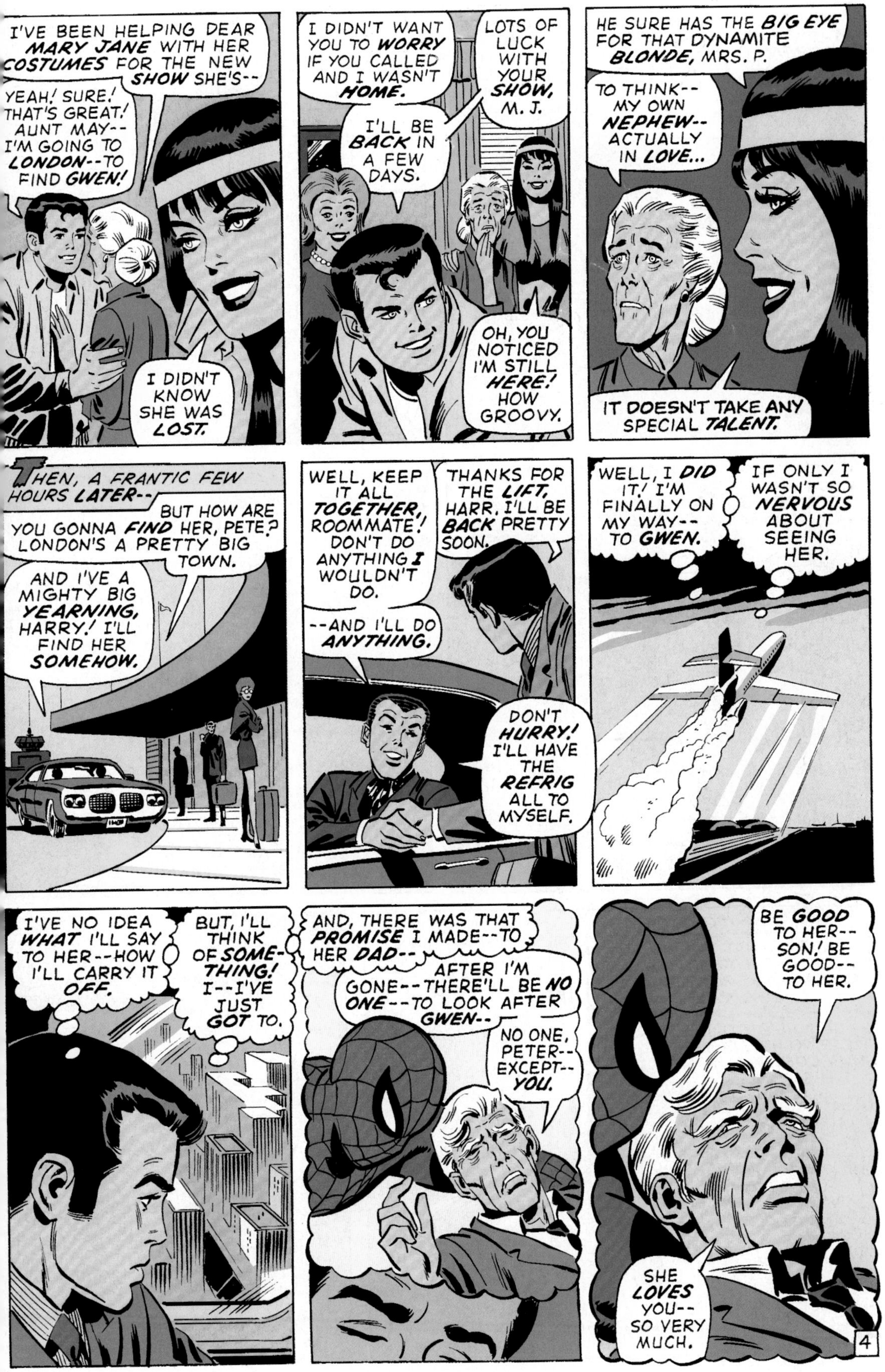
I'VE BEEN HELPING DEAR MARY JANE WITH HER COSTUMES FOR THE NEW SHOW SHE'S--
YEAH! SURE! THAT'S GREAT! AUNT MAY-- I'M GOING TO LONDON--TO FIND GWEN!
I DIDN'T KNOW SHE WAS LOST.
I DIDN'T WANT YOU TO WORRY IF YOU CALLED AND I WASN'T HOME.
LOTS OF LUCK WITH YOUR SHOW, M. J.
I'LL BE BACK IN A FEW DAYS.
OH, YOU NOTICED I'M STILL HERE! HOW GROOVY.
HE SURE HAS THE BIG EYE FOR THAT DYNAMITE BLONDE, MRS. P.
TO THINK-- MY OWN NEPHEW-- ACTUALLY IN LOVE...
IT DOESN'T TAKE ANY SPECIAL TALENT.
THEN, A FRANTIC FEW HOURS LATER--
BUT HOW ARE YOU GONNA FIND HER, PETE? LONDON'S A PRETTY BIG TOWN.
AND I'VE A MIGHTY BIG YEARNING, HARRY! I'LL FIND HER SOMEHOW.
WELL, KEEP IT ALL TOGETHER, ROOMMATE! DON'T DO ANYTHING I WOULDN'T DO.
THANKS FOR THE LIFT, HARR. I'LL BE BACK PRETTY SOON.
--AND I'LL DO ANYTHING.
DON'T HURRY! I'LL HAVE THE REFRIG ALL TO MYSELF.
WELL, I DID IT! I'M FINALLY ON MY WAY-- TO GWEN.
IF ONLY I WASN'T SO NERVOUS ABOUT SEEING HER.
I'VE NO IDEA WHAT I'LL SAY TO HER--HOW I'LL CARRY IT OFF.
BUT, I'LL THINK OF SOME-THING! I--I'VE JUST GOT TO.
AND, THERE WAS THAT PROMISE I MADE--TO HER DAD--
AFTER I'M GONE--THERE'LL BE NO ONE--TO LOOK AFTER GWEN--
NO ONE, PETER-- EXCEPT-- YOU.
BE GOOD TO HER-- SON! BE GOOD-- TO HER.
SHE LOVES YOU-- SO VERY MUCH.
4

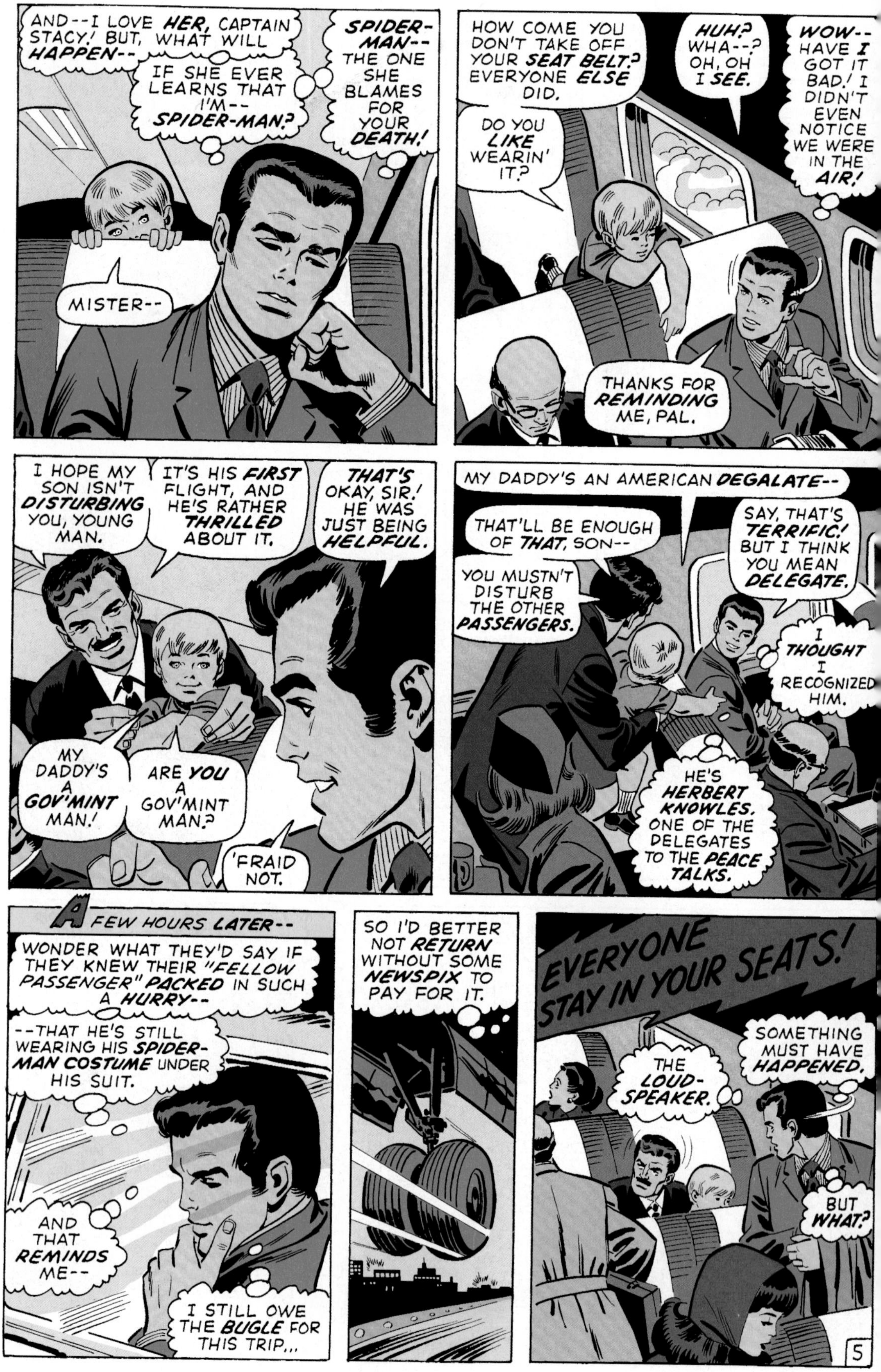

AND--I LOVE HER, CAPTAIN STACY! BUT, WHAT WILL HAPPEN--
IF SHE EVER LEARNS THAT I'M--SPIDER-MAN?
SPIDER-MAN--THE ONE SHE BLAMES FOR YOUR DEATH!
MISTER--
HOW COME YOU DON'T TAKE OFF YOUR SEAT BELT? EVERYONE ELSE DID.
DO YOU LIKE WEARIN' IT?
HUH? WHA--? OH, OH I SEE.
WOW--HAVE I GOT IT BAD! I DIDN'T EVEN NOTICE WE WERE IN THE AIR!
THANKS FOR REMINDING ME, PAL.
I HOPE MY SON ISN'T DISTURBING YOU, YOUNG MAN.
IT'S HIS FIRST FLIGHT, AND HE'S RATHER THRILLED ABOUT IT.
THAT'S OKAY, SIR! HE WAS JUST BEING HELPFUL.
MY DADDY'S A GOV'MINT MAN!
ARE YOU A GOV'MINT MAN?
'FRAID NOT.
MY DADDY'S AN AMERICAN DEGALATE--
THAT'LL BE ENOUGH OF THAT, SON--
YOU MUSTN'T DISTURB THE OTHER PASSENGERS.
SAY, THAT'S TERRIFIC! BUT I THINK YOU MEAN DELEGATE.
I THOUGHT I RECOGNIZED HIM.
HE'S HERBERT KNOWLES, ONE OF THE DELEGATES TO THE PEACE TALKS.
A FEW HOURS LATER--
WONDER WHAT THEY'D SAY IF THEY KNEW THEIR "FELLOW PASSENGER" PACKED IN SUCH A HURRY--
--THAT HE'S STILL WEARING HIS SPIDER-MAN COSTUME UNDER HIS SUIT.
AND THAT REMINDS ME--
I STILL OWE THE BUGLE FOR THIS TRIP...
SO I'D BETTER NOT RETURN WITHOUT SOME NEWSPIX TO PAY FOR IT.
EVERYONE STAY IN YOUR SEATS!
THE LOUD-SPEAKER.
SOMETHING MUST HAVE HAPPENED.
BUT WHAT?
5

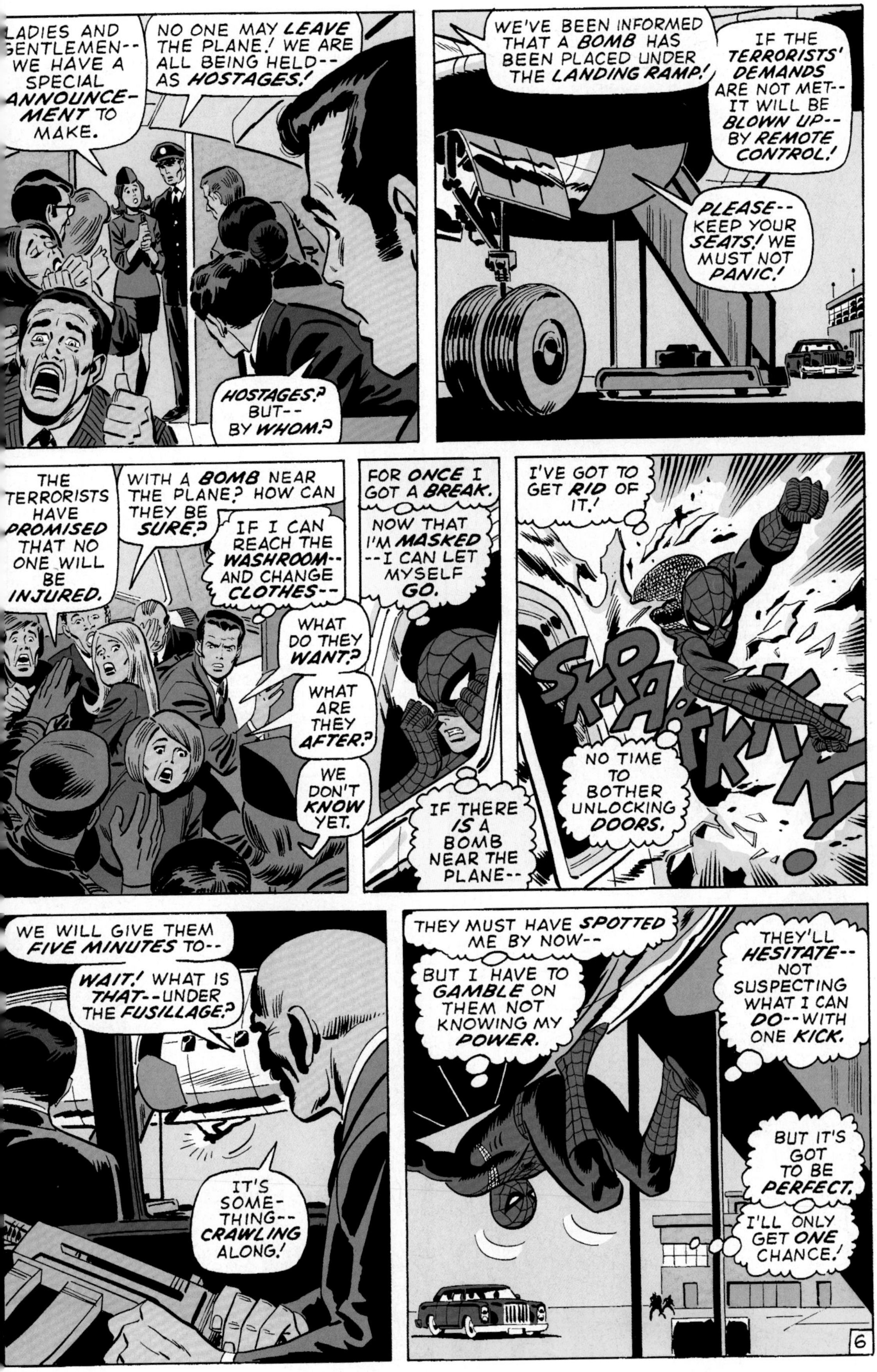

LADIES AND GENTLEMEN-- WE HAVE A SPECIAL ANNOUNCEMENT TO MAKE.
NO ONE MAY LEAVE THE PLANE! WE ARE ALL BEING HELD-- AS HOSTAGES!
HOSTAGES? BUT-- BY WHOM?
WE'VE BEEN INFORMED THAT A BOMB HAS BEEN PLACED UNDER THE LANDING RAMP!
IF THE TERRORISTS' DEMANDS ARE NOT MET-- IT WILL BE BLOWN UP-- BY REMOTE CONTROL!
PLEASE-- KEEP YOUR SEATS! WE MUST NOT PANIC!
THE TERRORISTS HAVE PROMISED THAT NO ONE WILL BE INJURED.
WITH A BOMB NEAR THE PLANE? HOW CAN THEY BE SURE?
IF I CAN REACH THE WASHROOM-- AND CHANGE CLOTHES--
WHAT DO THEY WANT?
WHAT ARE THEY AFTER?
WE DON'T KNOW YET.
FOR ONCE I GOT A BREAK.
NOW THAT I'M MASKED --I CAN LET MYSELF GO.
IF THERE IS A BOMB NEAR THE PLANE--
I'VE GOT TO GET RID OF IT.!
SKRAKKK
NO TIME TO BOTHER UNLOCKING DOORS.
WE WILL GIVE THEM FIVE MINUTES TO--
WAIT! WHAT IS THAT--UNDER THE FUSILLAGE?
IT'S SOME-THING-- CRAWLING ALONG!
THEY MUST HAVE SPOTTED ME BY NOW--
BUT I HAVE TO GAMBLE ON THEM NOT KNOWING MY POWER.
THEY'LL HESITATE-- NOT SUSPECTING WHAT I CAN DO--WITH ONE KICK.
BUT IT'S GOT TO BE PERFECT.
I'LL ONLY GET ONE CHANCE!

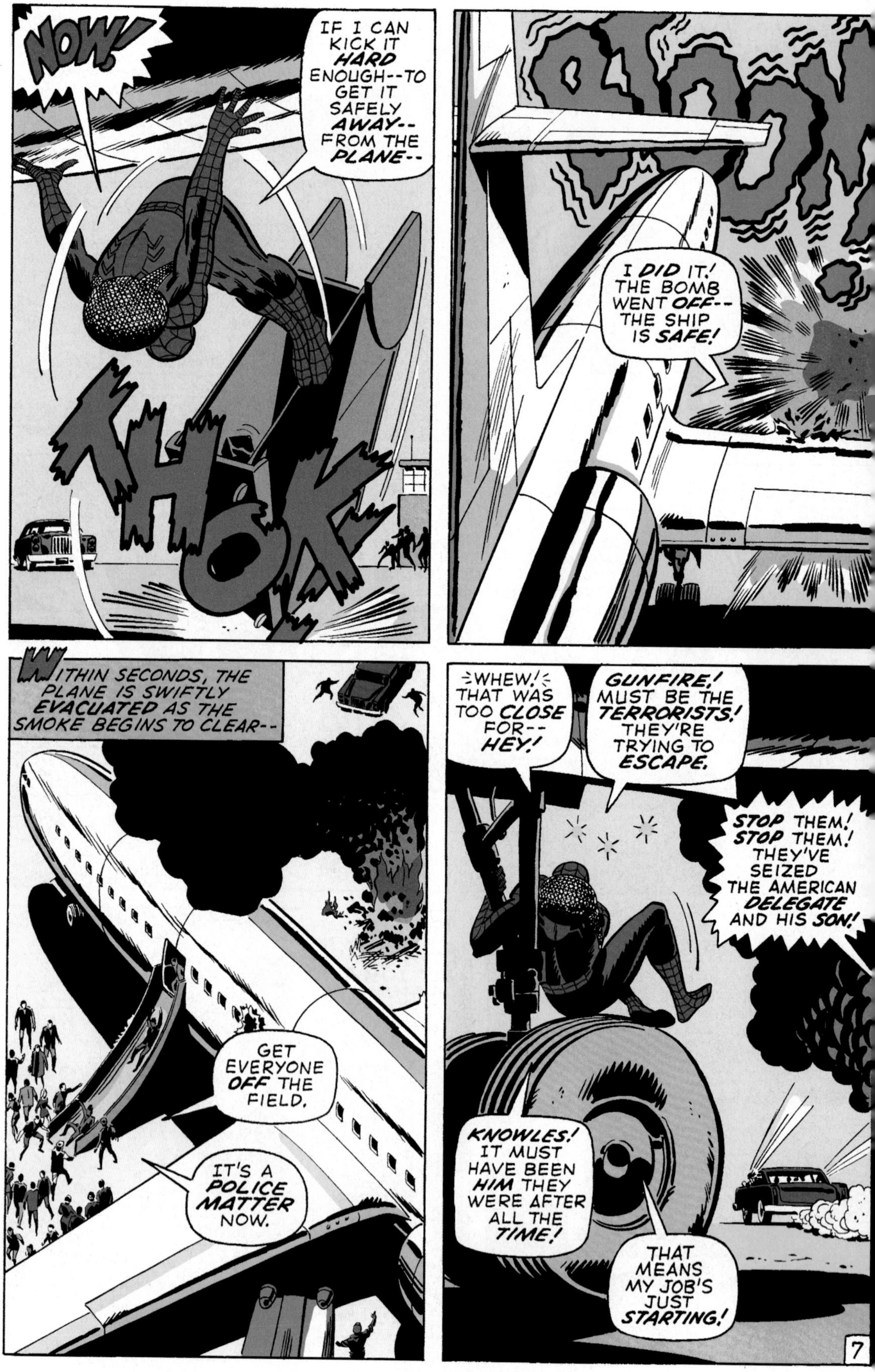
NOW!
IF I CAN KICK IT HARD ENOUGH--TO GET IT SAFELY AWAY-- FROM THE PLANE--
THOK
I DID IT! THE BOMB WENT OFF-- THE SHIP IS SAFE!
WITHIN SECONDS, THE PLANE IS SWIFTLY EVACUATED AS THE SMOKE BEGINS TO CLEAR--
GET EVERYONE OFF THE FIELD.
IT'S A POLICE MATTER NOW.
WHEW! THAT WAS TOO CLOSE FOR-- HEY!
GUNFIRE! MUST BE THE TERRORISTS! THEY'RE TRYING TO ESCAPE.
STOP THEM! STOP THEM! THEY'VE SEIZED THE AMERICAN DELEGATE AND HIS SON!
KNOWLES! IT MUST HAVE BEEN HIM THEY WERE AFTER ALL THE TIME!
THAT MEANS MY JOB'S JUST STARTING!
7

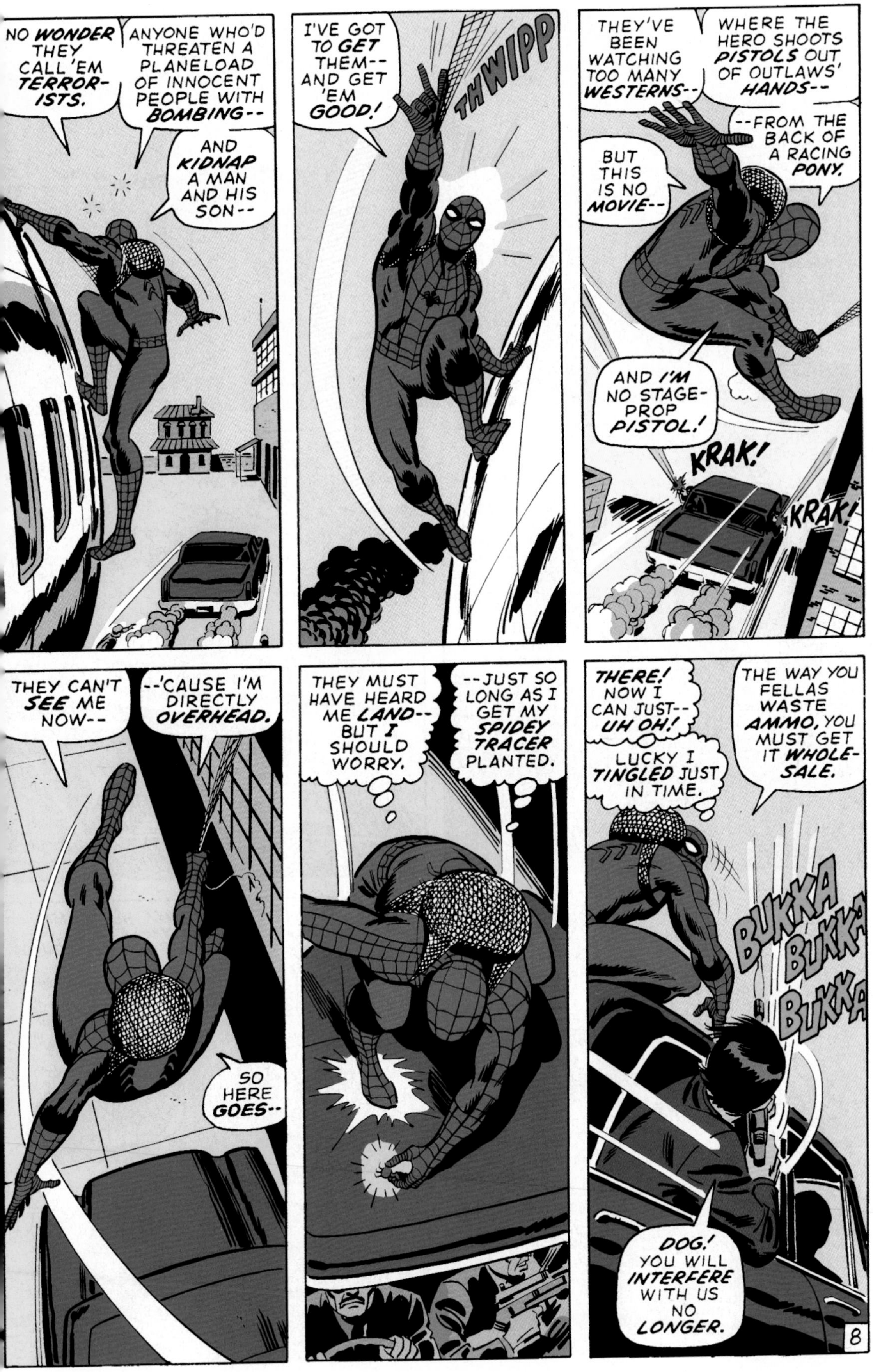

NO WONDER THEY CALL 'EM TERRORISTS.
ANYONE WHO'D THREATEN A PLANELOAD OF INNOCENT PEOPLE WITH BOMBING--
AND KIDNAP A MAN AND HIS SON--
I'VE GOT TO GET THEM--AND GET 'EM GOOD!
THWIPP
THEY'VE BEEN WATCHING TOO MANY WESTERNS--
WHERE THE HERO SHOOTS PISTOLS OUT OF OUTLAWS' HANDS--
--FROM THE BACK OF A RACING PONY.
BUT THIS IS NO MOVIE--
AND I'M NO STAGE-PROP PISTOL!
KRAK!
KRAK!
THEY CAN'T SEE ME NOW--
--'CAUSE I'M DIRECTLY OVERHEAD.
SO HERE GOES--
THEY MUST HAVE HEARD ME LAND--BUT I SHOULD WORRY.
--JUST SO LONG AS I GET MY SPIDEY TRACER PLANTED.
THERE! NOW I CAN JUST--UH OH!
LUCKY I TINGLED JUST IN TIME.
THE WAY YOU FELLAS WASTE AMMO, YOU MUST GET IT WHOLESALE.
BUKKA
BUKKA
BUKKA
DOG! YOU WILL INTERFERE WITH US NO LONGER.
8

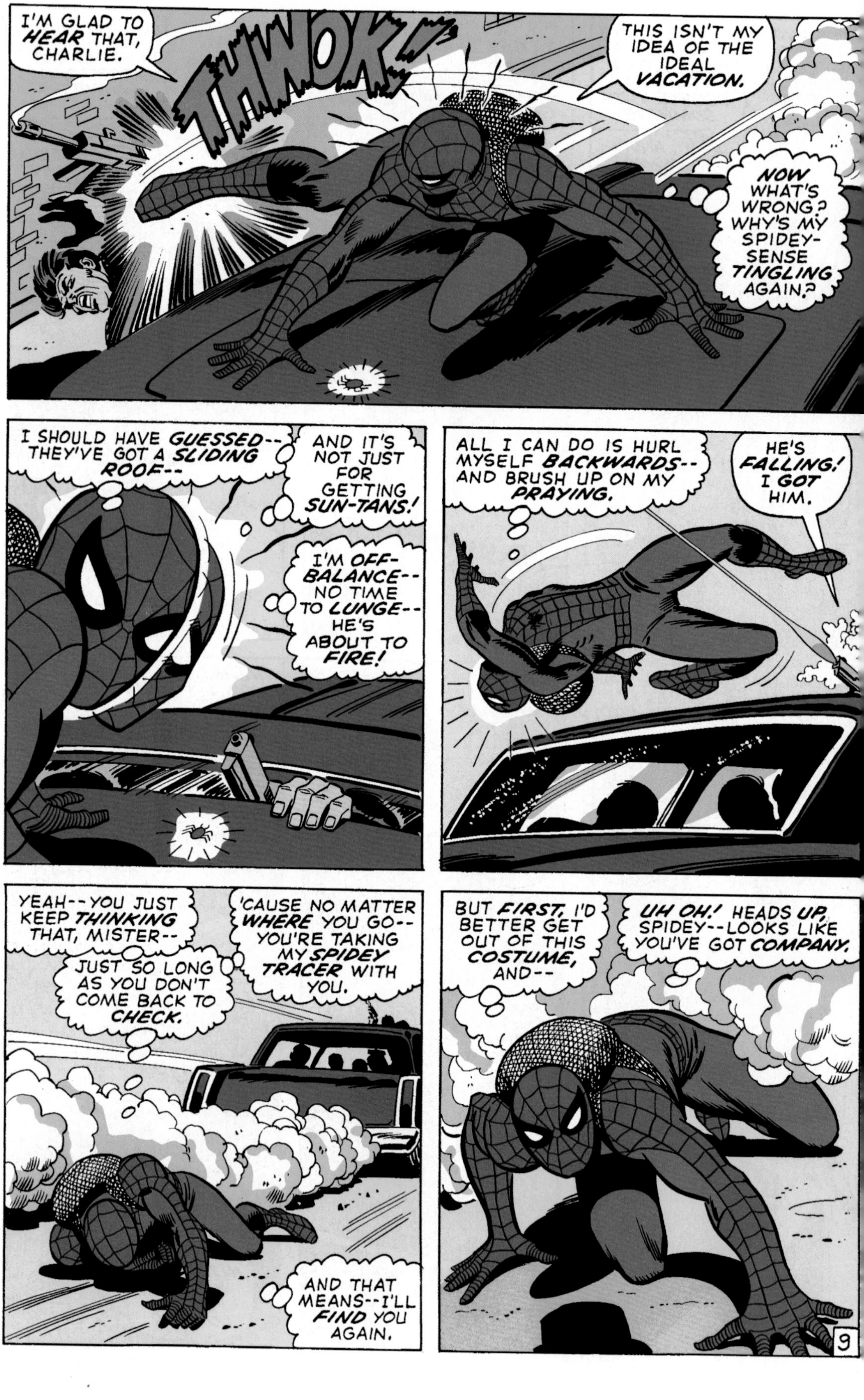
I'M GLAD TO HEAR THAT, CHARLIE.
THWOK!
THIS ISN'T MY IDEA OF THE IDEAL VACATION.
NOW WHAT'S WRONG? WHY'S MY SPIDEY-SENSE TINGLING AGAIN?
I SHOULD HAVE GUESSED-- THEY'VE GOT A SLIDING ROOF--
AND IT'S NOT JUST FOR GETTING SUN-TANS!
I'M OFF-BALANCE-- NO TIME TO LUNGE-- HE'S ABOUT TO FIRE!
ALL I CAN DO IS HURL MYSELF BACKWARDS-- AND BRUSH UP ON MY PRAYING.
HE'S FALLING! I GOT HIM.
YEAH--YOU JUST KEEP THINKING THAT, MISTER--
'CAUSE NO MATTER WHERE YOU GO-- YOU'RE TAKING MY SPIDEY TRACER WITH YOU.
JUST SO LONG AS YOU DON'T COME BACK TO CHECK.
AND THAT MEANS--I'LL FIND YOU AGAIN.
BUT FIRST, I'D BETTER GET OUT OF THIS COSTUME, AND--
UH OH! HEADS UP, SPIDEY--LOOKS LIKE YOU'VE GOT COMPANY.
9

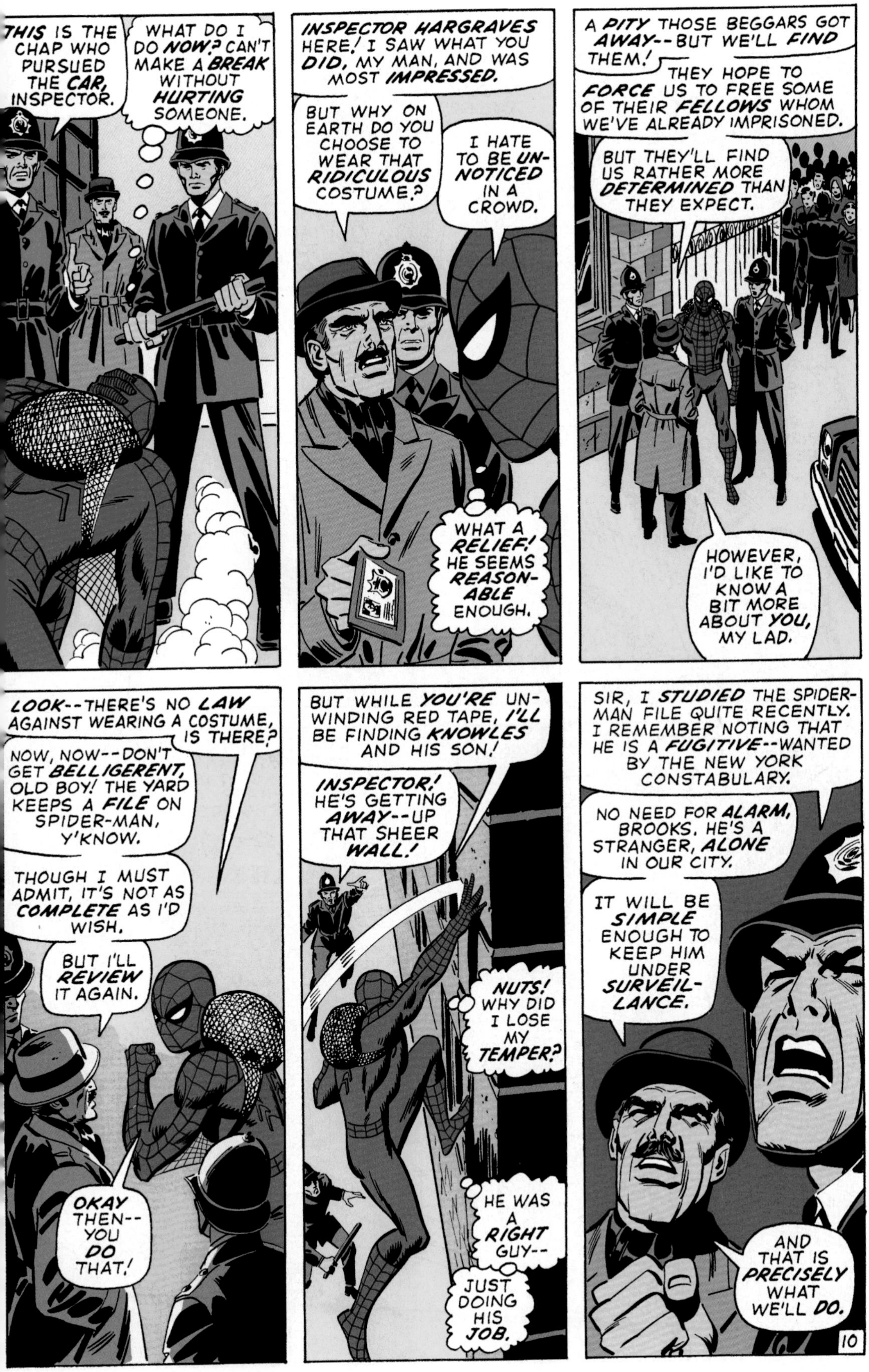

THIS IS THE CHAP WHO PURSUED THE CAR, INSPECTOR.
WHAT DO I DO NOW? CAN'T MAKE A BREAK WITHOUT HURTING SOMEONE.
INSPECTOR HARGRAVES HERE! I SAW WHAT YOU DID, MY MAN, AND WAS MOST IMPRESSED.
BUT WHY ON EARTH DO YOU CHOOSE TO WEAR THAT RIDICULOUS COSTUME?
I HATE TO BE UN-NOTICED IN A CROWD.
WHAT A RELIEF! HE SEEMS REASON-ABLE ENOUGH.
A PITY THOSE BEGGARS GOT AWAY--BUT WE'LL FIND THEM!
THEY HOPE TO FORCE US TO FREE SOME OF THEIR FELLOWS WHOM WE'VE ALREADY IMPRISONED.
BUT THEY'LL FIND US RATHER MORE DETERMINED THAN THEY EXPECT.
HOWEVER, I'D LIKE TO KNOW A BIT MORE ABOUT YOU, MY LAD.
LOOK--THERE'S NO LAW AGAINST WEARING A COSTUME, IS THERE?
NOW, NOW--DON'T GET BELLIGERENT, OLD BOY! THE YARD KEEPS A FILE ON SPIDER-MAN, Y'KNOW.
THOUGH I MUST ADMIT, IT'S NOT AS COMPLETE AS I'D WISH.
BUT I'LL REVIEW IT AGAIN.
OKAY THEN--YOU DO THAT!
BUT WHILE YOU'RE UN-WINDING RED TAPE, I'LL BE FINDING KNOWLES AND HIS SON!
INSPECTOR! HE'S GETTING AWAY--UP THAT SHEER WALL!
NUTS! WHY DID I LOSE MY TEMPER?
HE WAS A RIGHT GUY--
JUST DOING HIS JOB.
SIR, I STUDIED THE SPIDER-MAN FILE QUITE RECENTLY. I REMEMBER NOTING THAT HE IS A FUGITIVE--WANTED BY THE NEW YORK CONSTABULARY.
NO NEED FOR ALARM, BROOKS. HE'S A STRANGER, ALONE IN OUR CITY.
IT WILL BE SIMPLE ENOUGH TO KEEP HIM UNDER SURVEIL-LANCE.
AND THAT IS PRECISELY WHAT WE'LL DO.
10

THEN, FOR THE NEXT FEW HOURS--

I'VE GOT TO KEEP CRISS-CROSSING THE CITY...

...UNTIL I SENSE THE SIGNAL FROM MY SPIDEY-TRACER.

I JUST HOPE IT WON'T TAKE TOO LONG.

'CAUSE EVERY MINUTE THAT GOES BY--

--IS A MINUTE AWAY FROM GWENDY!

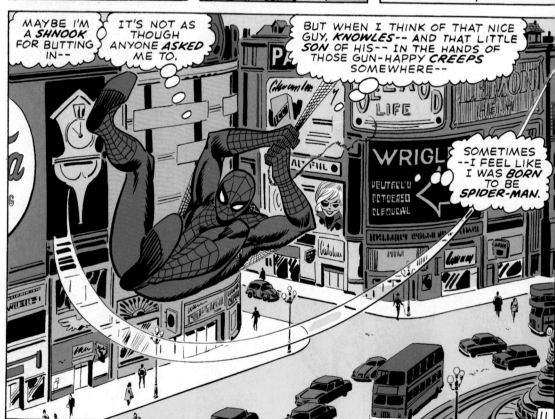

MAYBE I'M A SHNOOK FOR BUTTING IN--

IT'S NOT AS THOUGH ANYONE ASKED ME TO.

BUT WHEN I THINK OF THAT NICE GUY, KNOWLES-- AND THAT LITTLE SON OF HIS-- IN THE HANDS OF THOSE GUN-HAPPY CREEPS SOMEWHERE--

SOMETIMES --I FEEL LIKE I WAS BORN TO BE SPIDER-MAN.

11

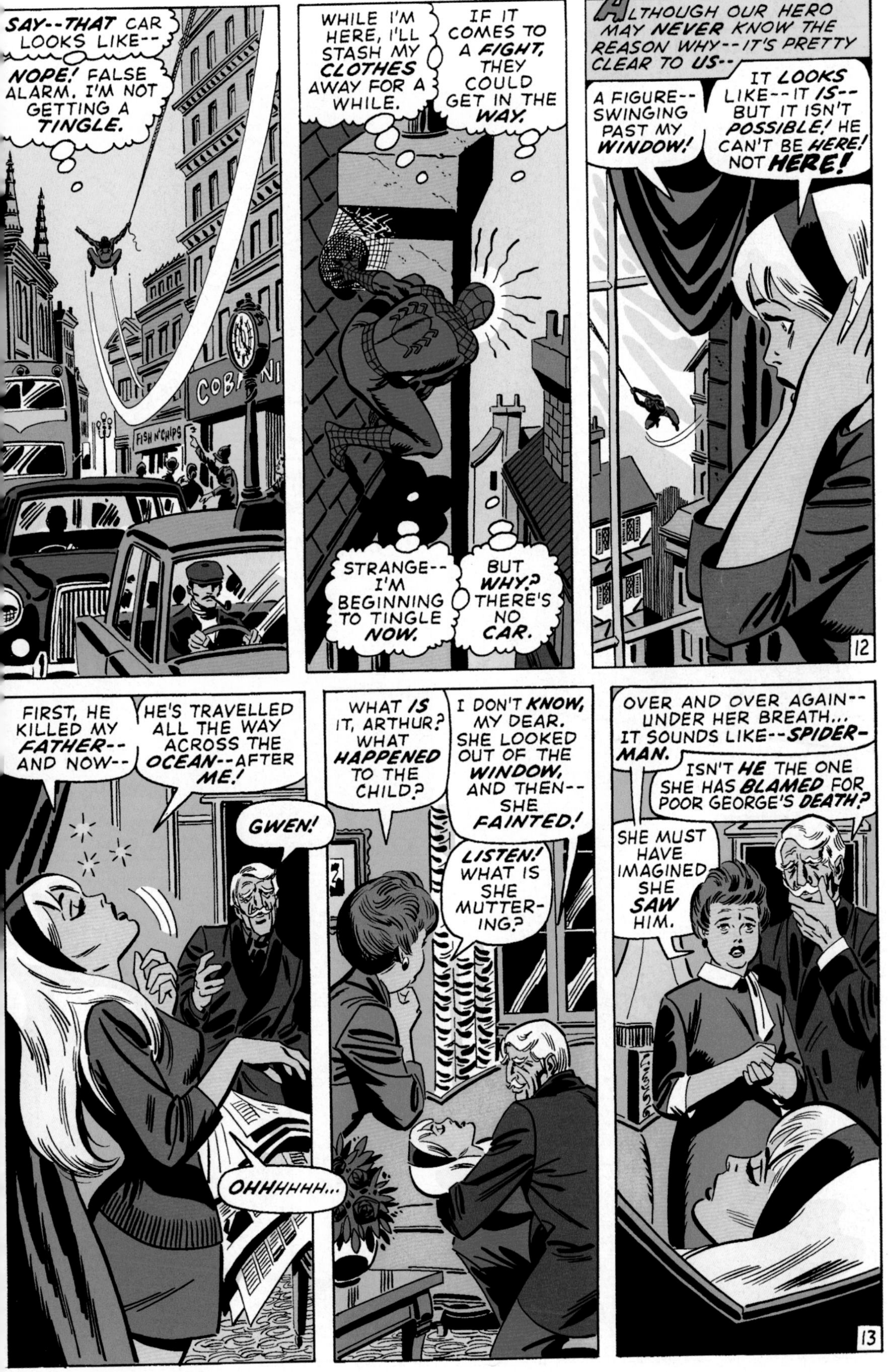
SAY--THAT CAR LOOKS LIKE--
NOPE! FALSE ALARM. I'M NOT GETTING A TINGLE.
COBANI
FISH N' CHIPS
WHILE I'M HERE, I'LL STASH MY CLOTHES AWAY FOR A WHILE.
IF IT COMES TO A FIGHT, THEY COULD GET IN THE WAY.
STRANGE--I'M BEGINNING TO TINGLE NOW.
BUT WHY? THERE'S NO CAR.
ALTHOUGH OUR HERO MAY NEVER KNOW THE REASON WHY--IT'S PRETTY CLEAR TO US--
A FIGURE--SWINGING PAST MY WINDOW!
IT LOOKS LIKE--IT IS--BUT IT ISN'T POSSIBLE! HE CAN'T BE HERE! NOT HERE!
12
FIRST, HE KILLED MY FATHER--AND NOW--
HE'S TRAVELLED ALL THE WAY ACROSS THE OCEAN--AFTER ME!
GWEN!
OHHHHHH...
WHAT IS IT, ARTHUR? WHAT HAPPENED TO THE CHILD?
I DON'T KNOW, MY DEAR. SHE LOOKED OUT OF THE WINDOW, AND THEN--SHE FAINTED!
LISTEN! WHAT IS SHE MUTTER-ING?
OVER AND OVER AGAIN--UNDER HER BREATH... IT SOUNDS LIKE--SPIDER-MAN.
ISN'T HE THE ONE SHE HAS BLAMED FOR POOR GEORGE'S DEATH?
SHE MUST HAVE IMAGINED SHE SAW HIM.
13

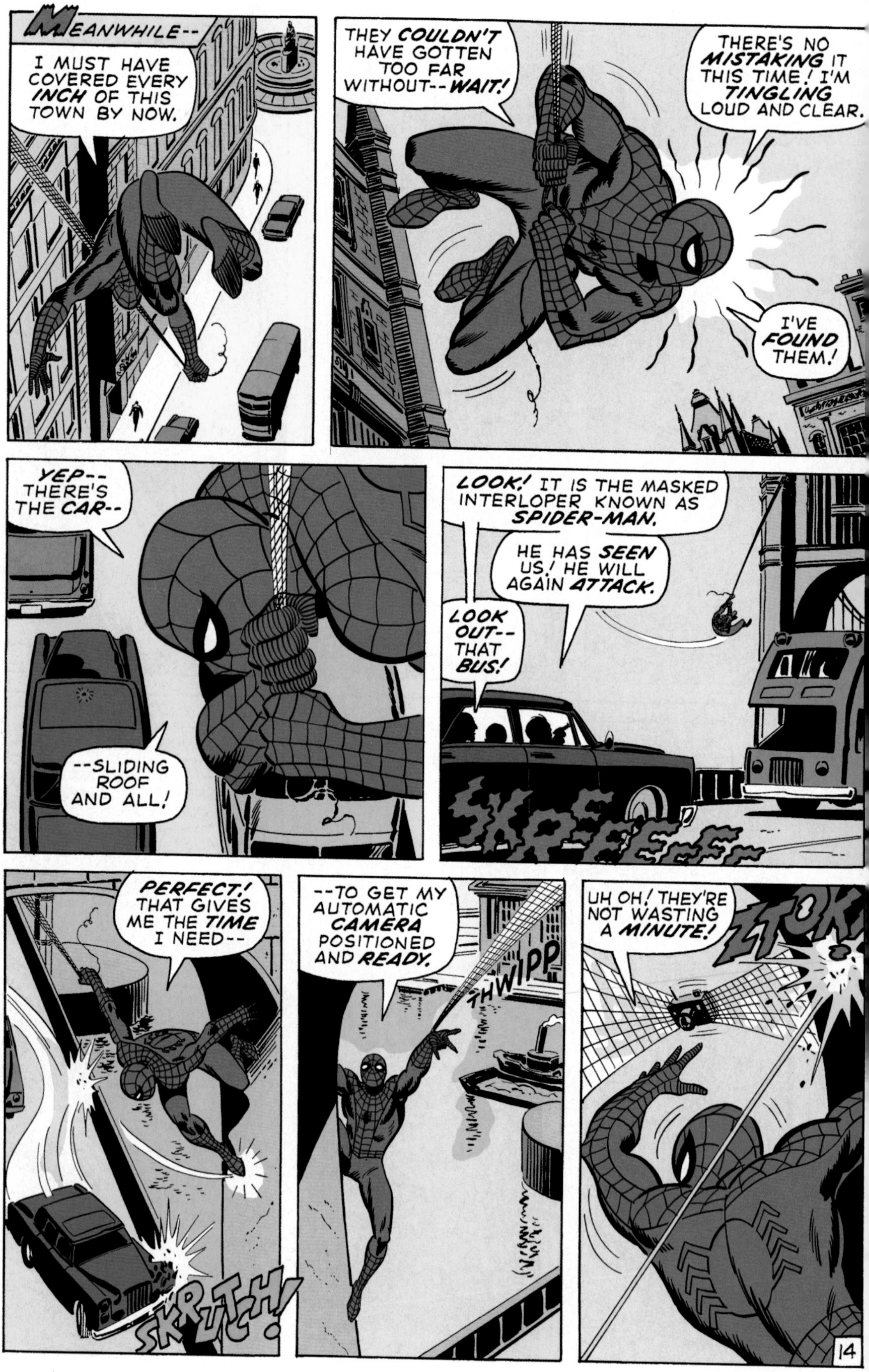
MEANWHILE--
I MUST HAVE COVERED EVERY INCH OF THIS TOWN BY NOW.
THEY COULDN'T HAVE GOTTEN TOO FAR WITHOUT--WAIT!
THERE'S NO MISTAKING IT THIS TIME! I'M TINGLING LOUD AND CLEAR.
I'VE FOUND THEM!
YEP--THERE'S THE CAR--
--SLIDING ROOF AND ALL!
LOOK! IT IS THE MASKED INTERLOPER KNOWN AS SPIDER-MAN.
HE HAS SEEN US! HE WILL AGAIN ATTACK.
LOOK OUT--THAT BUS!
SKREEEEE
PERFECT! THAT GIVES ME THE TIME I NEED--
SKRUTCH!
--TO GET MY AUTOMATIC CAMERA POSITIONED AND READY.
THWIPP
UH OH! THEY'RE NOT WASTING A MINUTE!

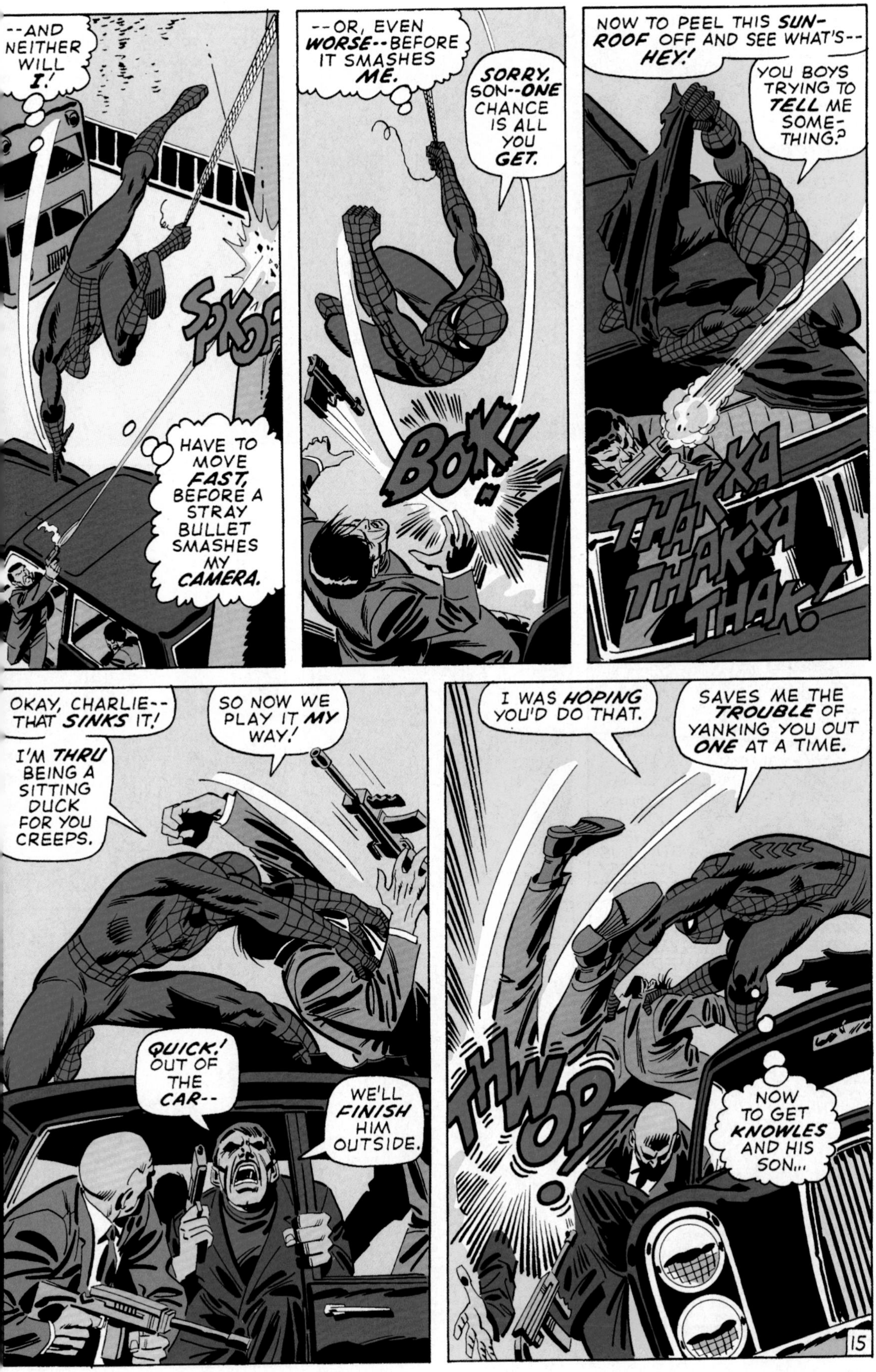

--AND NEITHER WILL I!
SPKOW
HAVE TO MOVE FAST, BEFORE A STRAY BULLET SMASHES MY CAMERA.
--OR, EVEN WORSE--BEFORE IT SMASHES ME.
SORRY, SON--ONE CHANCE IS ALL YOU GET.
BOK!
NOW TO PEEL THIS SUN-ROOF OFF AND SEE WHAT'S-- HEY!
YOU BOYS TRYING TO TELL ME SOMETHING?
THAKKA THAKKA THAK!
OKAY, CHARLIE--THAT SINKS IT!
I'M THRU BEING A SITTING DUCK FOR YOU CREEPS.
SO NOW WE PLAY IT MY WAY!
QUICK! OUT OF THE CAR--
WE'LL FINISH HIM OUTSIDE.
I WAS HOPING YOU'D DO THAT.
SAVES ME THE TROUBLE OF YANKING YOU OUT ONE AT A TIME.
THWOP
NOW TO GET KNOWLES AND HIS SON...

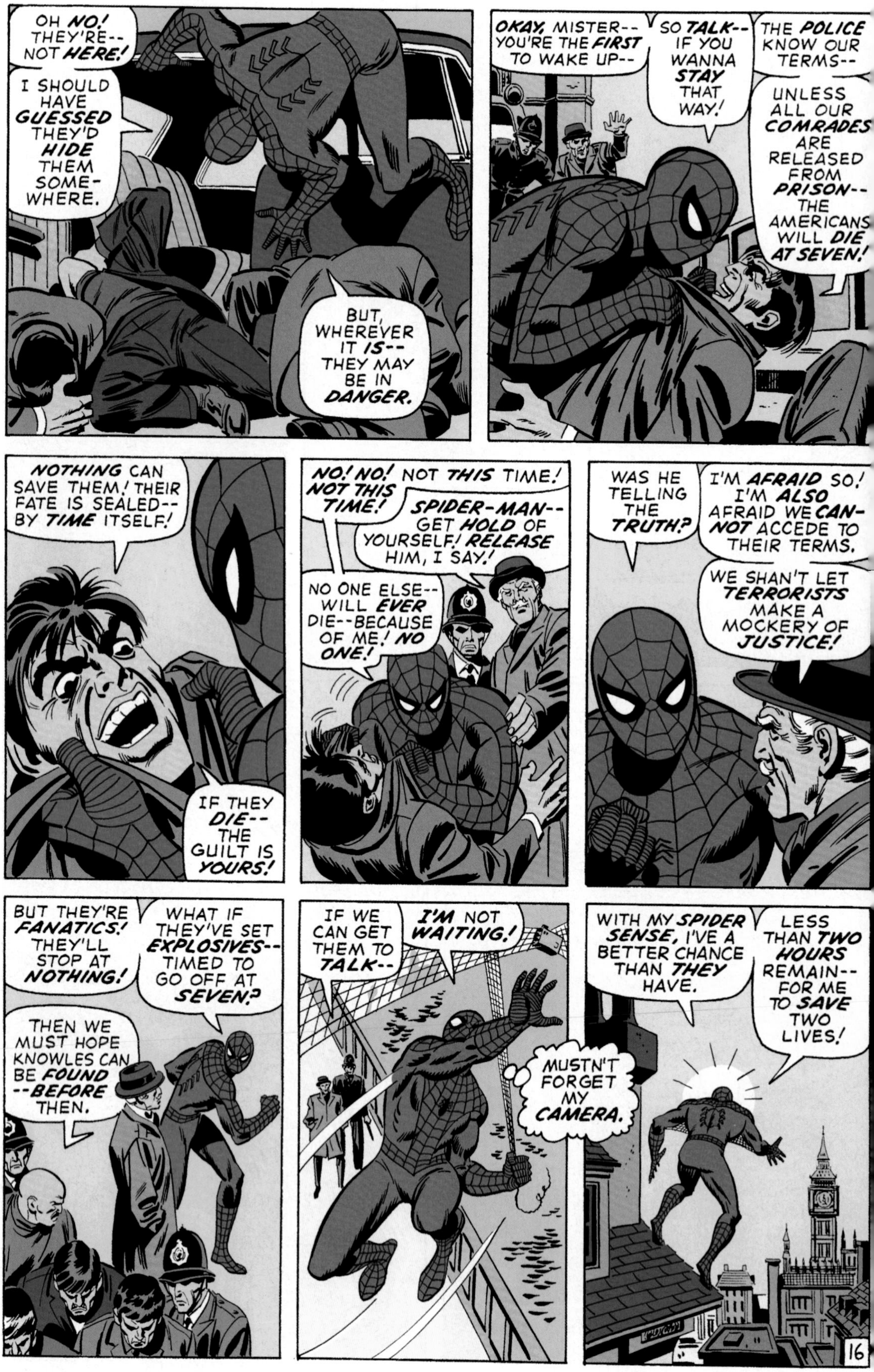

OH NO! THEY'RE-- NOT HERE!
I SHOULD HAVE GUESSED THEY'D HIDE THEM SOMEWHERE.
BUT, WHEREVER IT IS-- THEY MAY BE IN DANGER.
OKAY, MISTER-- YOU'RE THE FIRST TO WAKE UP--
SO TALK-- IF YOU WANNA STAY THAT WAY!
THE POLICE KNOW OUR TERMS--
UNLESS ALL OUR COMRADES ARE RELEASED FROM PRISON-- THE AMERICANS WILL DIE AT SEVEN!
NOTHING CAN SAVE THEM! THEIR FATE IS SEALED-- BY TIME ITSELF!
IF THEY DIE-- THE GUILT IS YOURS!
NO! NO! NOT THIS TIME! NOT THIS TIME!
SPIDER-MAN-- GET HOLD OF YOURSELF! RELEASE HIM, I SAY!
NO ONE ELSE-- WILL EVER DIE--BECAUSE OF ME! NO ONE!
WAS HE TELLING THE TRUTH?
I'M AFRAID SO! I'M ALSO AFRAID WE CANNOT ACCEDE TO THEIR TERMS.
WE SHAN'T LET TERRORISTS MAKE A MOCKERY OF JUSTICE!
BUT THEY'RE FANATICS! THEY'LL STOP AT NOTHING!
WHAT IF THEY'VE SET EXPLOSIVES-- TIMED TO GO OFF AT SEVEN?
THEN WE MUST HOPE KNOWLES CAN BE FOUND --BEFORE THEN.
IF WE CAN GET THEM TO TALK--
I'M NOT WAITING!
MUSTN'T FORGET MY CAMERA.
WITH MY SPIDER SENSE, I'VE A BETTER CHANCE THAN THEY HAVE.
LESS THAN TWO HOURS REMAIN-- FOR ME TO SAVE TWO LIVES!

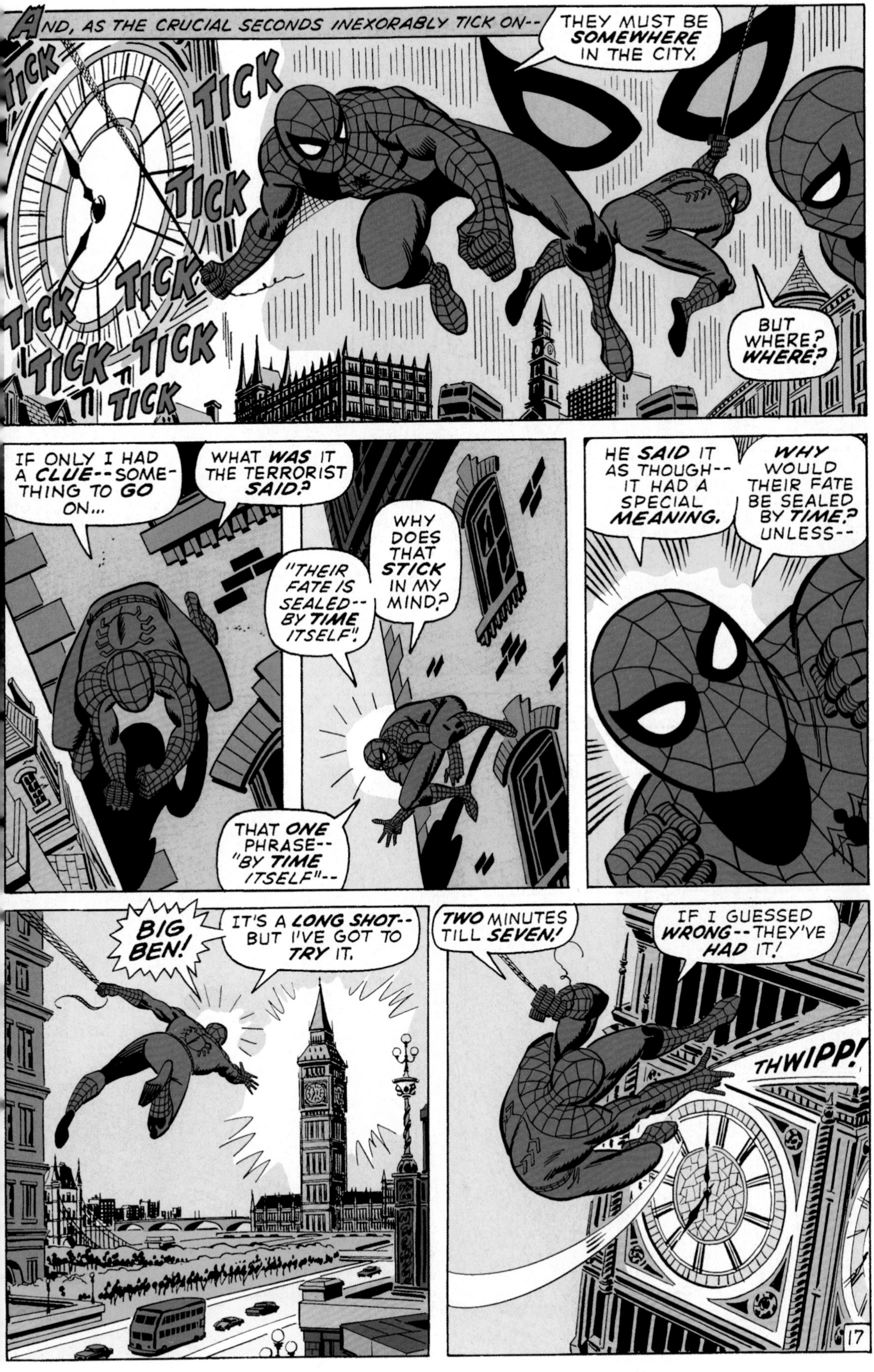
AND, AS THE CRUCIAL SECONDS INEXORABLY TICK ON--
THEY MUST BE SOMEWHERE IN THE CITY.
TICK TICK TICK TICK TICK TICK TICK TICK
BUT WHERE? WHERE?
IF ONLY I HAD A CLUE--SOMETHING TO GO ON...
WHAT WAS IT THE TERRORIST SAID?
"THEIR FATE IS SEALED--BY TIME ITSELF"!
WHY DOES THAT STICK IN MY MIND?
THAT ONE PHRASE--"BY TIME ITSELF"--
HE SAID IT AS THOUGH--IT HAD A SPECIAL MEANING.
WHY WOULD THEIR FATE BE SEALED BY TIME? UNLESS--
BIG BEN!
IT'S A LONG SHOT--BUT I'VE GOT TO TRY IT.
TWO MINUTES TILL SEVEN!
IF I GUESSED WRONG--THEY'VE HAD IT!
THWIPP!

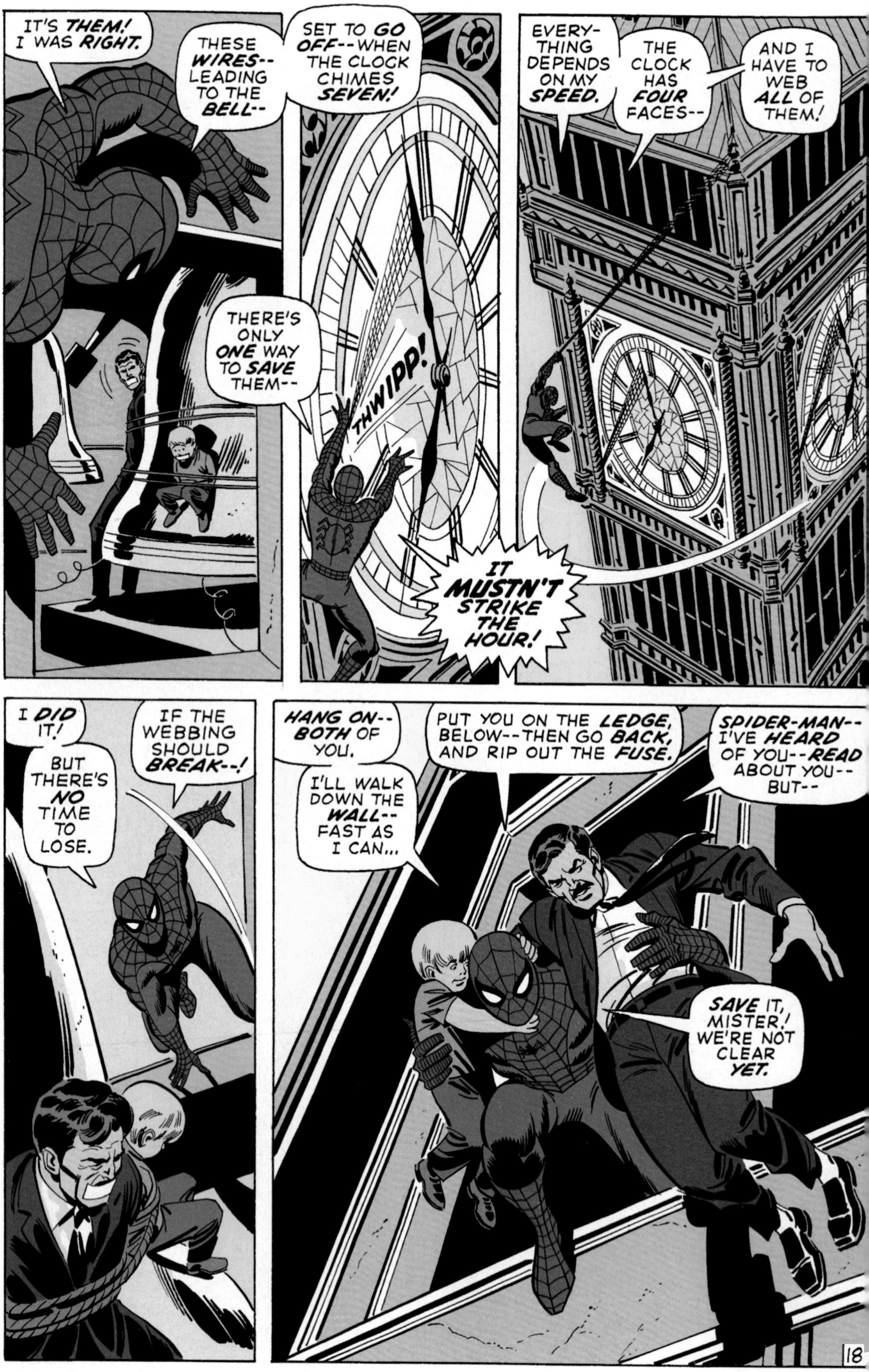
IT'S THEM! I WAS RIGHT.
THESE WIRES-- LEADING TO THE BELL--
SET TO GO OFF--WHEN THE CLOCK CHIMES SEVEN!
THERE'S ONLY ONE WAY TO SAVE THEM--
THWIPP!
EVERY-THING DEPENDS ON MY SPEED.
THE CLOCK HAS FOUR FACES--
AND I HAVE TO WEB ALL OF THEM!
IT MUSTN'T STRIKE THE HOUR!
I DID IT!
BUT THERE'S NO TIME TO LOSE.
IF THE WEBBING SHOULD BREAK--!
HANG ON-- BOTH OF YOU.
I'LL WALK DOWN THE WALL-- FAST AS I CAN...
PUT YOU ON THE LEDGE, BELOW--THEN GO BACK, AND RIP OUT THE FUSE.
SPIDER-MAN-- I'VE HEARD OF YOU--READ ABOUT YOU-- BUT--
SAVE IT, MISTER! WE'RE NOT CLEAR YET.
18

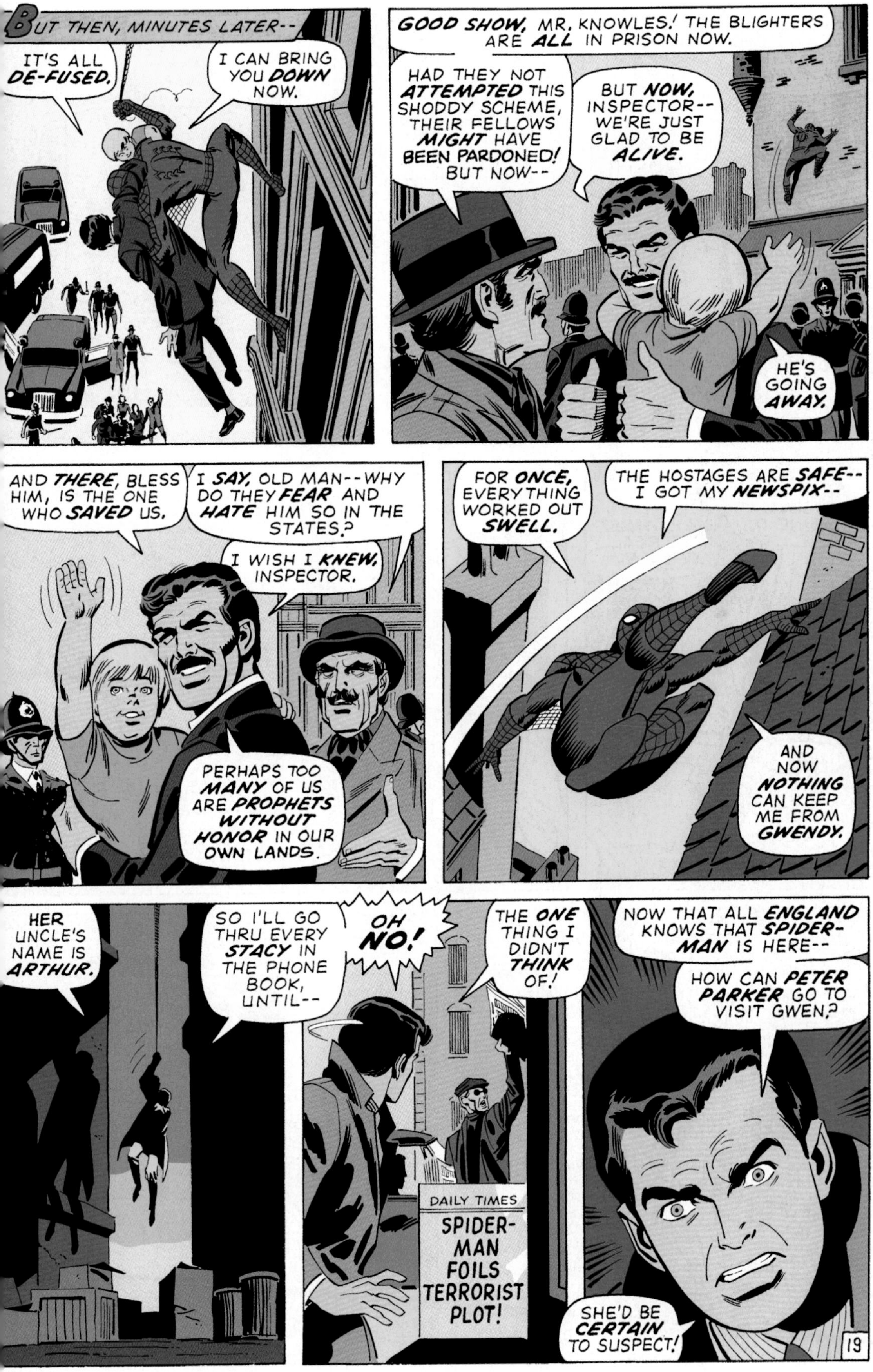
BUT THEN, MINUTES LATER--
IT'S ALL DE-FUSED.
I CAN BRING YOU DOWN NOW.
GOOD SHOW, MR. KNOWLES! THE BLIGHTERS ARE ALL IN PRISON NOW.
HAD THEY NOT ATTEMPTED THIS SHODDY SCHEME, THEIR FELLOWS MIGHT HAVE BEEN PARDONED! BUT NOW--
BUT NOW, INSPECTOR-- WE'RE JUST GLAD TO BE ALIVE.
HE'S GOING AWAY.
AND THERE, BLESS HIM, IS THE ONE WHO SAVED US.
I SAY, OLD MAN--WHY DO THEY FEAR AND HATE HIM SO IN THE STATES?
I WISH I KNEW, INSPECTOR.
PERHAPS TOO MANY OF US ARE PROPHETS WITHOUT HONOR IN OUR OWN LANDS.
FOR ONCE, EVERYTHING WORKED OUT SWELL.
THE HOSTAGES ARE SAFE-- I GOT MY NEWSPIX--
AND NOW NOTHING CAN KEEP ME FROM GWENDY.
HER UNCLE'S NAME IS ARTHUR.
SO I'LL GO THRU EVERY STACY IN THE PHONE BOOK, UNTIL--
OH NO!
THE ONE THING I DIDN'T THINK OF!
DAILY TIMES
SPIDER-MAN FOILS TERRORIST PLOT!
NOW THAT ALL ENGLAND KNOWS THAT SPIDER-MAN IS HERE--
HOW CAN PETER PARKER GO TO VISIT GWEN?
SHE'D BE CERTAIN TO SUSPECT!
19

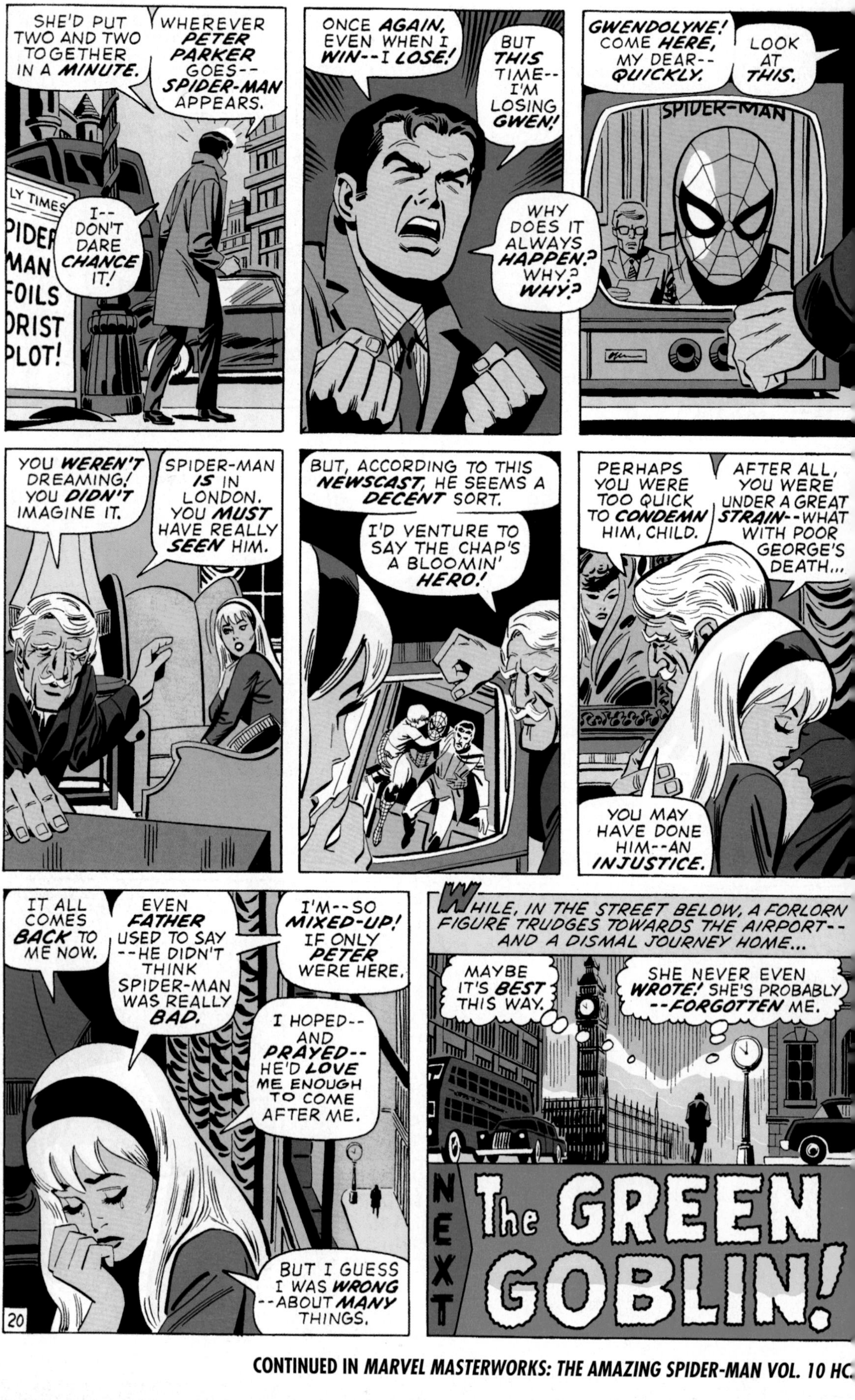
SHE'D PUT TWO AND TWO TOGETHER IN A MINUTE.
WHEREVER PETER PARKER GOES-- SPIDER-MAN APPEARS.
LY TIMES
SPIDER MAN FOILS ORIST PLOT!
I-- DON'T DARE CHANCE IT!
ONCE AGAIN, EVEN WHEN I WIN--I LOSE!
BUT THIS TIME-- I'M LOSING GWEN!
WHY DOES IT ALWAYS HAPPEN? WHY? WHY?
GWENDOLYNE! COME HERE, MY DEAR-- QUICKLY.
LOOK AT THIS.
SPIDER-MAN
YOU WEREN'T DREAMING! YOU DIDN'T IMAGINE IT.
SPIDER-MAN IS IN LONDON. YOU MUST HAVE REALLY SEEN HIM.
BUT, ACCORDING TO THIS NEWSCAST, HE SEEMS A DECENT SORT.
I'D VENTURE TO SAY THE CHAP'S A BLOOMIN' HERO!
PERHAPS YOU WERE TOO QUICK TO CONDEMN HIM, CHILD.
AFTER ALL, YOU WERE UNDER A GREAT STRAIN--WHAT WITH POOR GEORGE'S DEATH...
YOU MAY HAVE DONE HIM--AN INJUSTICE.
IT ALL COMES BACK TO ME NOW.
EVEN FATHER USED TO SAY --HE DIDN'T THINK SPIDER-MAN WAS REALLY BAD.
I'M--SO MIXED-UP! IF ONLY PETER WERE HERE.
I HOPED-- AND PRAYED-- HE'D LOVE ME ENOUGH TO COME AFTER ME.
BUT I GUESS I WAS WRONG --ABOUT MANY THINGS.
20
WHILE, IN THE STREET BELOW, A FORLORN FIGURE TRUDGES TOWARDS THE AIRPORT-- AND A DISMAL JOURNEY HOME...
MAYBE IT'S BEST THIS WAY.
SHE NEVER EVEN WROTE! SHE'S PROBABLY --FORGOTTEN ME.
NEXT
The GREEN GOBLIN!

CONTINUED IN *MARVEL MASTERWORKS: THE AMAZING SPIDER-MAN VOL. 10 HC.*

IT'S A BATTLE OF ILLUSIONS AS SPIDER-MAN ONCE AGAIN FINDS HIMSELF FACING SPECIAL-EFFECTS-DESIGNER-TURNED-SUPER-VILLAIN, MYSTERIO!

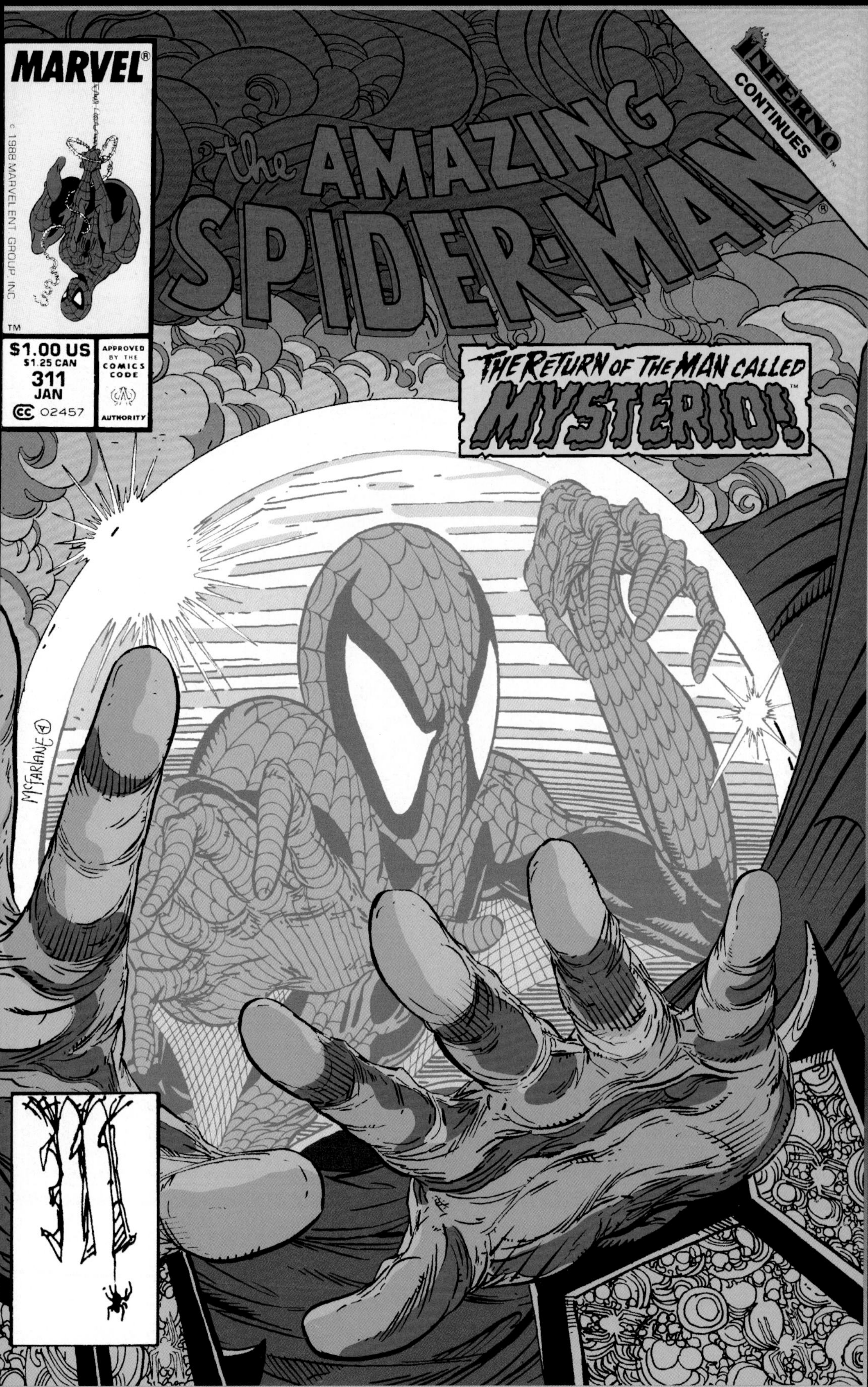

MARVEL®
© 1988 MARVEL ENT. GROUP, INC.
TM
$1.00 US
$1.25 CAN
311
JAN
02457
APPROVED BY THE COMICS CODE AUTHORITY
INFERNO CONTINUES
the AMAZING SPIDER-MAN®
THE RETURN OF THE MAN CALLED MYSTERIO!™
McFARLANE

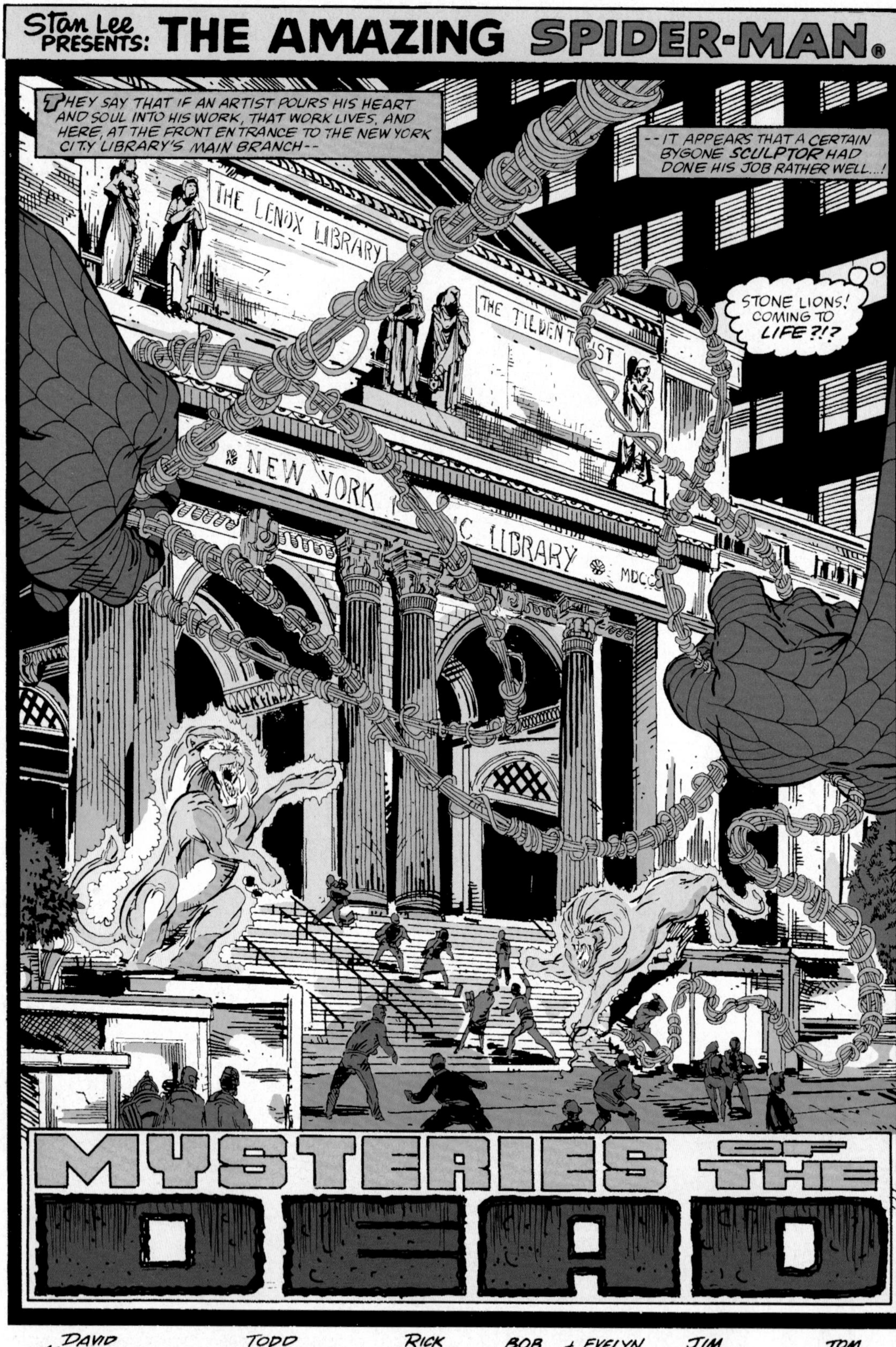
Stan Lee PRESENTS: THE AMAZING SPIDER-MAN®
THEY SAY THAT IF AN ARTIST POURS HIS HEART AND SOUL INTO HIS WORK, THAT WORK LIVES, AND HERE, AT THE FRONT ENTRANCE TO THE NEW YORK CITY LIBRARY'S MAIN BRANCH--
--IT APPEARS THAT A CERTAIN BYGONE SCULPTOR HAD DONE HIS JOB RATHER WELL...!
THE LENOX LIBRARY
THE TILDEN TRUST
NEW YORK
LIBRARY
STONE LIONS! COMING TO LIFE?!?
MYSTERIES OF THE DEAD

DAVID MICHELINIE WRITER · TODD McFARLANE ARTIST · RICK PARKER LETTERS · BOB SHAREN & EVELYN STEIN COLOR · JIM SALICRUP EDITOR · TOM DeFALCO EDITOR IN CHIEF

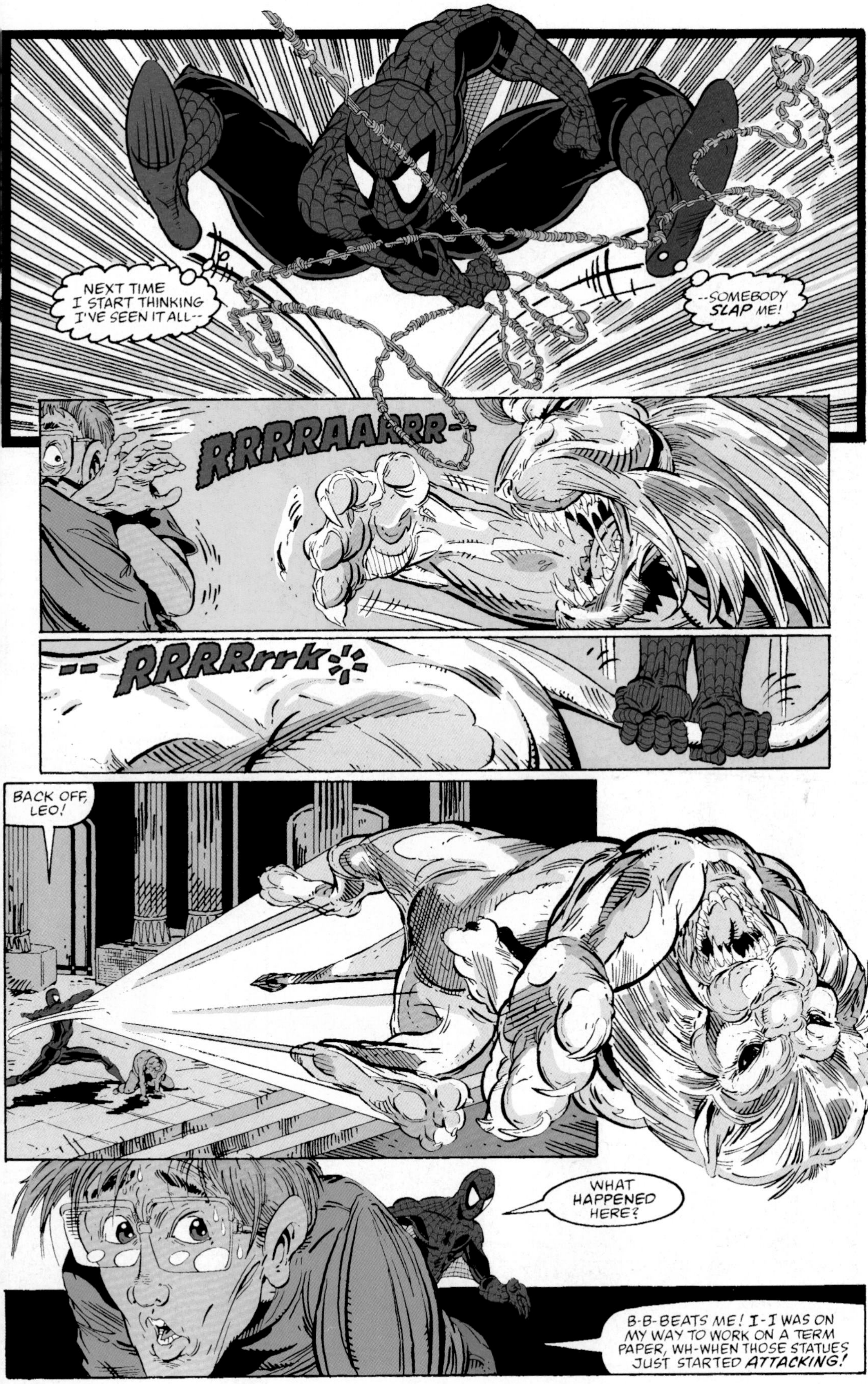
NEXT TIME I START THINKING I'VE SEEN IT ALL--
--SOMEBODY SLAP ME!
RRRRAARRR-
--RRRRrrk
BACK OFF, LEO!
WHAT HAPPENED HERE?
B-B-BEATS ME! I-I WAS ON MY WAY TO WORK ON A TERM PAPER, WH-WHEN THOSE STATUES JUST STARTED ATTACKING!

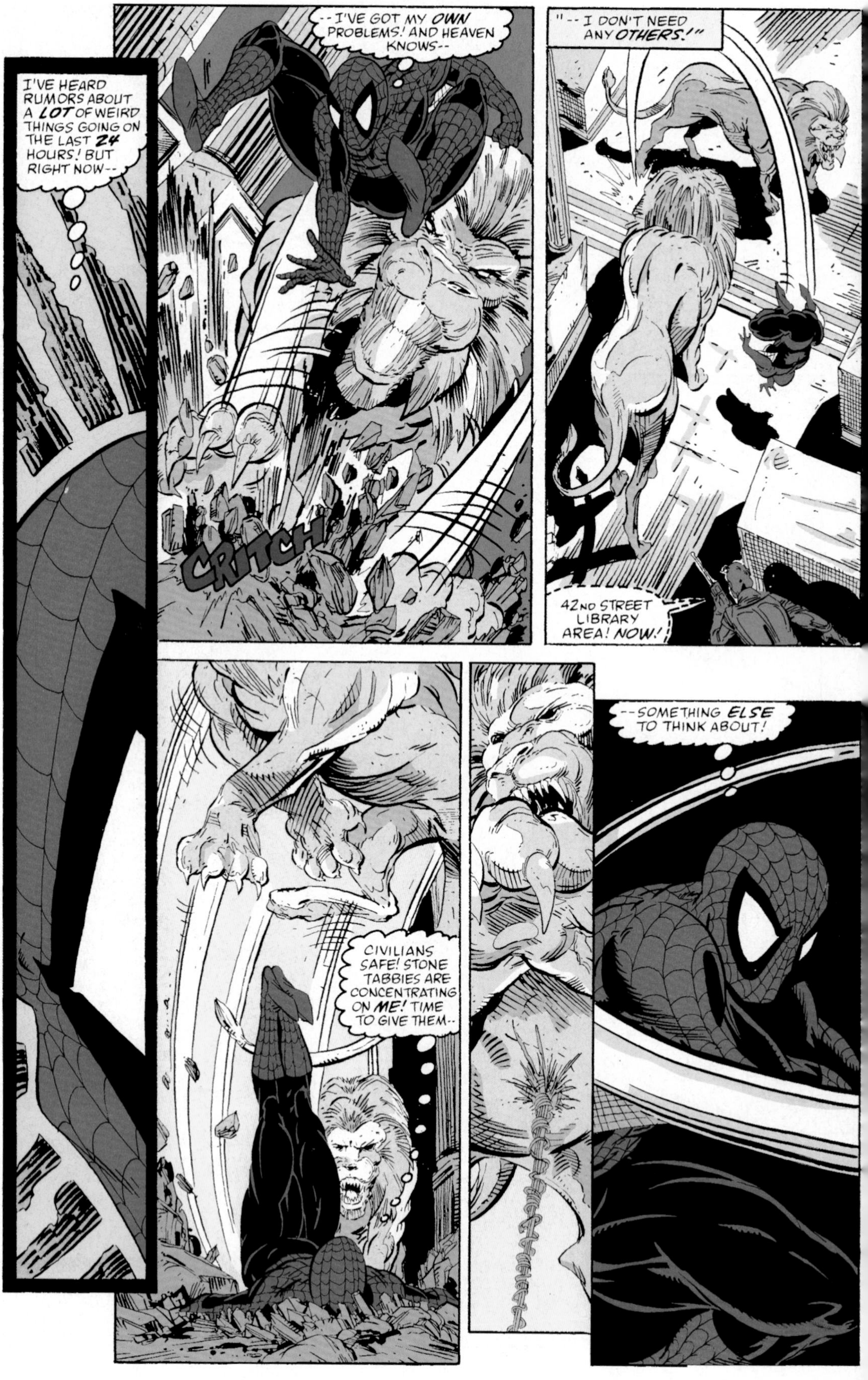

I'VE HEARD RUMORS ABOUT A LOT OF WEIRD THINGS GOING ON THE LAST 24 HOURS! BUT RIGHT NOW--
--I'VE GOT MY OWN PROBLEMS! AND HEAVEN KNOWS--
CRITCH
"--I DON'T NEED ANY OTHERS!"
42ND STREET LIBRARY AREA! NOW!
CIVILIANS SAFE! STONE TABBIES ARE CONCENTRATING ON ME! TIME TO GIVE THEM--
--SOMETHING ELSE TO THINK ABOUT!

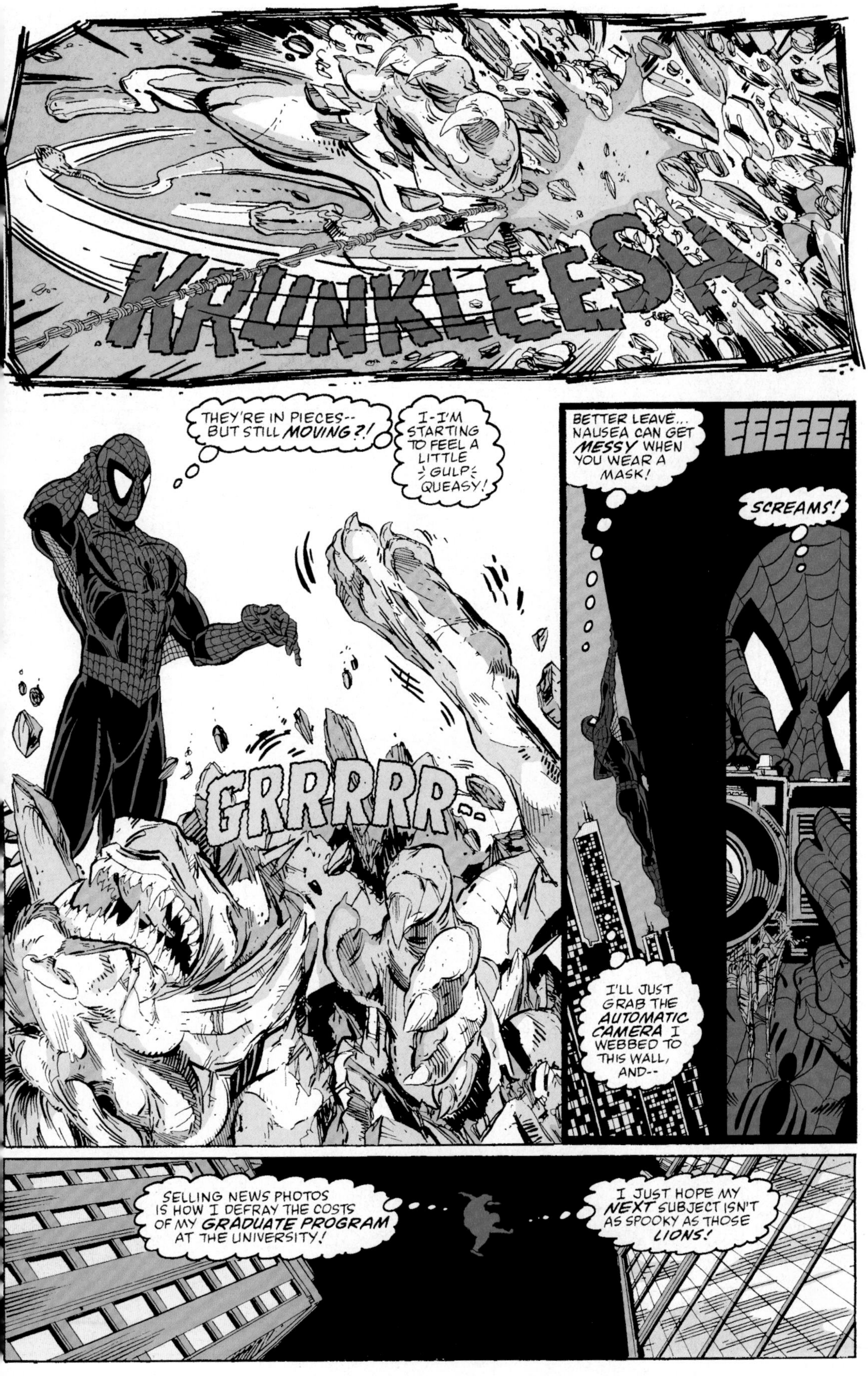
KRUNKLEESH
THEY'RE IN PIECES-- BUT STILL MOVING?!
I-I'M STARTING TO FEEL A LITTLE -GULP- QUEASY!
GRRRRR
BETTER LEAVE... NAUSEA CAN GET MESSY WHEN YOU WEAR A MASK!
EEEEEE!
SCREAMS!
I'LL JUST GRAB THE AUTOMATIC CAMERA I WEBBED TO THIS WALL, AND--
SELLING NEWS PHOTOS IS HOW I DEFRAY THE COSTS OF MY GRADUATE PROGRAM AT THE UNIVERSITY!
I JUST HOPE MY NEXT SUBJECT ISN'T AS SPOOKY AS THOSE LIONS!

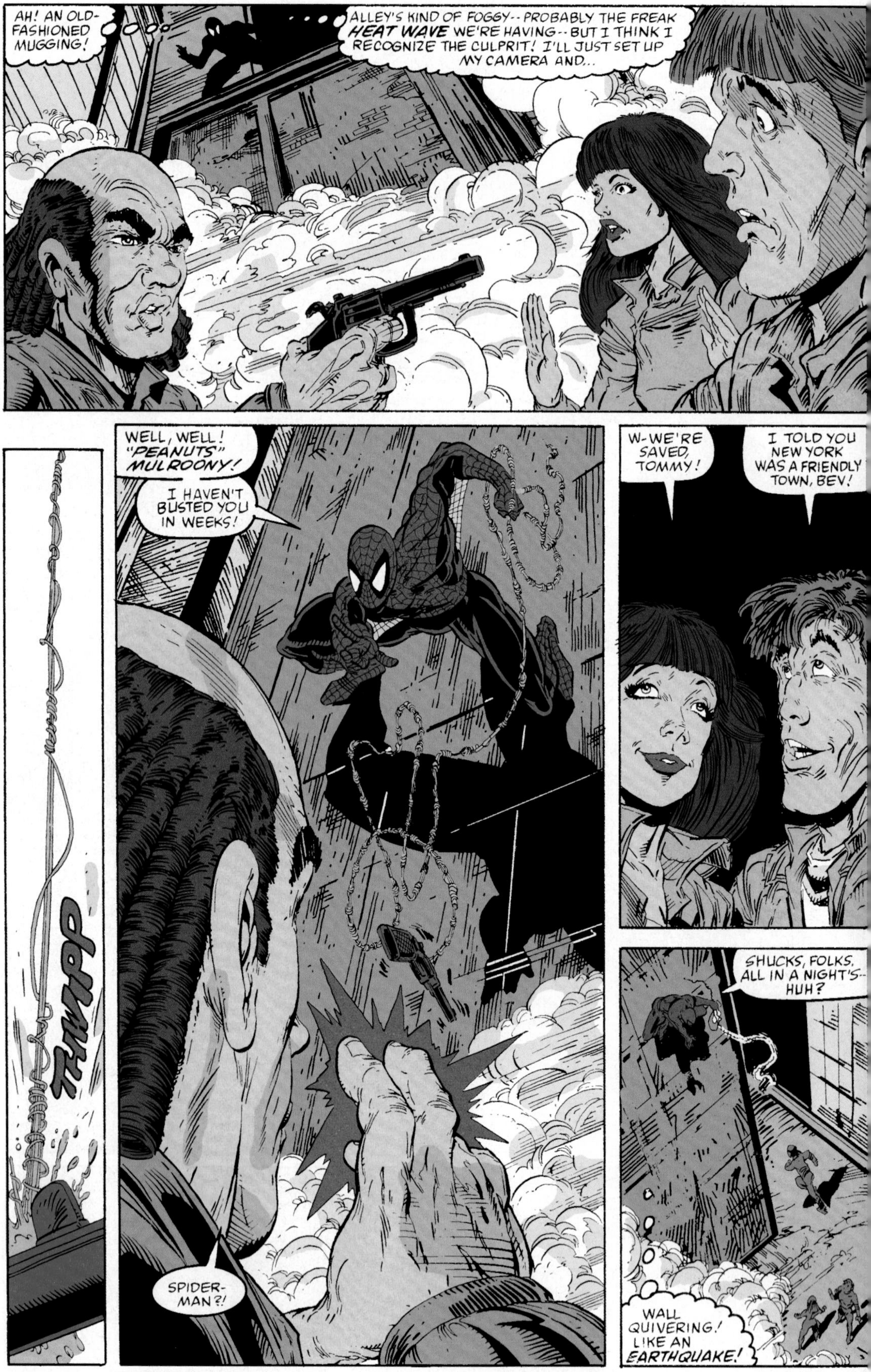

AH! AN OLD-FASHIONED MUGGING!
ALLEY'S KIND OF FOGGY-- PROBABLY THE FREAK HEAT WAVE WE'RE HAVING-- BUT I THINK I RECOGNIZE THE CULPRIT! I'LL JUST SET UP MY CAMERA AND...
THWIPP
WELL, WELL! "PEANUTS" MULROONY!
I HAVEN'T BUSTED YOU IN WEEKS!
SPIDER-MAN?!
W-WE'RE SAVED, TOMMY!
I TOLD YOU NEW YORK WAS A FRIENDLY TOWN, BEV!
SHUCKS, FOLKS. ALL IN A NIGHT'S-- HUH?
WALL QUIVERING! LIKE AN EARTHQUAKE!

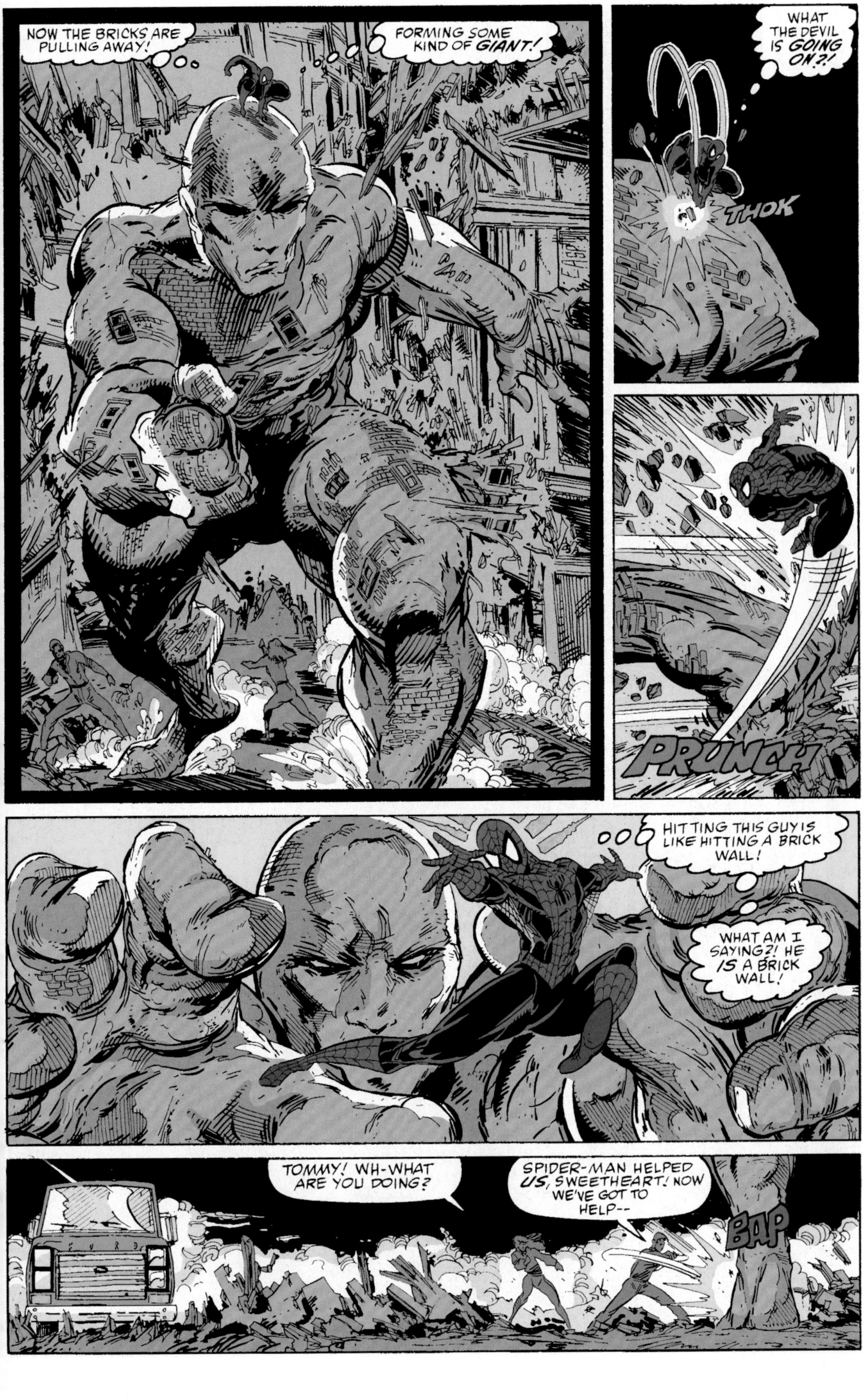

NOW THE BRICKS ARE PULLING AWAY!
FORMING SOME KIND OF GIANT!
WHAT THE DEVIL IS GOING ON?!
THOK
PRUNCH
HITTING THIS GUY IS LIKE HITTING A BRICK WALL!
WHAT AM I SAYING?! HE IS A BRICK WALL!
TOMMY! WH-WHAT ARE YOU DOING?
SPIDER-MAN HELPED US, SWEETHEART! NOW WE'VE GOT TO HELP--
BAP

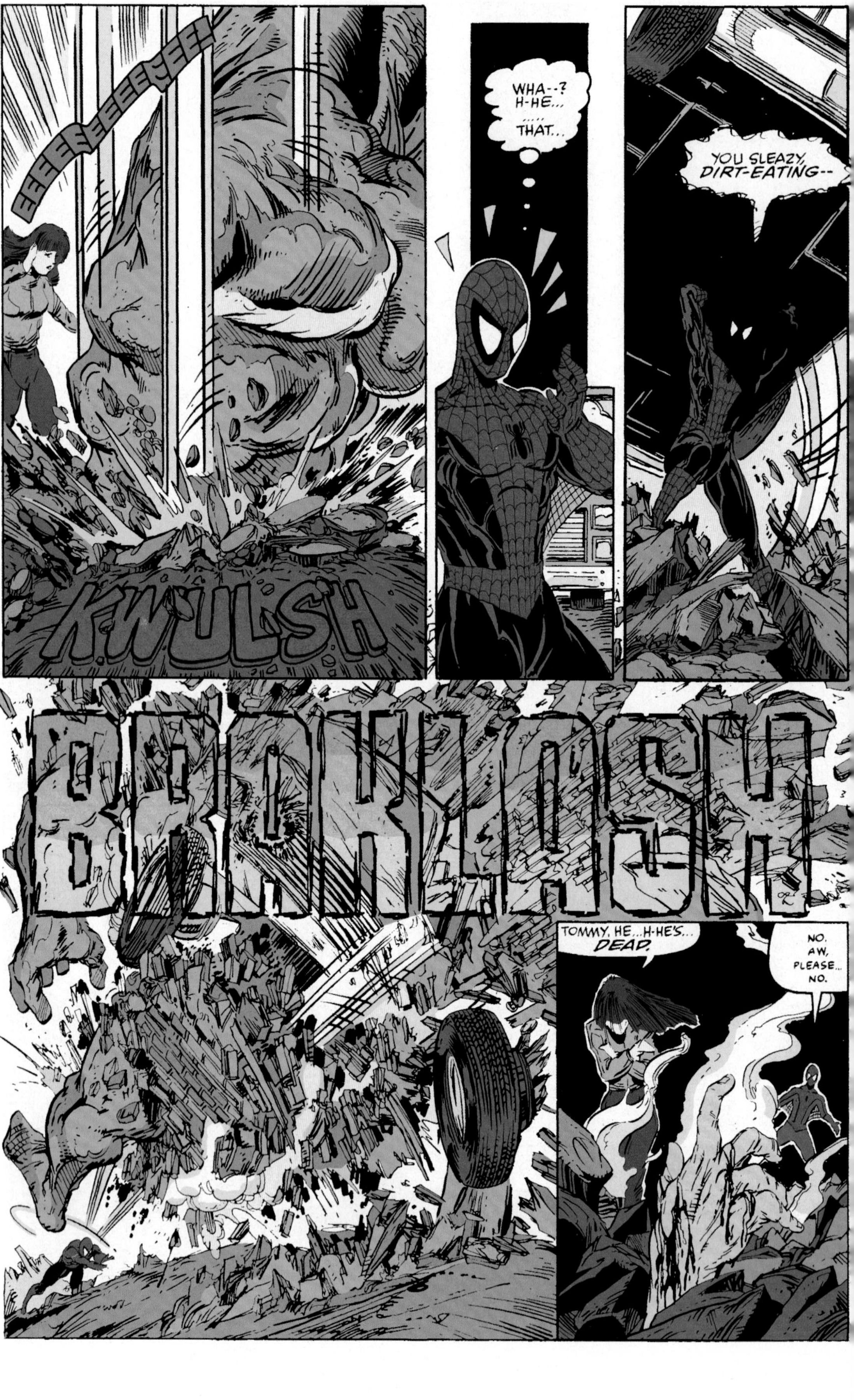
K-WULSH
WHA--? H-HE... ...... THAT...
YOU SLEAZY, DIRT-EATING--
TOMMY, HE...H-HE'S... DEAD.
NO. AW, PLEASE... NO.

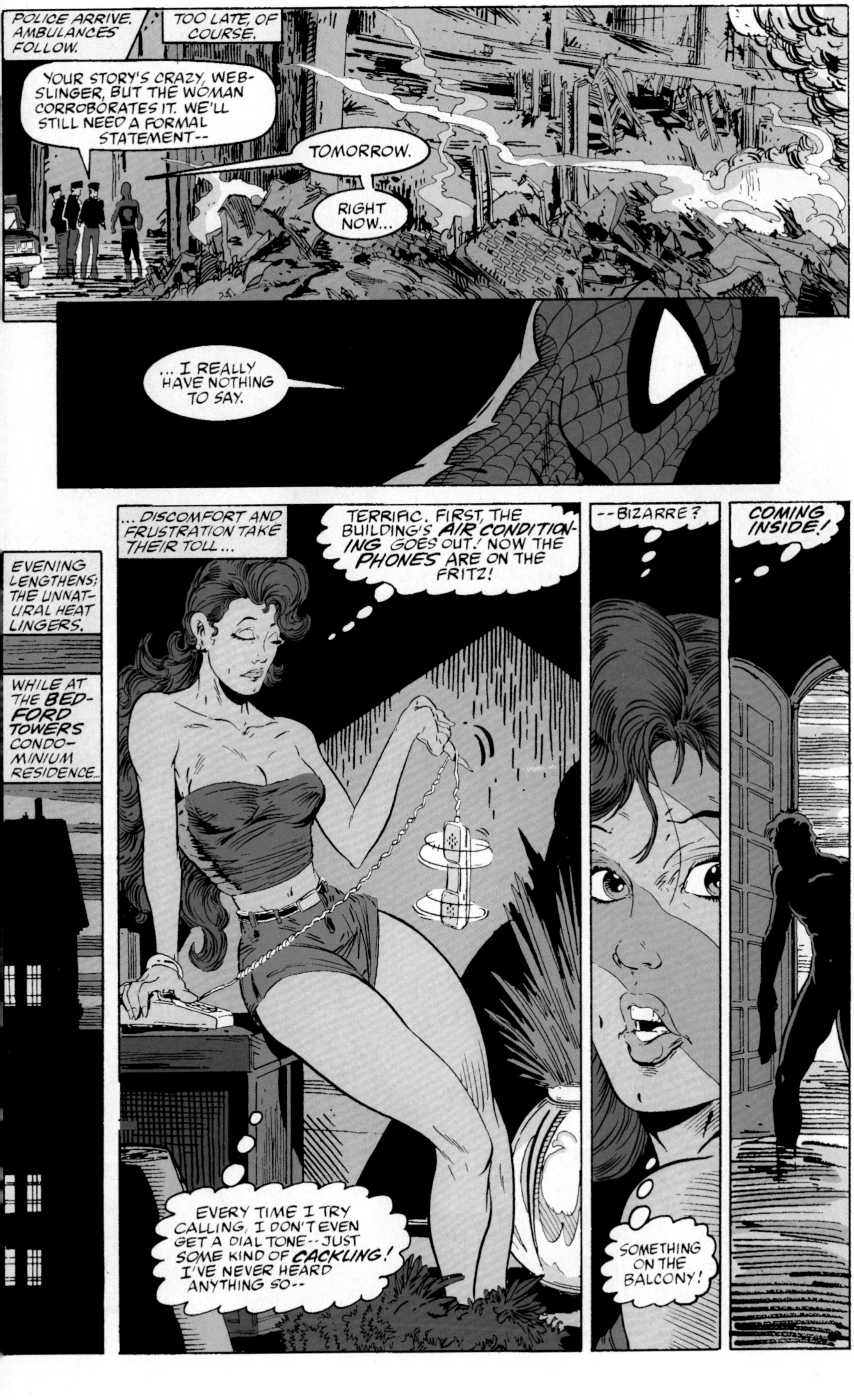

POLICE ARRIVE. AMBULANCES FOLLOW.
TOO LATE, OF COURSE.
YOUR STORY'S CRAZY, WEB-SLINGER, BUT THE WOMAN CORROBORATES IT. WE'LL STILL NEED A FORMAL STATEMENT--
TOMORROW.
RIGHT NOW...
... I REALLY HAVE NOTHING TO SAY.
EVENING LENGTHENS; THE UNNATURAL HEAT LINGERS.
WHILE AT THE BEDFORD TOWERS CONDOMINIUM RESIDENCE...
...DISCOMFORT AND FRUSTRATION TAKE THEIR TOLL...
TERRIFIC. FIRST, THE BUILDING'S AIR CONDITIONING GOES OUT! NOW THE PHONES ARE ON THE FRITZ!
EVERY TIME I TRY CALLING, I DON'T EVEN GET A DIAL TONE--JUST SOME KIND OF CACKLING! I'VE NEVER HEARD ANYTHING SO--
--BIZARRE?
SOMETHING ON THE BALCONY!
COMING INSIDE!

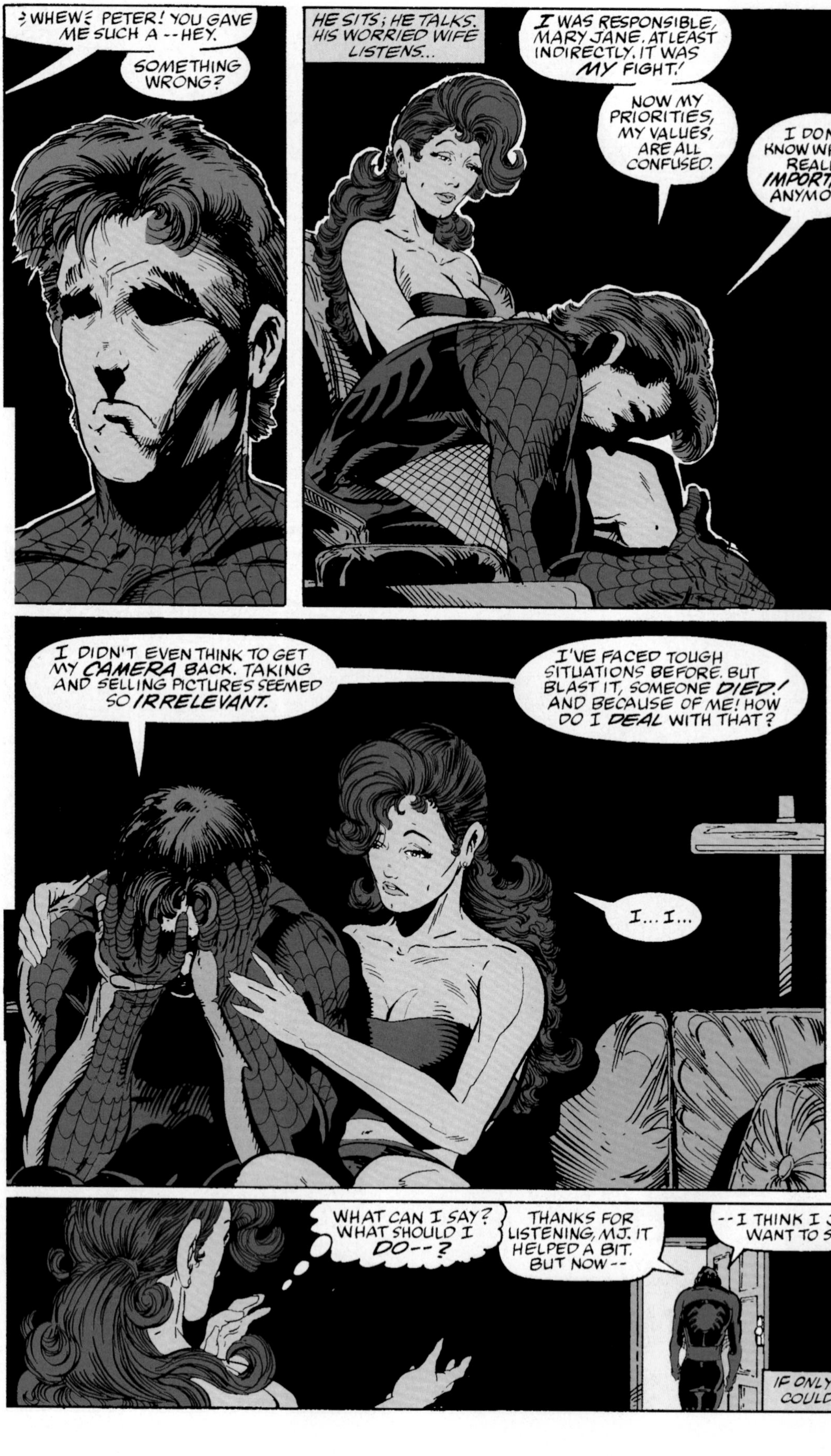

WHEW! PETER! YOU GAVE ME SUCH A --HEY.
SOMETHING WRONG?
HE SITS; HE TALKS. HIS WORRIED WIFE LISTENS...
I WAS RESPONSIBLE, MARY JANE. AT LEAST INDIRECTLY. IT WAS MY FIGHT!
NOW MY PRIORITIES, MY VALUES, ARE ALL CONFUSED.
I DON'T KNOW WHAT'S REALLY IMPORTANT ANYMORE.
I DIDN'T EVEN THINK TO GET MY CAMERA BACK. TAKING AND SELLING PICTURES SEEMED SO IRRELEVANT.
I'VE FACED TOUGH SITUATIONS BEFORE. BUT BLAST IT, SOMEONE DIED! AND BECAUSE OF ME! HOW DO I DEAL WITH THAT?
I... I...
WHAT CAN I SAY? WHAT SHOULD I DO--?
THANKS FOR LISTENING, MJ. IT HELPED A BIT. BUT NOW --
-- I THINK I JUST WANT TO SLEEP.
IF ONLY HE COULD.

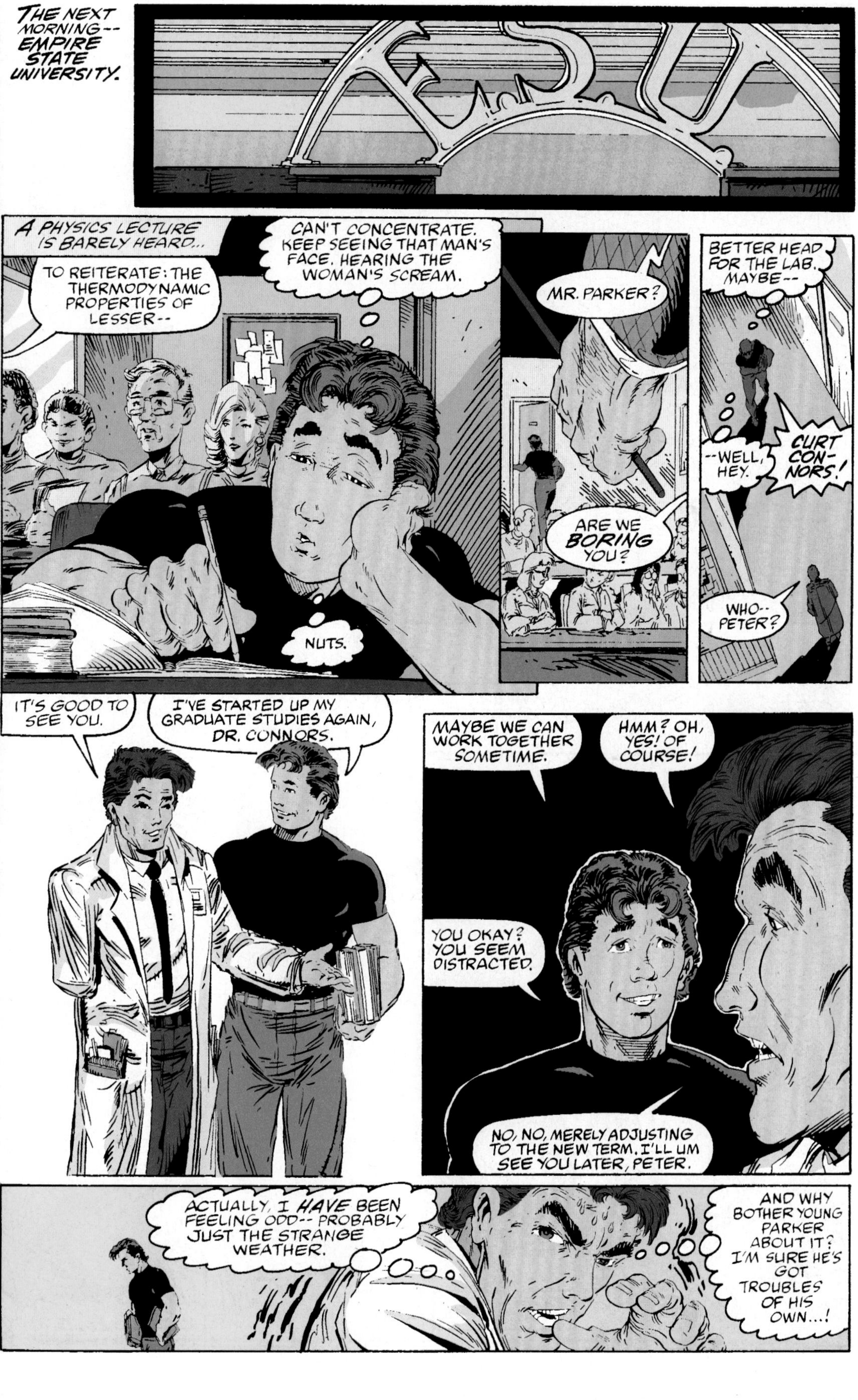

THE NEXT MORNING-- EMPIRE STATE UNIVERSITY.
E.S.U.
A PHYSICS LECTURE IS BARELY HEARD...
TO REITERATE: THE THERMODYNAMIC PROPERTIES OF LESSER--
CAN'T CONCENTRATE. KEEP SEEING THAT MAN'S FACE. HEARING THE WOMAN'S SCREAM.
NUTS.
MR. PARKER?
ARE WE BORING YOU?
BETTER HEAD FOR THE LAB. MAYBE--
--WELL, HEY.
CURT CONNORS!
WHO--PETER?
IT'S GOOD TO SEE YOU.
I'VE STARTED UP MY GRADUATE STUDIES AGAIN, DR. CONNORS.
MAYBE WE CAN WORK TOGETHER SOMETIME.
HMM? OH, YES! OF COURSE!
YOU OKAY? YOU SEEM DISTRACTED.
NO, NO, MERELY ADJUSTING TO THE NEW TERM. I'LL UM SEE YOU LATER, PETER.
ACTUALLY, I HAVE BEEN FEELING ODD-- PROBABLY JUST THE STRANGE WEATHER.
AND WHY BOTHER YOUNG PARKER ABOUT IT? I'M SURE HE'S GOT TROUBLES OF HIS OWN...!

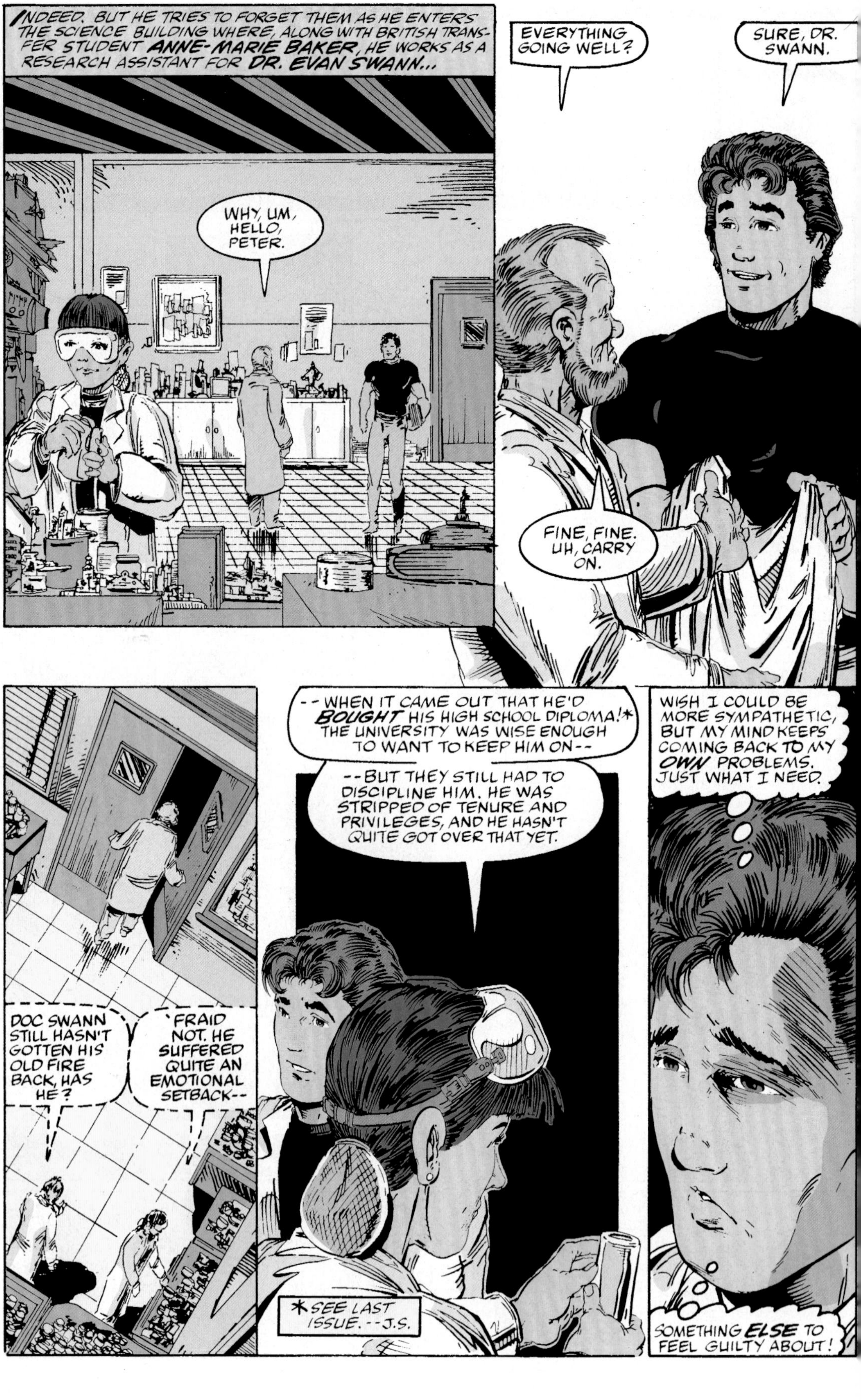
INDEED. BUT HE TRIES TO FORGET THEM AS HE ENTERS THE SCIENCE BUILDING WHERE, ALONG WITH BRITISH TRANSFER STUDENT ANNE-MARIE BAKER, HE WORKS AS A RESEARCH ASSISTANT FOR DR. EVAN SWANN...
WHY, UM, HELLO, PETER.
EVERYTHING GOING WELL?
SURE, DR. SWANN.
FINE, FINE. UH, CARRY ON.
DOC SWANN STILL HASN'T GOTTEN HIS OLD FIRE BACK, HAS HE?
'FRAID NOT. HE SUFFERED QUITE AN EMOTIONAL SETBACK--
--WHEN IT CAME OUT THAT HE'D BOUGHT HIS HIGH SCHOOL DIPLOMA!* THE UNIVERSITY WAS WISE ENOUGH TO WANT TO KEEP HIM ON--
--BUT THEY STILL HAD TO DISCIPLINE HIM. HE WAS STRIPPED OF TENURE AND PRIVILEGES, AND HE HASN'T QUITE GOT OVER THAT YET.
*SEE LAST ISSUE. --J.S.
WISH I COULD BE MORE SYMPATHETIC, BUT MY MIND KEEPS COMING BACK TO MY OWN PROBLEMS. JUST WHAT I NEED.
SOMETHING ELSE TO FEEL GUILTY ABOUT!

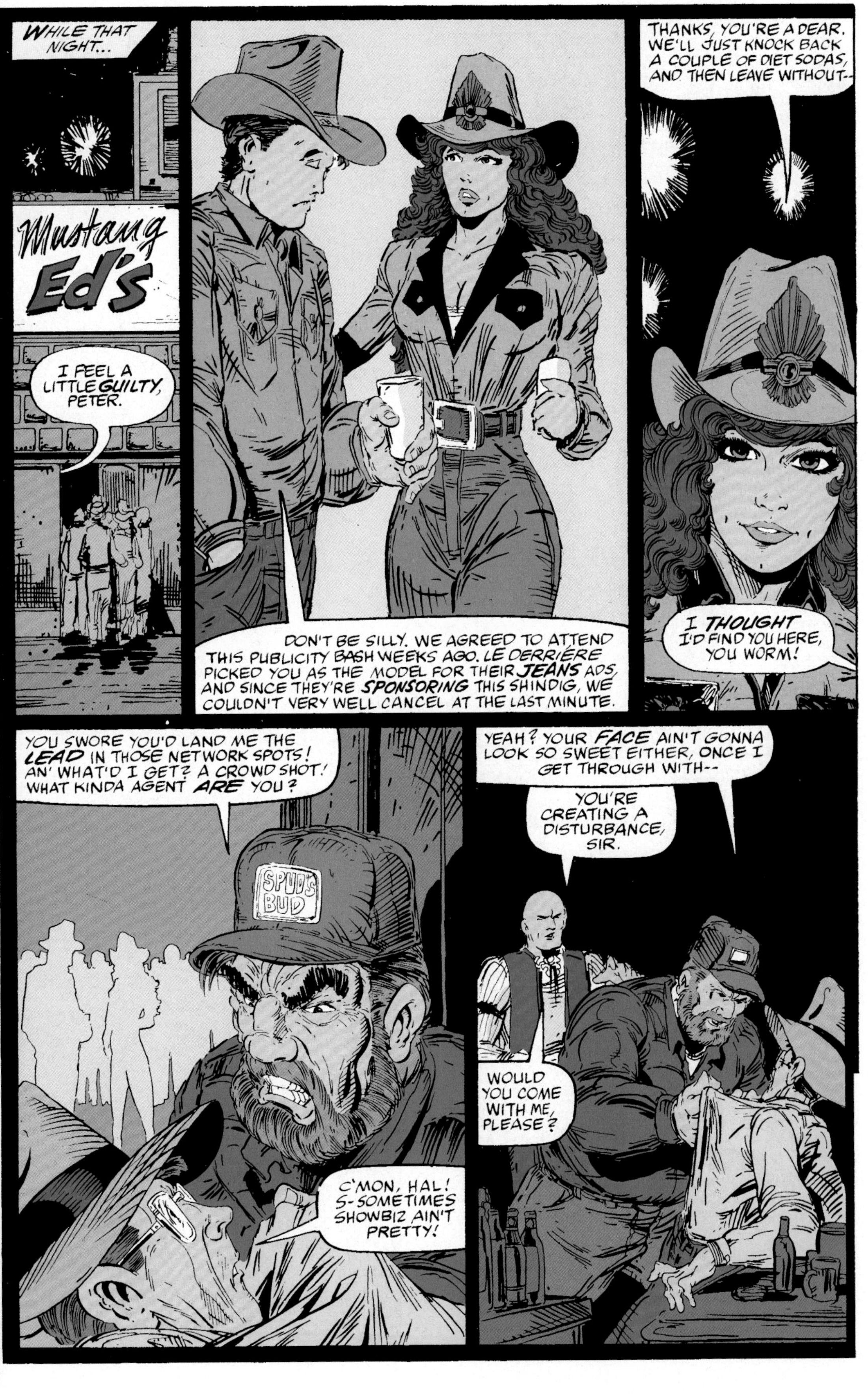
WHILE THAT NIGHT...
Mustang Ed's
I FEEL A LITTLE GUILTY, PETER.
DON'T BE SILLY. WE AGREED TO ATTEND THIS PUBLICITY BASH WEEKS AGO. LE DERRIÉRE PICKED YOU AS THE MODEL FOR THEIR JEANS ADS, AND SINCE THEY'RE SPONSORING THIS SHINDIG, WE COULDN'T VERY WELL CANCEL AT THE LAST MINUTE.
THANKS, YOU'RE A DEAR. WE'LL JUST KNOCK BACK A COUPLE OF DIET SODAS, AND THEN LEAVE WITHOUT--
I THOUGHT I'D FIND YOU HERE, YOU WORM!
YOU SWORE YOU'D LAND ME THE LEAD IN THOSE NETWORK SPOTS! AN' WHAT'D I GET? A CROWD SHOT! WHAT KINDA AGENT ARE YOU?
SPUD'S BUD
C'MON, HAL! S-SOMETIMES SHOWBIZ AIN'T PRETTY!
YEAH? YOUR FACE AIN'T GONNA LOOK SO SWEET EITHER, ONCE I GET THROUGH WITH--
YOU'RE CREATING A DISTURBANCE, SIR.
WOULD YOU COME WITH ME, PLEASE?

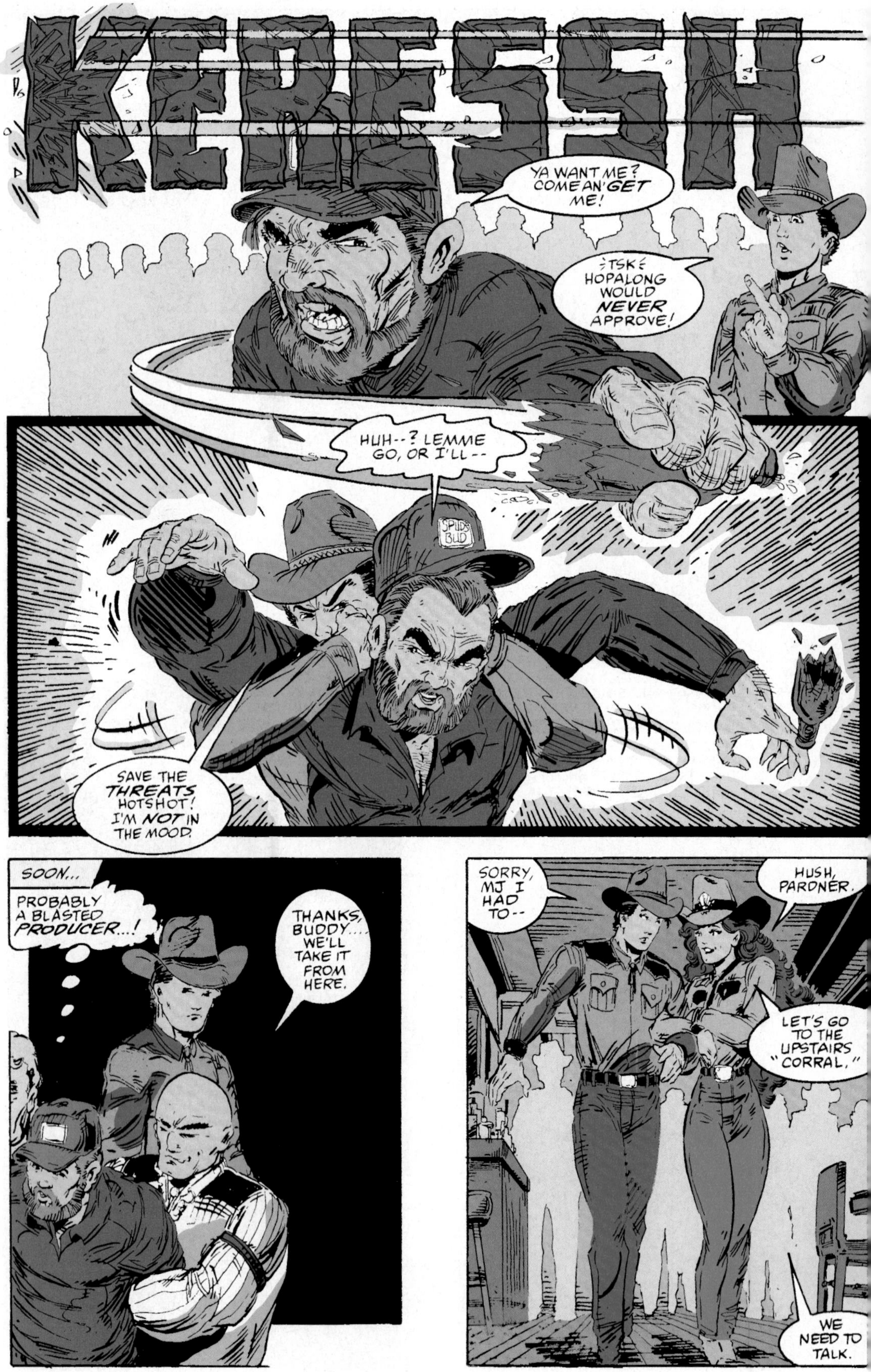
KERESSH
YA WANT ME? COME AN' GET ME!
TSK HOPALONG WOULD NEVER APPROVE!
HUH--? LEMME GO, OR I'LL--
SPUDS BUD
SAVE THE THREATS HOTSHOT! I'M NOT IN THE MOOD.
SOON...
PROBABLY A BLASTED PRODUCER...!
THANKS, BUDDY... WE'LL TAKE IT FROM HERE.
SORRY, MJ I HAD TO--
HUSH, PARDNER.
LET'S GO TO THE UPSTAIRS "CORRAL."
WE NEED TO TALK.

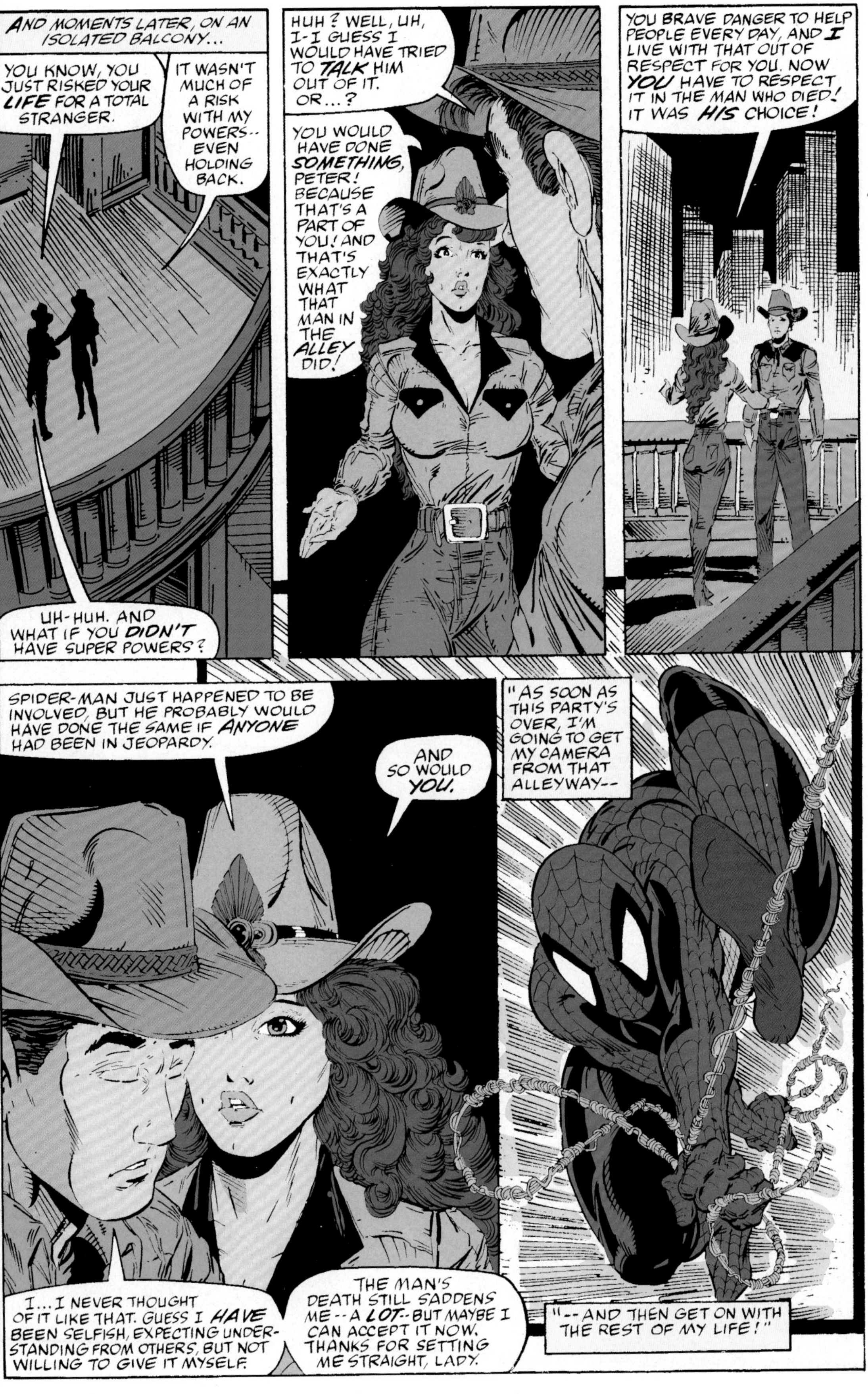
AND MOMENTS LATER, ON AN ISOLATED BALCONY...
YOU KNOW, YOU JUST RISKED YOUR LIFE FOR A TOTAL STRANGER.
IT WASN'T MUCH OF A RISK WITH MY POWERS-- EVEN HOLDING BACK.
UH-HUH. AND WHAT IF YOU DIDN'T HAVE SUPER POWERS?
HUH? WELL, UH, I-I GUESS I WOULD HAVE TRIED TO TALK HIM OUT OF IT. OR...?
YOU WOULD HAVE DONE SOMETHING, PETER! BECAUSE THAT'S A PART OF YOU! AND THAT'S EXACTLY WHAT THAT MAN IN THE ALLEY DID!
YOU BRAVE DANGER TO HELP PEOPLE EVERY DAY, AND I LIVE WITH THAT OUT OF RESPECT FOR YOU. NOW YOU HAVE TO RESPECT IT IN THE MAN WHO DIED! IT WAS HIS CHOICE!
SPIDER-MAN JUST HAPPENED TO BE INVOLVED, BUT HE PROBABLY WOULD HAVE DONE THE SAME IF ANYONE HAD BEEN IN JEOPARDY.
AND SO WOULD YOU.
I... I NEVER THOUGHT OF IT LIKE THAT. GUESS I HAVE BEEN SELFISH, EXPECTING UNDERSTANDING FROM OTHERS, BUT NOT WILLING TO GIVE IT MYSELF.
THE MAN'S DEATH STILL SADDENS ME -- A LOT -- BUT MAYBE I CAN ACCEPT IT NOW. THANKS FOR SETTING ME STRAIGHT, LADY.
"AS SOON AS THIS PARTY'S OVER, I'M GOING TO GET MY CAMERA FROM THAT ALLEYWAY--
"--AND THEN GET ON WITH THE REST OF MY LIFE!"

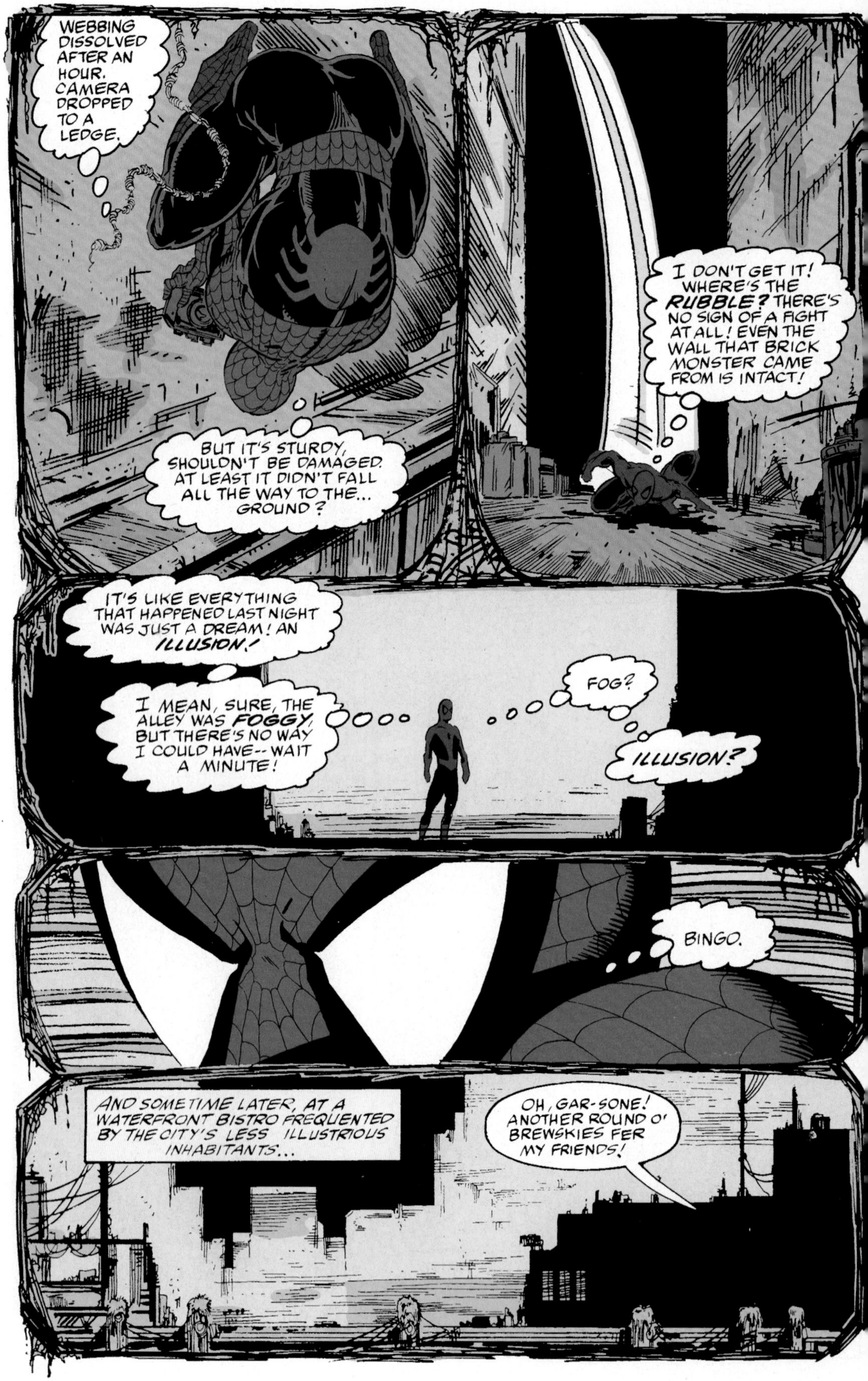

WEBBING DISSOLVED AFTER AN HOUR. CAMERA DROPPED TO A LEDGE.
BUT IT'S STURDY, SHOULDN'T BE DAMAGED. AT LEAST IT DIDN'T FALL ALL THE WAY TO THE... GROUND?
I DON'T GET IT! WHERE'S THE RUBBLE? THERE'S NO SIGN OF A FIGHT AT ALL! EVEN THE WALL THAT BRICK MONSTER CAME FROM IS INTACT!
IT'S LIKE EVERYTHING THAT HAPPENED LAST NIGHT WAS JUST A DREAM! AN ILLUSION!
I MEAN, SURE, THE ALLEY WAS FOGGY, BUT THERE'S NO WAY I COULD HAVE-- WAIT A MINUTE!
FOG?
ILLUSION?
BINGO.
AND SOMETIME LATER, AT A WATERFRONT BISTRO FREQUENTED BY THE CITY'S LESS ILLUSTRIOUS INHABITANTS...
OH, GAR-SONE! ANOTHER ROUND O' BREWSKIES FER MY FRIENDS!

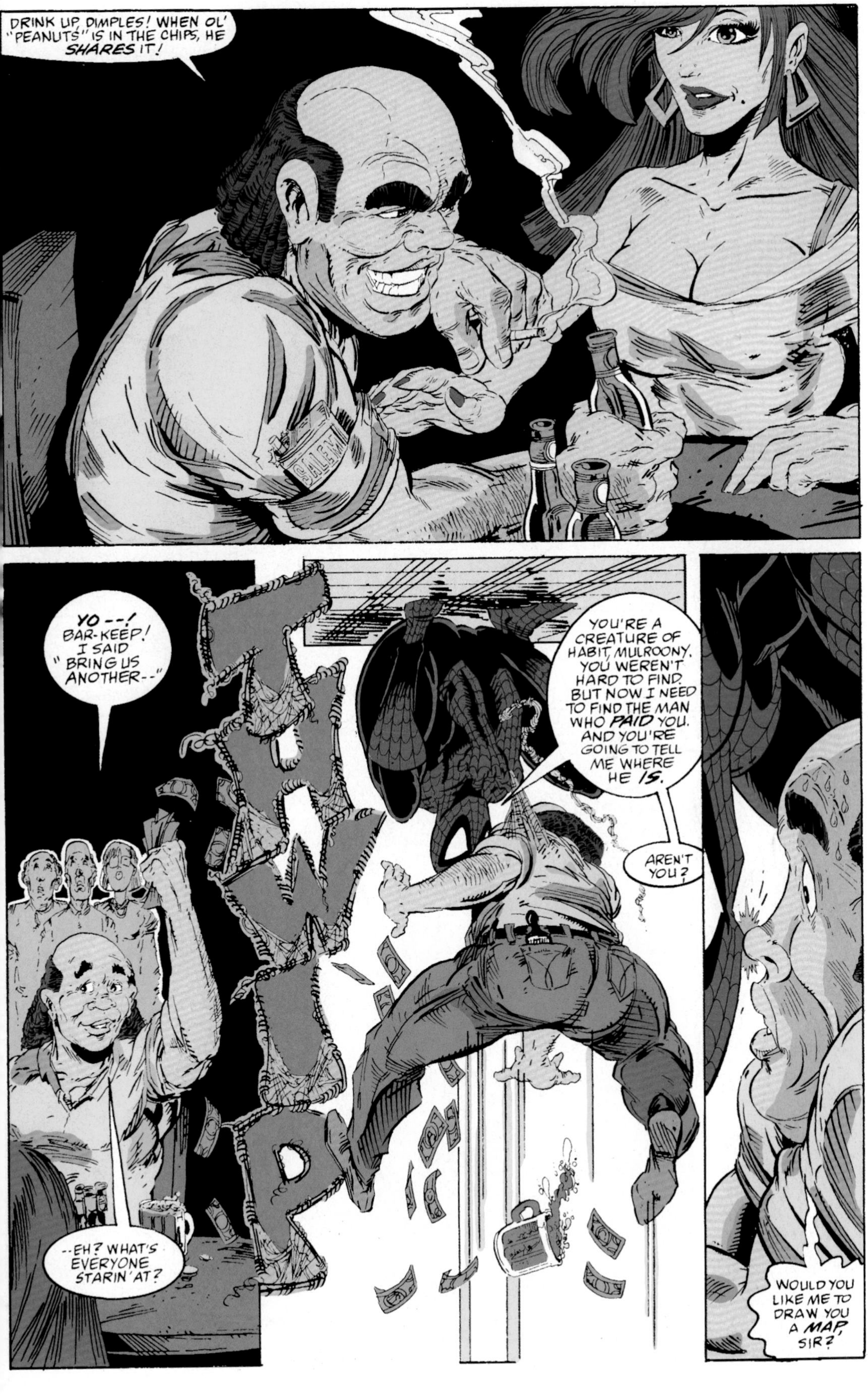
DRINK UP, DIMPLES! WHEN OL' "PEANUTS" IS IN THE CHIPS, HE SHARES IT!
SALEM
YO--! BAR-KEEP! I SAID "BRING US ANOTHER--"
--EH? WHAT'S EVERYONE STARIN' AT?
YOU'RE A CREATURE OF HABIT, MULROONY. YOU WEREN'T HARD TO FIND. BUT NOW I NEED TO FIND THE MAN WHO PAID YOU. AND YOU'RE GOING TO TELL ME WHERE HE IS.
AREN'T YOU?
WOULD YOU LIKE ME TO DRAW YOU A MAP, SIR?

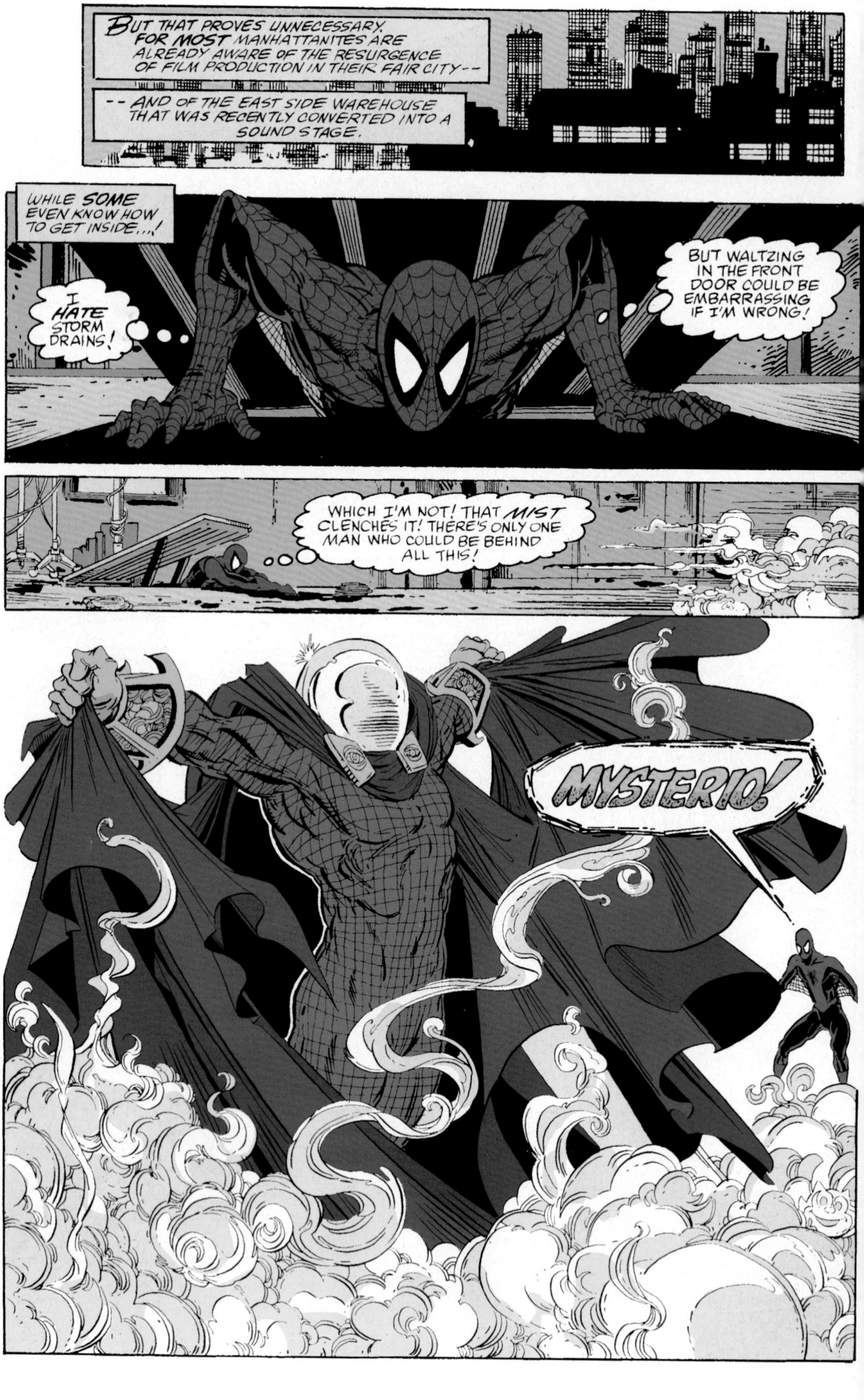
BUT THAT PROVES UNNECESSARY. FOR MOST MANHATTANITES ARE ALREADY AWARE OF THE RESURGENCE OF FILM PRODUCTION IN THEIR FAIR CITY--
--AND OF THE EAST SIDE WAREHOUSE THAT WAS RECENTLY CONVERTED INTO A SOUND STAGE.
WHILE SOME EVEN KNOW HOW TO GET INSIDE...!
I HATE STORM DRAINS!
BUT WALTZING IN THE FRONT DOOR COULD BE EMBARRASSING IF I'M WRONG!
WHICH I'M NOT! THAT MIST CLENCHES IT! THERE'S ONLY ONE MAN WHO COULD BE BEHIND ALL THIS!
MYSTERIO!

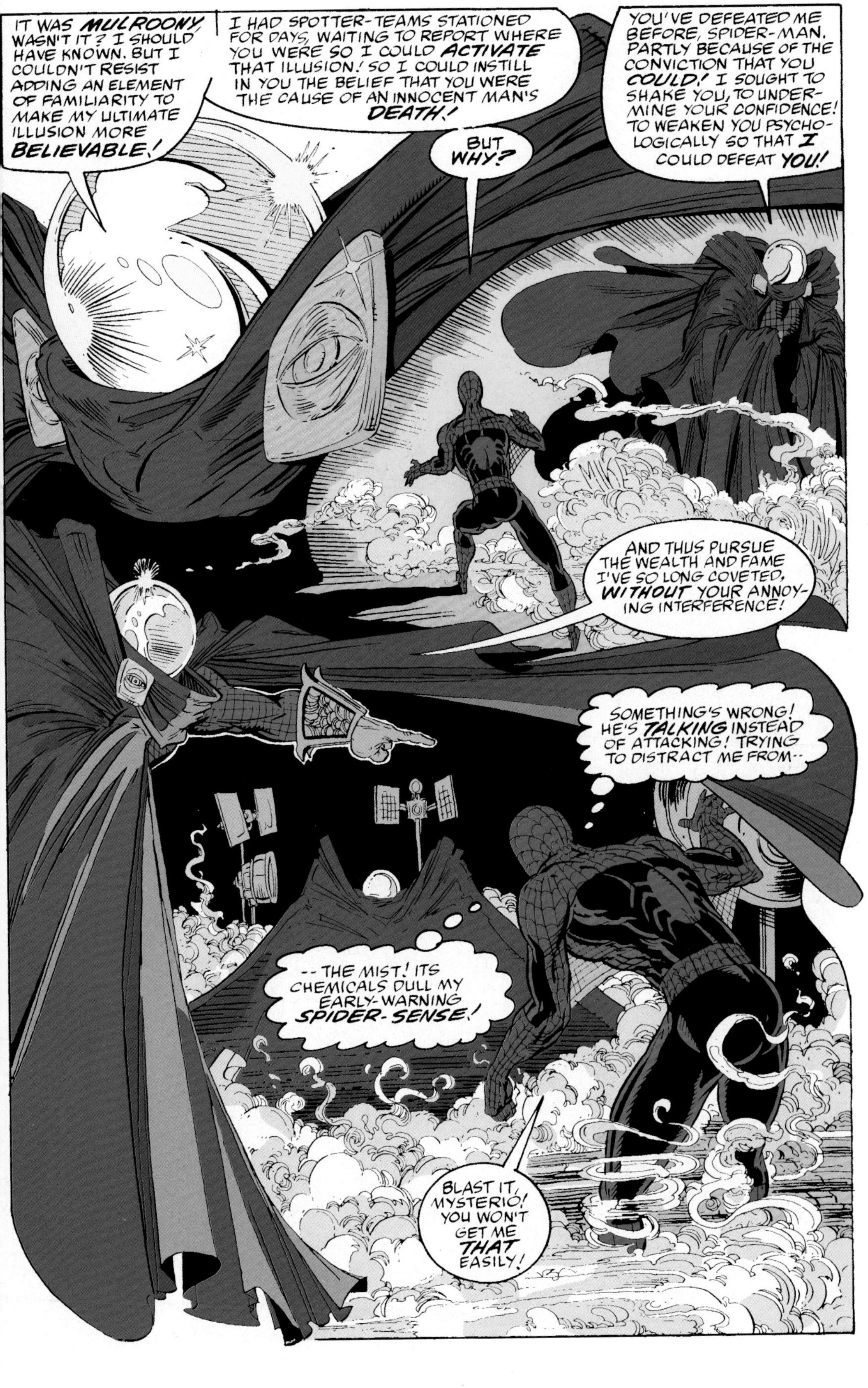
IT WAS MULROONY, WASN'T IT? I SHOULD HAVE KNOWN. BUT I COULDN'T RESIST ADDING AN ELEMENT OF FAMILIARITY TO MAKE MY ULTIMATE ILLUSION MORE BELIEVABLE!
I HAD SPOTTER-TEAMS STATIONED FOR DAYS, WAITING TO REPORT WHERE YOU WERE SO I COULD ACTIVATE THAT ILLUSION! SO I COULD INSTILL IN YOU THE BELIEF THAT YOU WERE THE CAUSE OF AN INNOCENT MAN'S DEATH!
BUT WHY?
YOU'VE DEFEATED ME BEFORE, SPIDER-MAN. PARTLY BECAUSE OF THE CONVICTION THAT YOU COULD! I SOUGHT TO SHAKE YOU, TO UNDERMINE YOUR CONFIDENCE! TO WEAKEN YOU PSYCHOLOGICALLY SO THAT I COULD DEFEAT YOU!
AND THUS PURSUE THE WEALTH AND FAME I'VE SO LONG COVETED, WITHOUT YOUR ANNOYING INTERFERENCE!
SOMETHING'S WRONG! HE'S TALKING INSTEAD OF ATTACKING! TRYING TO DISTRACT ME FROM--
--THE MIST! ITS CHEMICALS DULL MY EARLY-WARNING SPIDER-SENSE!
BLAST IT, MYSTERIO! YOU WON'T GET ME THAT EASILY!

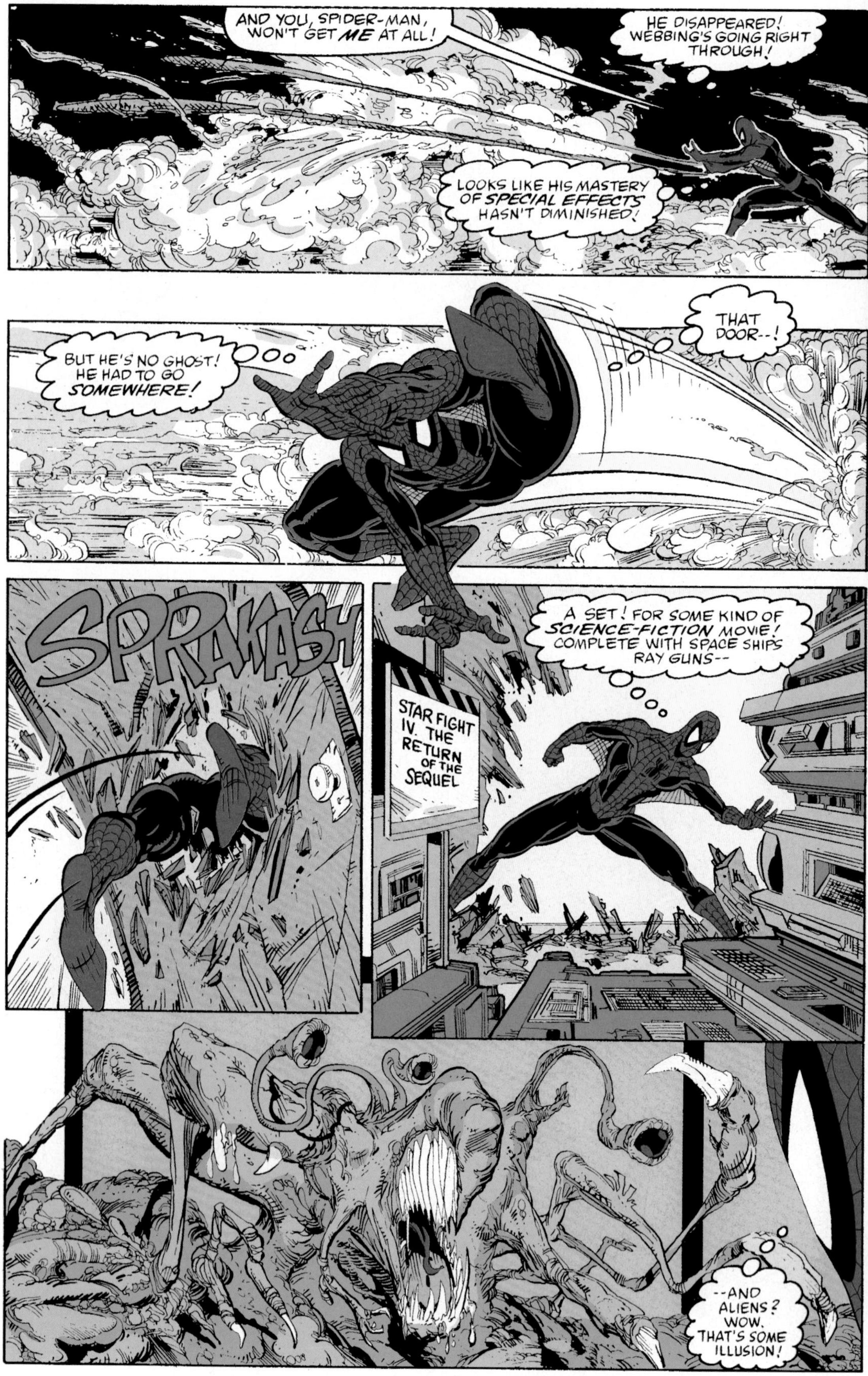

AND YOU, SPIDER-MAN, WON'T GET ME AT ALL!
HE DISAPPEARED! WEBBING'S GOING RIGHT THROUGH!
LOOKS LIKE HIS MASTERY OF SPECIAL EFFECTS HASN'T DIMINISHED!
BUT HE'S NO GHOST! HE HAD TO GO SOMEWHERE!
THAT DOOR--!
SPRAKASH
A SET! FOR SOME KIND OF SCIENCE-FICTION MOVIE! COMPLETE WITH SPACE SHIPS RAY GUNS--
STAR FIGHT IV. THE RETURN OF THE SEQUEL
--AND ALIENS? WOW. THAT'S SOME ILLUSION!

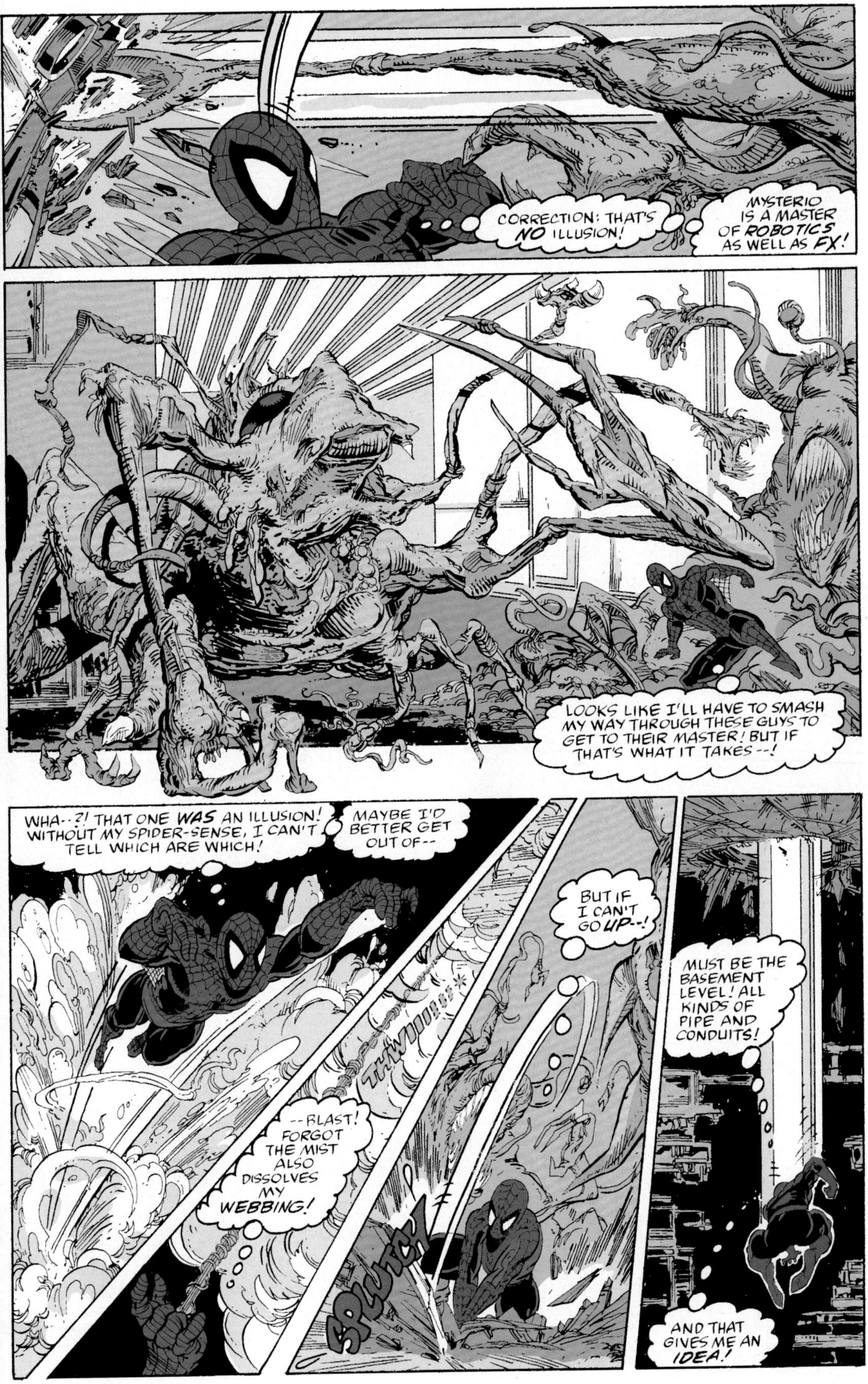

CORRECTION: THAT'S NO ILLUSION!
MYSTERIO IS A MASTER OF ROBOTICS AS WELL AS FX!
LOOKS LIKE I'LL HAVE TO SMASH MY WAY THROUGH THESE GUYS TO GET TO THEIR MASTER! BUT IF THAT'S WHAT IT TAKES--!
WHA--?! THAT ONE WAS AN ILLUSION! WITHOUT MY SPIDER-SENSE, I CAN'T TELL WHICH ARE WHICH!
MAYBE I'D BETTER GET OUT OF--
THWIIIIIIII*
--BLAST! FORGOT THE MIST ALSO DISSOLVES MY WEBBING!
BUT IF I CAN'T GO UP--!
SPLUTCH
MUST BE THE BASEMENT LEVEL! ALL KINDS OF PIPE AND CONDUITS!
AND THAT GIVES ME AN IDEA!

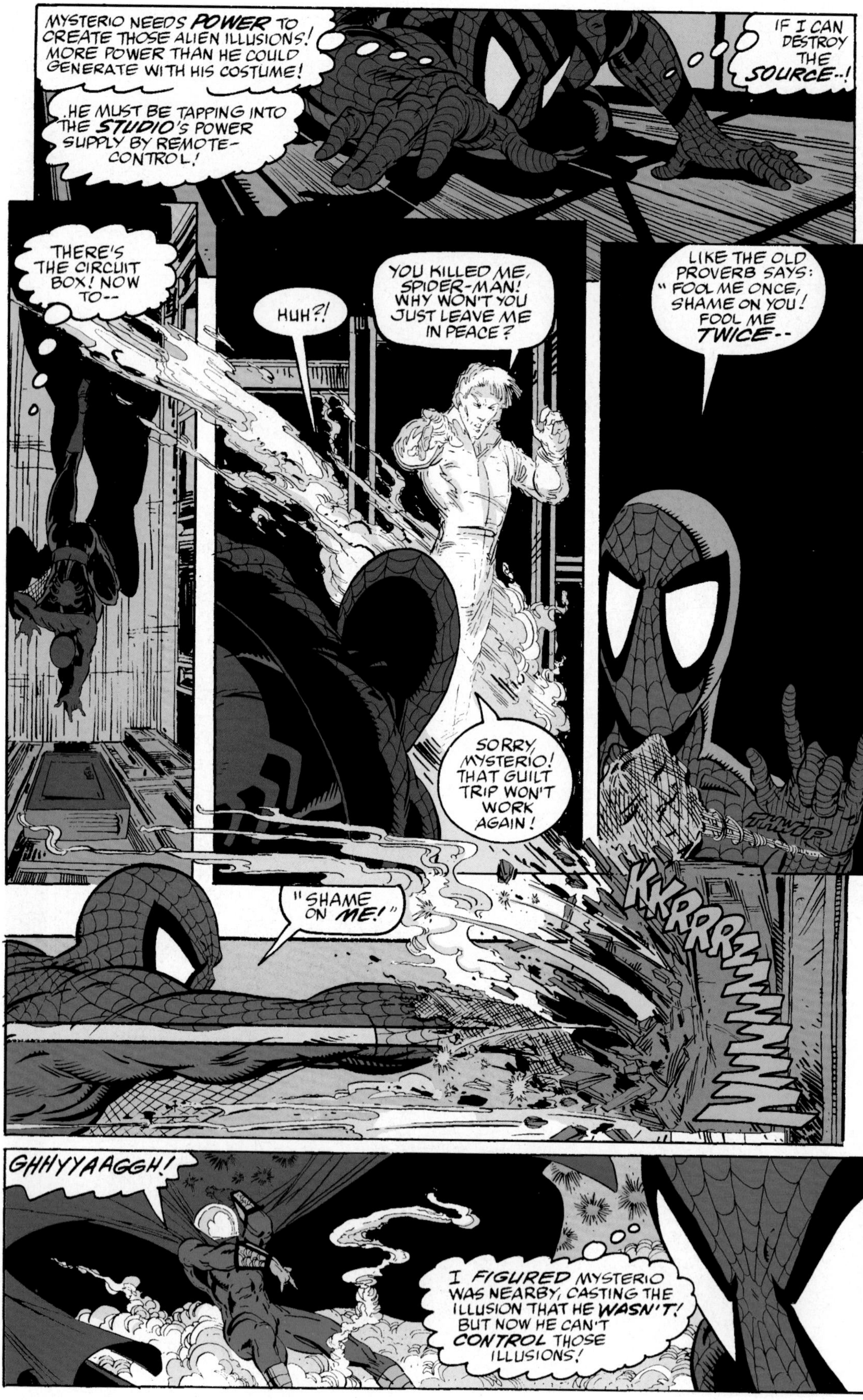
MYSTERIO NEEDS POWER TO CREATE THOSE ALIEN ILLUSIONS! MORE POWER THAN HE COULD GENERATE WITH HIS COSTUME!
..HE MUST BE TAPPING INTO THE STUDIO'S POWER SUPPLY BY REMOTE-CONTROL!
IF I CAN DESTROY THE SOURCE..!
THERE'S THE CIRCUIT BOX! NOW TO--
HUH?!
YOU KILLED ME, SPIDER-MAN! WHY WON'T YOU JUST LEAVE ME IN PEACE?
SORRY, MYSTERIO! THAT GUILT TRIP WON'T WORK AGAIN!
LIKE THE OLD PROVERB SAYS: "FOOL ME ONCE, SHAME ON YOU! FOOL ME TWICE--
THWIP
"SHAME ON ME!"
KKRRRRWWWWM
GHHYYAAGGH!
I FIGURED MYSTERIO WAS NEARBY, CASTING THE ILLUSION THAT HE WASN'T! BUT NOW HE CAN'T CONTROL THOSE ILLUSIONS!

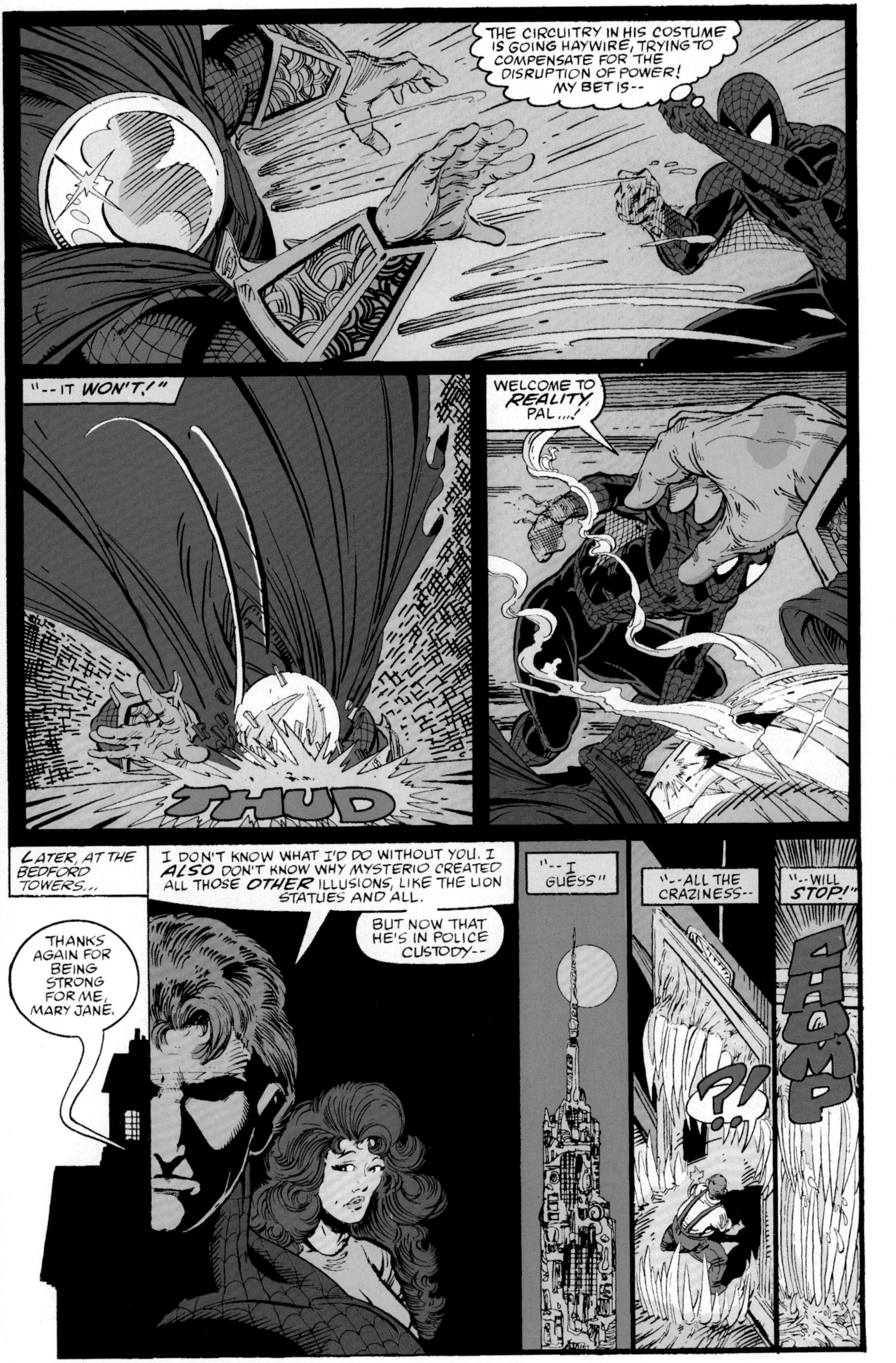
THE CIRCUITRY IN HIS COSTUME IS GOING HAYWIRE, TRYING TO COMPENSATE FOR THE DISRUPTION OF POWER! MY BET IS--
"--IT WON'T!"
THUD
WELCOME TO REALITY, PAL....!
LATER, AT THE BEDFORD TOWERS...
THANKS AGAIN FOR BEING STRONG FOR ME, MARY JANE.
I DON'T KNOW WHAT I'D DO WITHOUT YOU. I ALSO DON'T KNOW WHY MYSTERIO CREATED ALL THOSE OTHER ILLUSIONS, LIKE THE LION STATUES AND ALL.
BUT NOW THAT HE'S IN POLICE CUSTODY--
"--I GUESS"
"--ALL THE CRAZINESS--
"--WILL STOP!"
?!
CHOMP

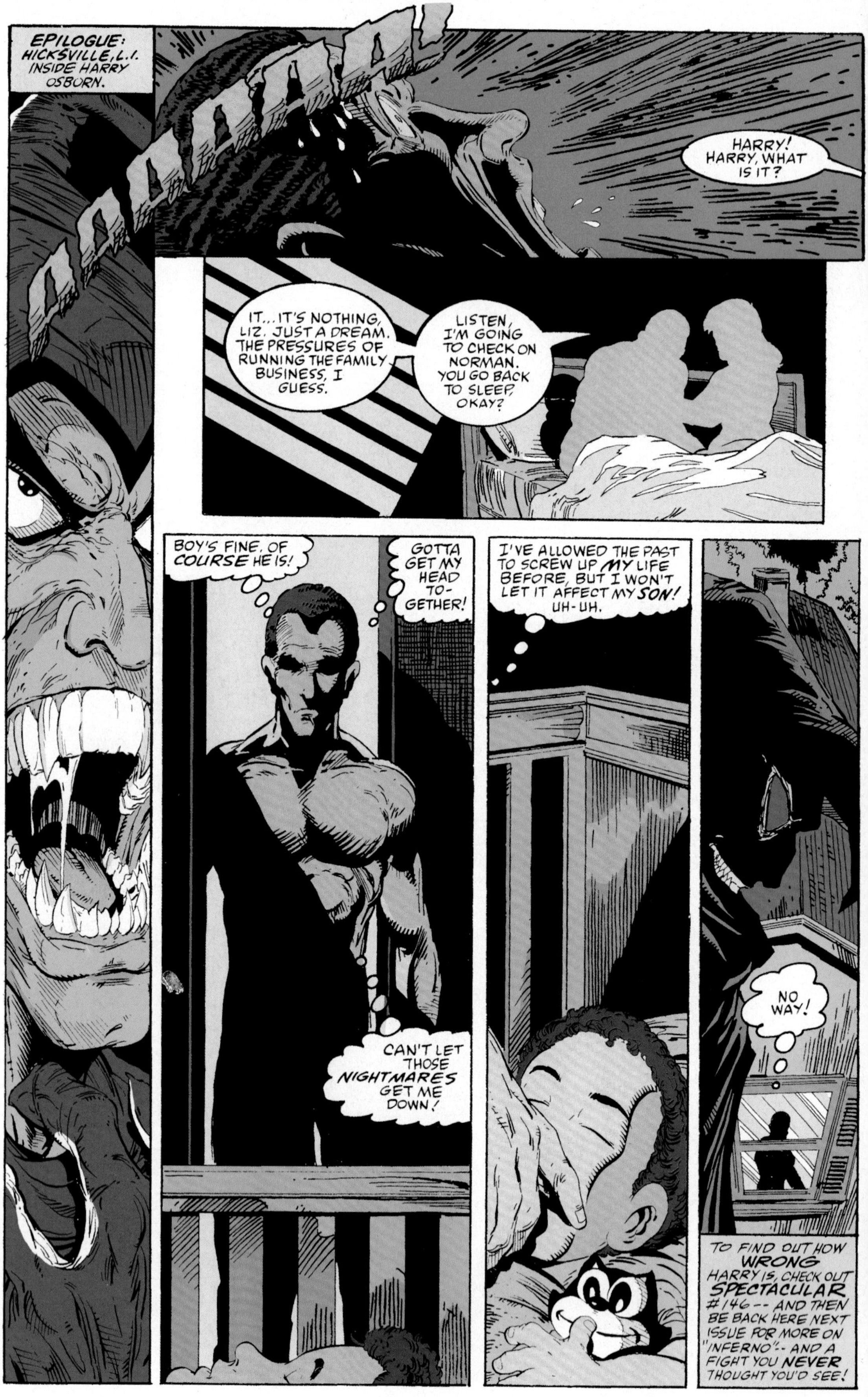
EPILOGUE: HICKSVILLE, L.I. INSIDE HARRY OSBORN.
HARRY! HARRY, WHAT IS IT?
IT... IT'S NOTHING, LIZ. JUST A DREAM. THE PRESSURES OF RUNNING THE FAMILY BUSINESS, I GUESS.
LISTEN, I'M GOING TO CHECK ON NORMAN. YOU GO BACK TO SLEEP, OKAY?
BOY'S FINE. OF COURSE HE IS!
GOTTA GET MY HEAD TO-GETHER!
CAN'T LET THOSE NIGHTMARES GET ME DOWN!
I'VE ALLOWED THE PAST TO SCREW UP MY LIFE BEFORE, BUT I WON'T LET IT AFFECT MY SON! UH-UH.
NO WAY!
TO FIND OUT HOW WRONG HARRY IS, CHECK OUT SPECTACULAR #146 -- AND THEN BE BACK HERE NEXT ISSUE FOR MORE ON "INFERNO"- AND A FIGHT YOU NEVER THOUGHT YOU'D SEE!

CONTINUED IN *AMAZING SPIDER-MAN EPIC COLLECTION: ASSASSIN NATION* TPB.

THE NEWEST INCARNATION OF SUPER VILLAIN TEAM THE ZODIAC HAS SPIDER-MAN
TEAMING UP WITH NICK FURY TO STOP THEIR SINISTER PLANS.

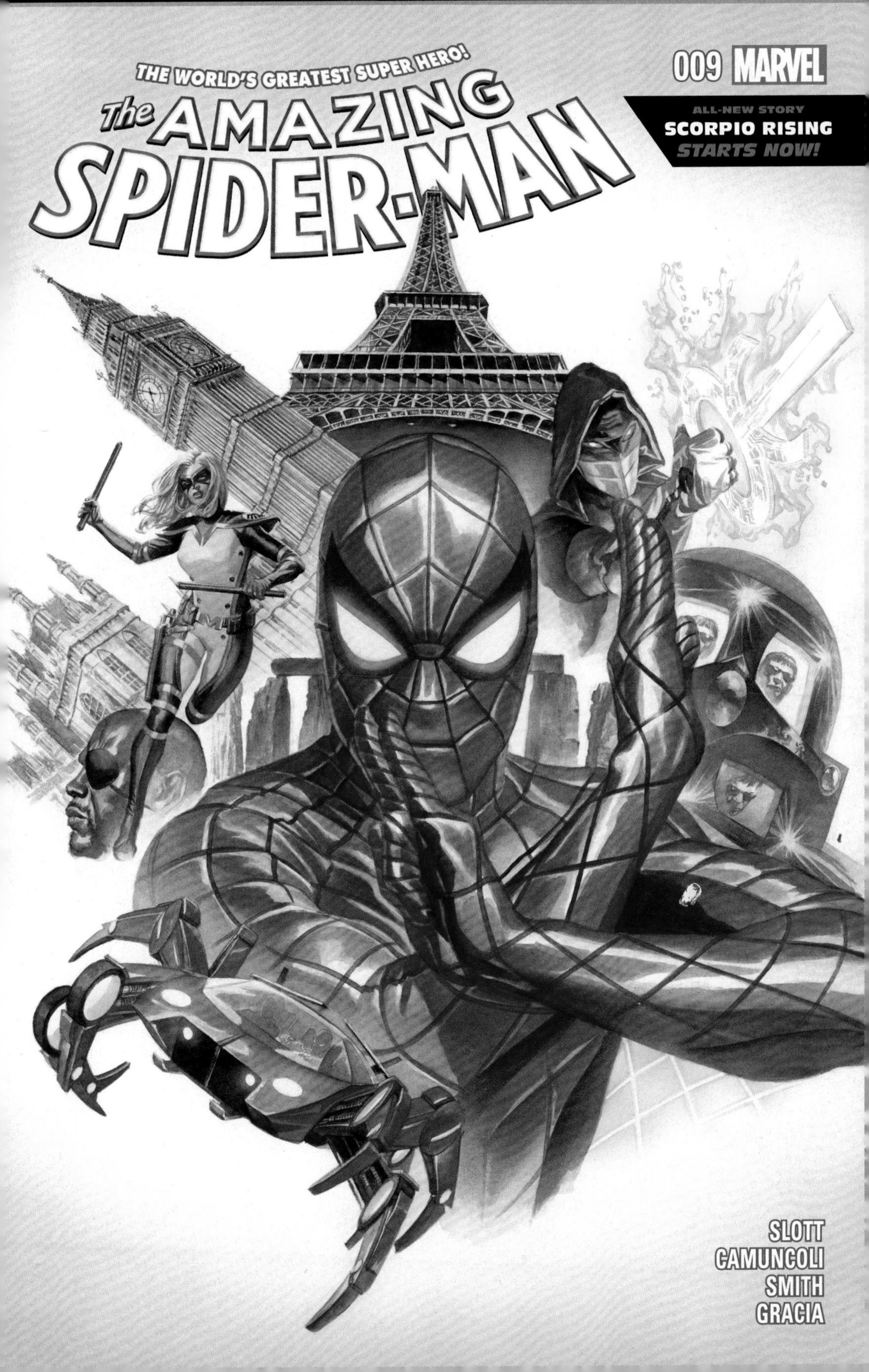
THE WORLD'S GREATEST SUPER HERO!
The AMAZING SPIDER-MAN
009
MARVEL
ALL-NEW STORY
SCORPIO RISING
STARTS NOW!
SLOTT
CAMUNCOLI
SMITH
GRACIA

WHEN **PETER PARKER** WAS BITTEN BY A RADIOACTIVE SPIDER, HE GAINED THE PROPORTIONAL SPEED, STRENGTH, AND AGILITY OF A SPIDER
ADHESIVE FINGERTIPS AND TOES; AND THE UNIQUE PRECOGNITIVE AWARENESS OF DANGER CALLED "SPIDER-SENSE!" AFTER LEARNING THAT
WITH GREAT POWER THERE MUST ALSO COME GREAT RESPONSIBILTY, HE BECAME THE CRIME-FIGHTING SUPER HERO CALLED...

The AMAZING SPIDER-MAN

THE AMAZING SPIDER-MAN'S "FRIENDLY NEIGHBORHOOD" HAS GOTTEN A WHOLE LOT BIGGER! PETER PARKER'S COMPANY, PARKER INDUSTRIES, IS CHANGING THE WORLD WITH CUTTING-EDGE TECHNOLOGY AND HAS OFFICES ACROSS THE GLOBE.

BUT PETER'S SUCCESS HAS BROUGHT ENEMIES TO HIS COMPANY'S DOORSTEP. RECENTLY, THE TERRORIST GROUP ZODIAC ROBBED PARKER INDUSTRIES AND USED THE TECH THEY STOLE TO INFILTRATE S.H.I.E.L.D.'S DEFENSIVE SATTELITES! USING THE HIJACKED SYSTEM, ZODIAC WAS ABLE TO LOCATE THE ORRERY, AN ANCIENT AND MYSTERIOUS ARTIFACT.

S.H.I.E.L.D. MOBILIZED QUICKLY IN A COUNTEROFFENSIVE AND WERE ABLE TO FIND AND CAPTURE MOST OF ZODIAC'S TOP MEMBERS. THE GROUP'S LEADER, SCORPIO, REMAINS AT LARGE, THOUGH. FOR DAYS, PETER PARKER AND SPIDER-MAN HAVE HAD MORE IMMEDIATE THREATS TO DEAL WITH, BUT THAT ENDS TONIGHT...

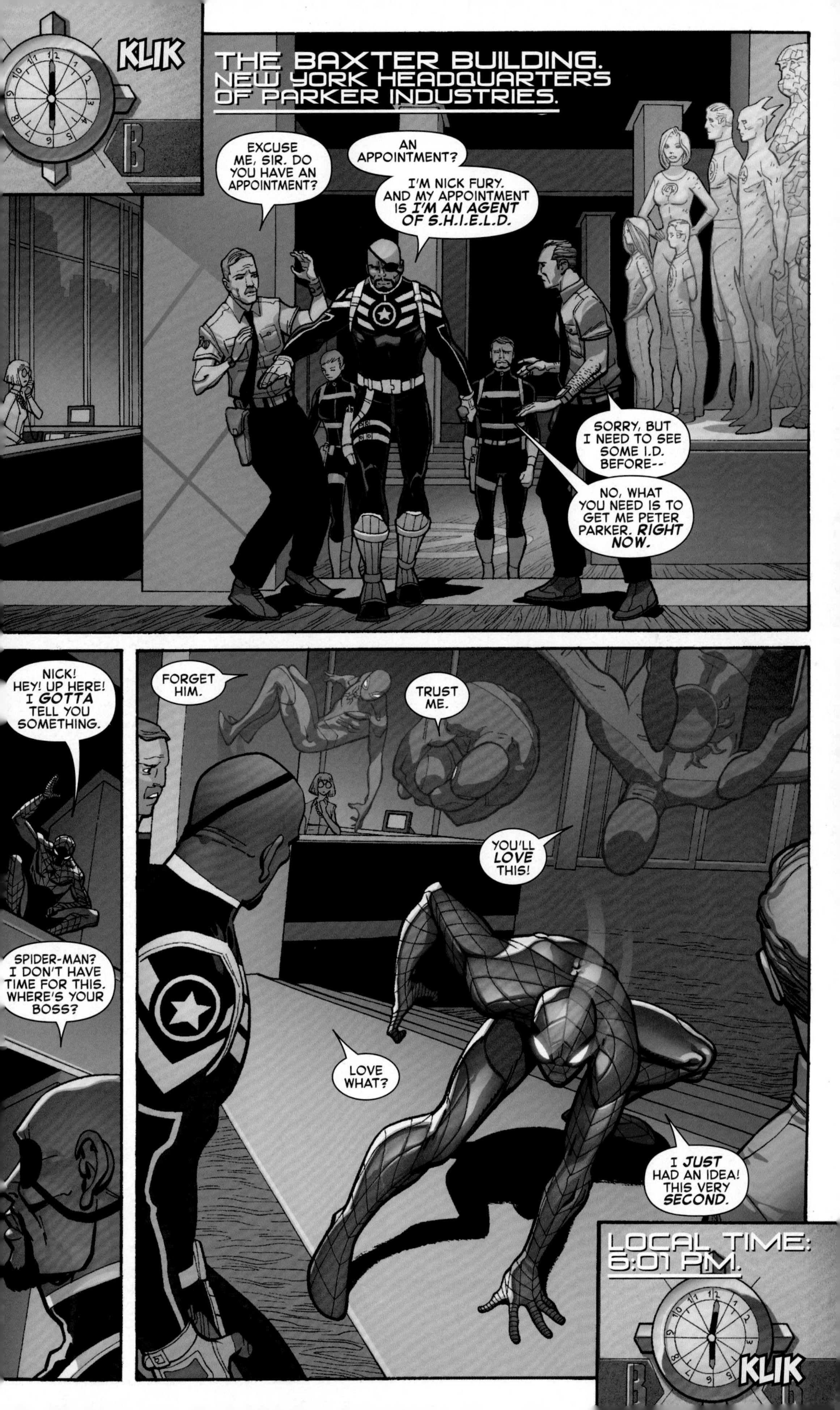

KLIK
THE BAXTER BUILDING. NEW YORK HEADQUARTERS OF PARKER INDUSTRIES.
EXCUSE ME, SIR. DO YOU HAVE AN APPOINTMENT?
AN APPOINTMENT?
I'M NICK FURY. AND MY APPOINTMENT IS I'M AN AGENT OF S.H.I.E.L.D.
SORRY, BUT I NEED TO SEE SOME I.D. BEFORE--
NO, WHAT YOU NEED IS TO GET ME PETER PARKER. RIGHT NOW.
NICK! HEY! UP HERE! I GOTTA TELL YOU SOMETHING.
SPIDER-MAN? I DON'T HAVE TIME FOR THIS. WHERE'S YOUR BOSS?
FORGET HIM.
TRUST ME.
YOU'LL LOVE THIS!
LOVE WHAT?
I JUST HAD AN IDEA! THIS VERY SECOND.
LOCAL TIME: 6:01 PM.
KLIK

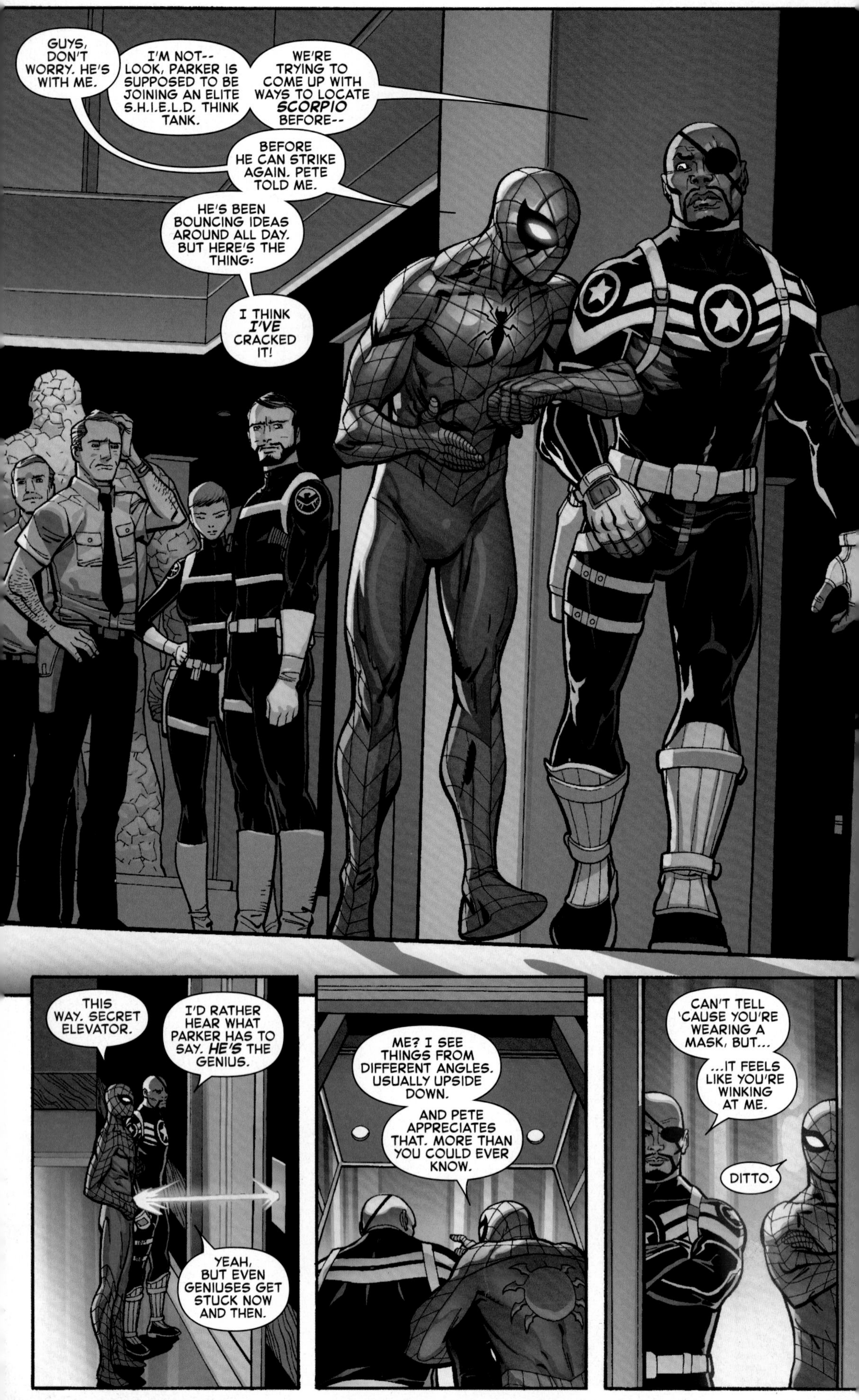
GUYS, DON'T WORRY. HE'S WITH ME.
I'M NOT-- LOOK, PARKER IS SUPPOSED TO BE JOINING AN ELITE S.H.I.E.L.D. THINK TANK.
WE'RE TRYING TO COME UP WITH WAYS TO LOCATE SCORPIO BEFORE--
BEFORE HE CAN STRIKE AGAIN. PETE TOLD ME.
HE'S BEEN BOUNCING IDEAS AROUND ALL DAY. BUT HERE'S THE THING:
I THINK I'VE CRACKED IT!
THIS WAY. SECRET ELEVATOR.
I'D RATHER HEAR WHAT PARKER HAS TO SAY. HE'S THE GENIUS.
YEAH, BUT EVEN GENIUSES GET STUCK NOW AND THEN.
ME? I SEE THINGS FROM DIFFERENT ANGLES. USUALLY UPSIDE DOWN.
AND PETE APPRECIATES THAT. MORE THAN YOU COULD EVER KNOW.
CAN'T TELL 'CAUSE YOU'RE WEARING A MASK, BUT...
...IT FEELS LIKE YOU'RE WINKING AT ME.
DITTO.

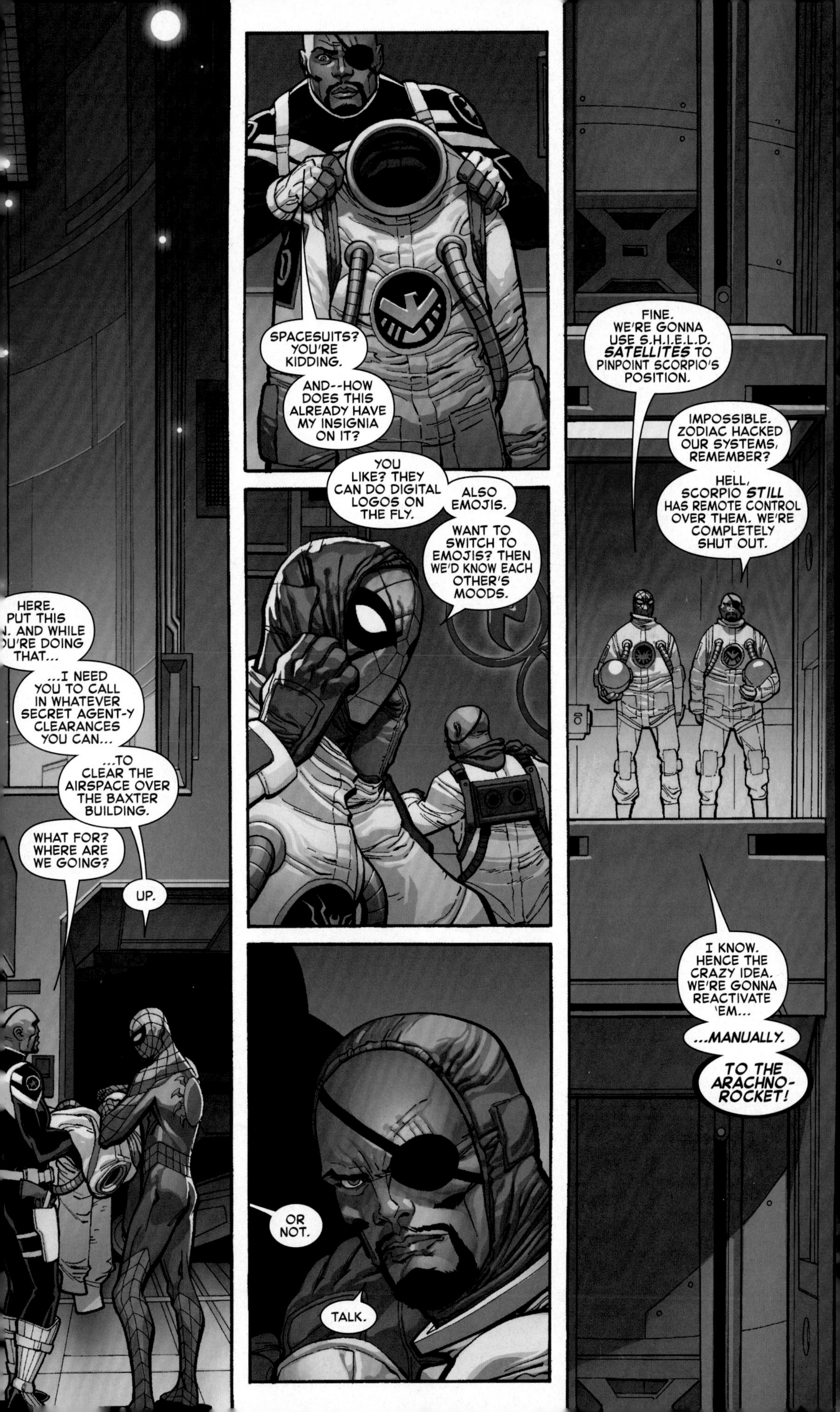
HERE. PUT THIS ...N. AND WHILE ...OU'RE DOING THAT...
...I NEED YOU TO CALL IN WHATEVER SECRET AGENT-Y CLEARANCES YOU CAN...
...TO CLEAR THE AIRSPACE OVER THE BAXTER BUILDING.
WHAT FOR? WHERE ARE WE GOING?
UP.
SPACESUITS? YOU'RE KIDDING.
AND--HOW DOES THIS ALREADY HAVE MY INSIGNIA ON IT?
YOU LIKE? THEY CAN DO DIGITAL LOGOS ON THE FLY.
ALSO EMOJIS.
WANT TO SWITCH TO EMOJIS? THEN WE'D KNOW EACH OTHER'S MOODS.
OR NOT.
TALK.
FINE. WE'RE GONNA USE S.H.I.E.L.D. SATELLITES TO PINPOINT SCORPIO'S POSITION.
IMPOSSIBLE. ZODIAC HACKED OUR SYSTEMS, REMEMBER?
HELL, SCORPIO STILL HAS REMOTE CONTROL OVER THEM. WE'RE COMPLETELY SHUT OUT.
I KNOW. HENCE THE CRAZY IDEA. WE'RE GONNA REACTIVATE 'EM...
...MANUALLY.
TO THE ARACHNO-ROCKET!

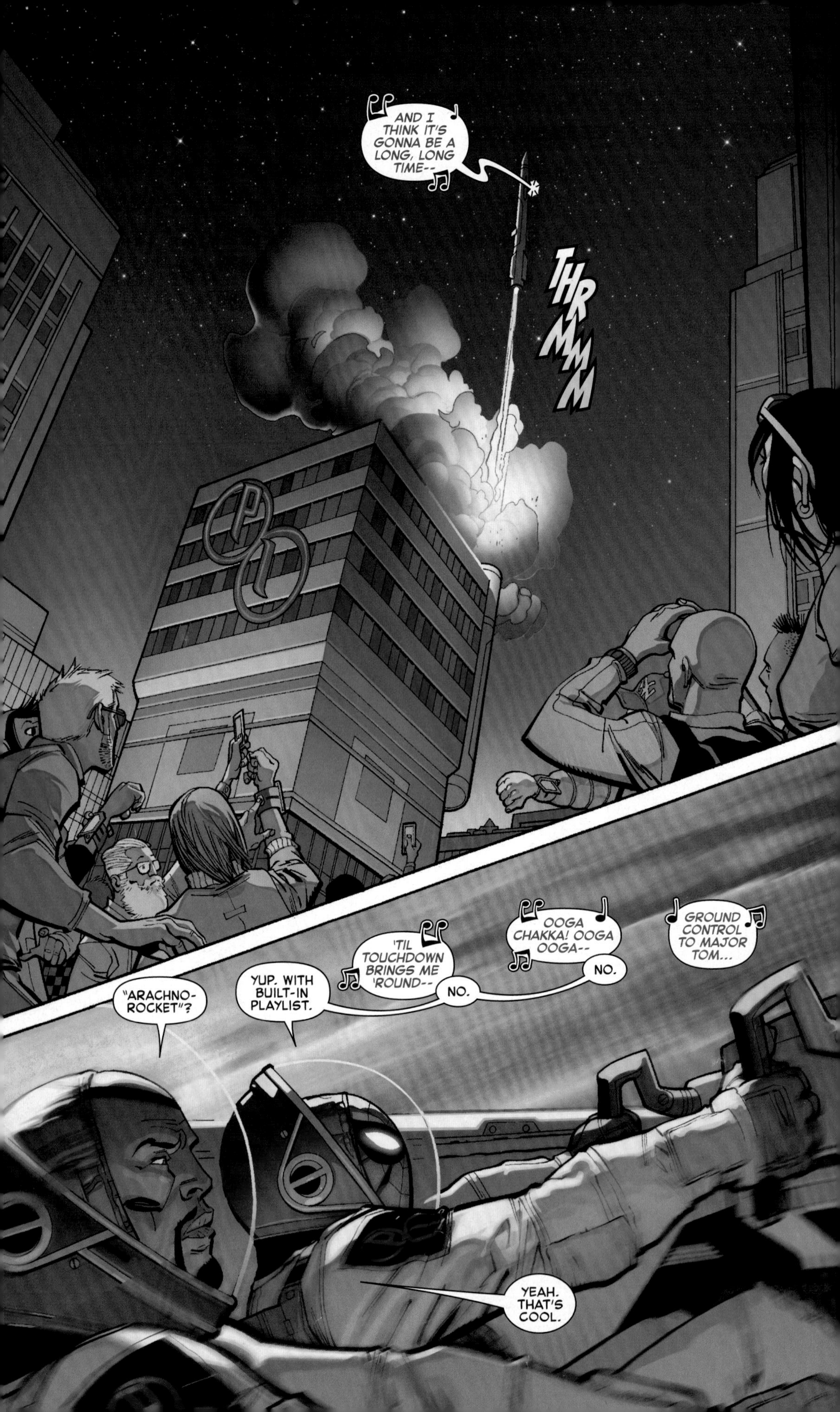
AND I THINK IT'S GONNA BE A LONG, LONG TIME--
THRMMMM
"ARACHNO-ROCKET"?
YUP. WITH BUILT-IN PLAYLIST.
'TIL TOUCHDOWN BRINGS ME 'ROUND--
NO.
OOGA CHAKKA! OOGA OOGA--
NO.
GROUND CONTROL TO MAJOR TOM...
YEAH. THAT'S COOL.

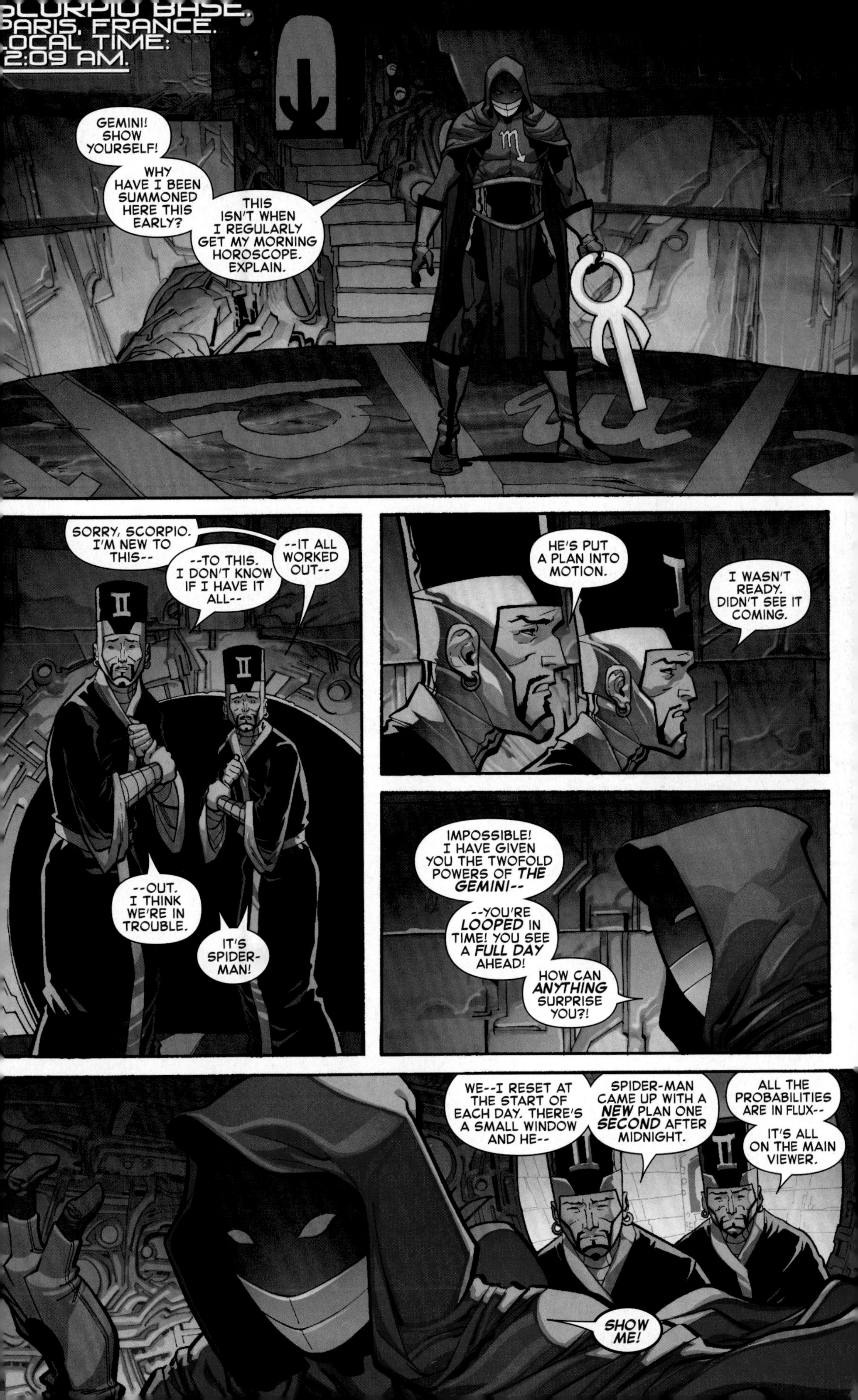
CORPIO BASE.
PARIS, FRANCE.
OCAL TIME:
2:09 AM.
GEMINI! SHOW YOURSELF!
WHY HAVE I BEEN SUMMONED HERE THIS EARLY?
THIS ISN'T WHEN I REGULARLY GET MY MORNING HOROSCOPE. EXPLAIN.
SORRY, SCORPIO. I'M NEW TO THIS--
--TO THIS. I DON'T KNOW IF I HAVE IT ALL--
--IT ALL WORKED OUT--
--OUT. I THINK WE'RE IN TROUBLE.
IT'S SPIDER-MAN!
HE'S PUT A PLAN INTO MOTION.
I WASN'T READY. DIDN'T SEE IT COMING.
IMPOSSIBLE! I HAVE GIVEN YOU THE TWOFOLD POWERS OF THE GEMINI--
--YOU'RE LOOPED IN TIME! YOU SEE A FULL DAY AHEAD!
HOW CAN ANYTHING SURPRISE YOU?!
WE--I RESET AT THE START OF EACH DAY. THERE'S A SMALL WINDOW AND HE--
SPIDER-MAN CAME UP WITH A NEW PLAN ONE SECOND AFTER MIDNIGHT.
ALL THE PROBABILITIES ARE IN FLUX--
IT'S ALL ON THE MAIN VIEWER.
SHOW ME!

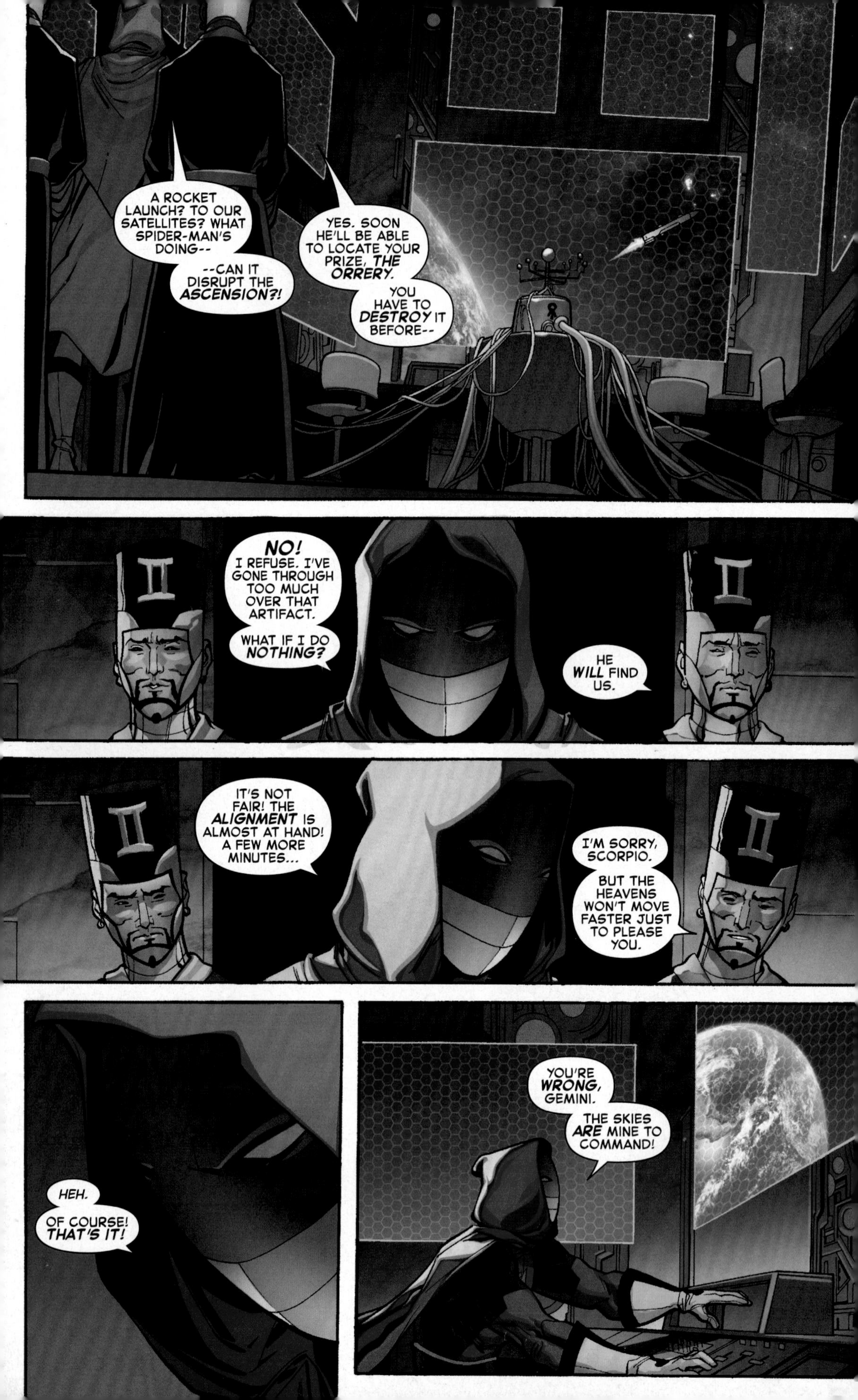
A ROCKET LAUNCH? TO OUR SATELLITES? WHAT SPIDER-MAN'S DOING--
--CAN IT DISRUPT THE ASCENSION?!
YES. SOON HE'LL BE ABLE TO LOCATE YOUR PRIZE, THE ORRERY.
YOU HAVE TO DESTROY IT BEFORE--
NO! I REFUSE. I'VE GONE THROUGH TOO MUCH OVER THAT ARTIFACT.
WHAT IF I DO NOTHING?
HE WILL FIND US.
IT'S NOT FAIR! THE ALIGNMENT IS ALMOST AT HAND! A FEW MORE MINUTES...
I'M SORRY, SCORPIO.
BUT THE HEAVENS WON'T MOVE FASTER JUST TO PLEASE YOU.
HEH.
OF COURSE! THAT'S IT!
YOU'RE WRONG, GEMINI.
THE SKIES ARE MINE TO COMMAND!

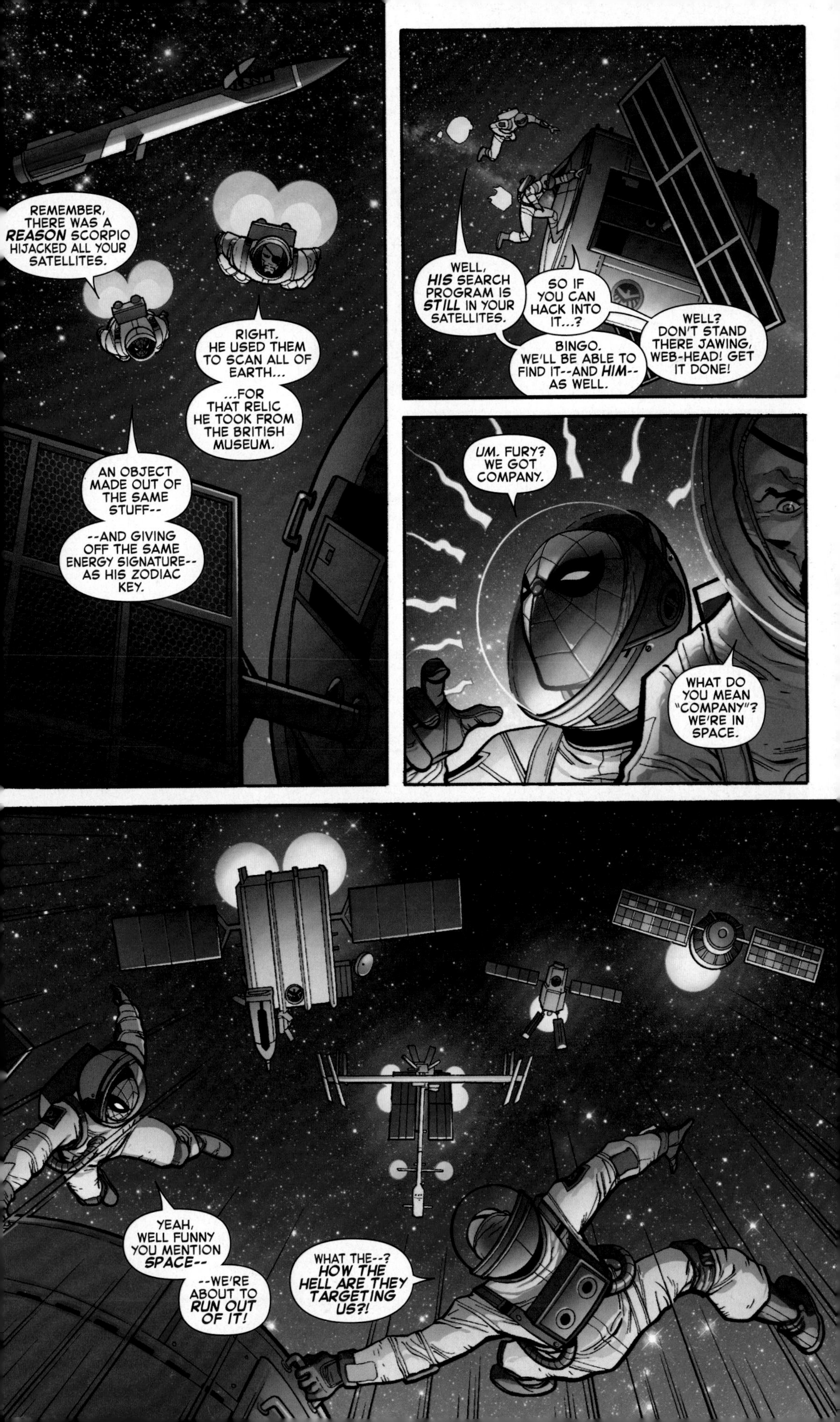
REMEMBER, THERE WAS A REASON SCORPIO HIJACKED ALL YOUR SATELLITES.
RIGHT. HE USED THEM TO SCAN ALL OF EARTH...
...FOR THAT RELIC HE TOOK FROM THE BRITISH MUSEUM.
AN OBJECT MADE OUT OF THE SAME STUFF--
--AND GIVING OFF THE SAME ENERGY SIGNATURE--AS HIS ZODIAC KEY.
WELL, HIS SEARCH PROGRAM IS STILL IN YOUR SATELLITES.
SO IF YOU CAN HACK INTO IT...?
BINGO. WE'LL BE ABLE TO FIND IT--AND HIM--AS WELL.
WELL? DON'T STAND THERE JAWING, WEB-HEAD! GET IT DONE!
UM. FURY? WE GOT COMPANY.
WHAT DO YOU MEAN "COMPANY"? WE'RE IN SPACE.
YEAH, WELL FUNNY YOU MENTION SPACE--
--WE'RE ABOUT TO RUN OUT OF IT!
WHAT THE--? HOW THE HELL ARE THEY TARGETING US?!

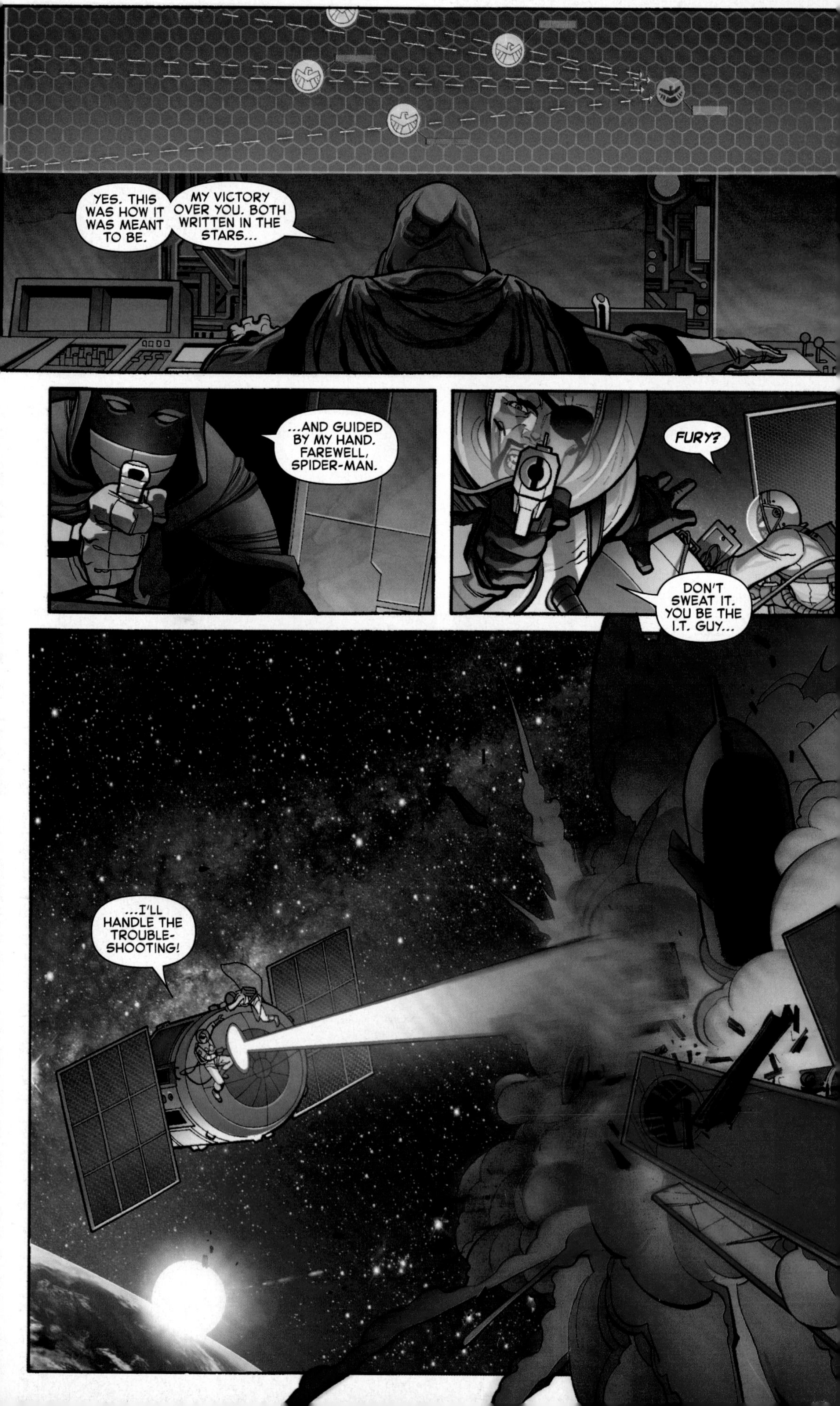

YES. THIS WAS HOW IT WAS MEANT TO BE.
MY VICTORY OVER YOU. BOTH WRITTEN IN THE STARS...
...AND GUIDED BY MY HAND. FAREWELL, SPIDER-MAN.
FURY?
DON'T SWEAT IT. YOU BE THE I.T. GUY...
...I'LL HANDLE THE TROUBLE-SHOOTING!

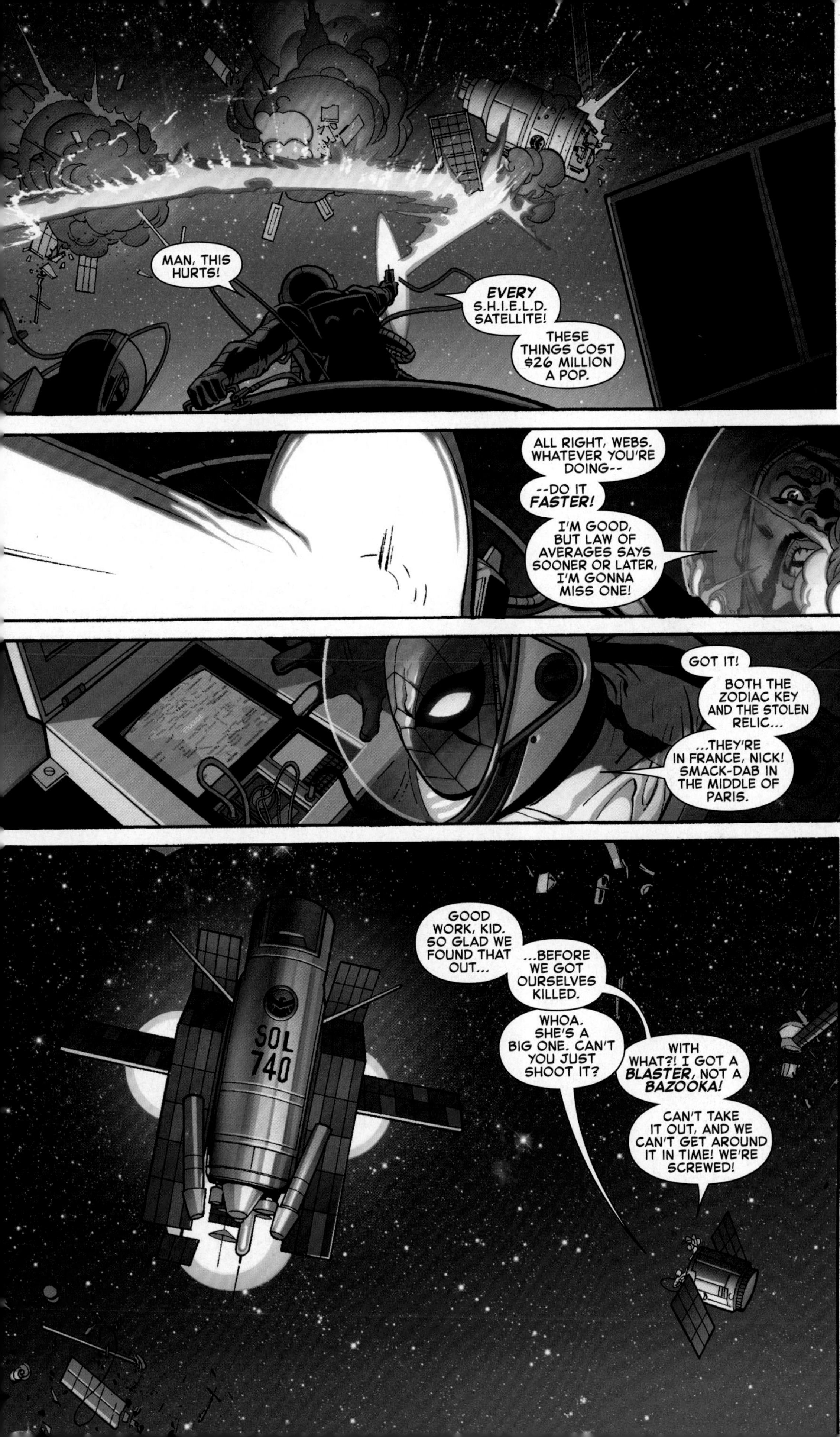
MAN, THIS HURTS!
EVERY S.H.I.E.L.D. SATELLITE!
THESE THINGS COST $26 MILLION A POP.
ALL RIGHT, WEBS. WHATEVER YOU'RE DOING--
--DO IT FASTER!
I'M GOOD, BUT LAW OF AVERAGES SAYS SOONER OR LATER, I'M GONNA MISS ONE!
GOT IT!
BOTH THE ZODIAC KEY AND THE STOLEN RELIC...
...THEY'RE IN FRANCE, NICK! SMACK-DAB IN THE MIDDLE OF PARIS.
GOOD WORK, KID. SO GLAD WE FOUND THAT OUT...
...BEFORE WE GOT OURSELVES KILLED.
WHOA. SHE'S A BIG ONE. CAN'T YOU JUST SHOOT IT?
WITH WHAT?! I GOT A BLASTER, NOT A BAZOOKA!
CAN'T TAKE IT OUT, AND WE CAN'T GET AROUND IT IN TIME! WE'RE SCREWED!
SOL 740

ONE SEC. I STILL GOT A TRICK UP MY SLEEVE.

HOW? CAN YOUR WEB-SHOOTERS EVEN WORK IN SPACE?

OH, THIS'S WAYYY BIGGER THAN A WEB-SHOOTER, NICK.

"ARACHNO-ROCKET TO THE RESCUE!"

♪ THERE'S A STARMAN WAITING IN THE SKY. ♪

♪ HE'D LIKE TO COME AND MEET US... ♪

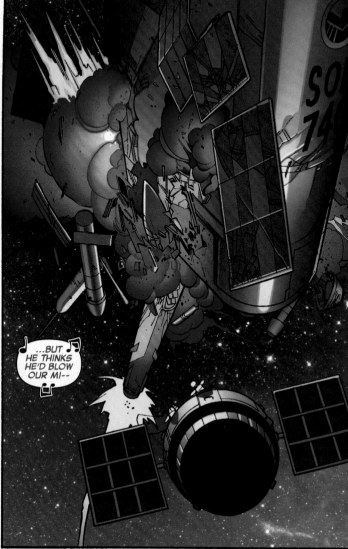

♪ ...BUT HE THINKS HE'D BLOW OUR MI-- ♪

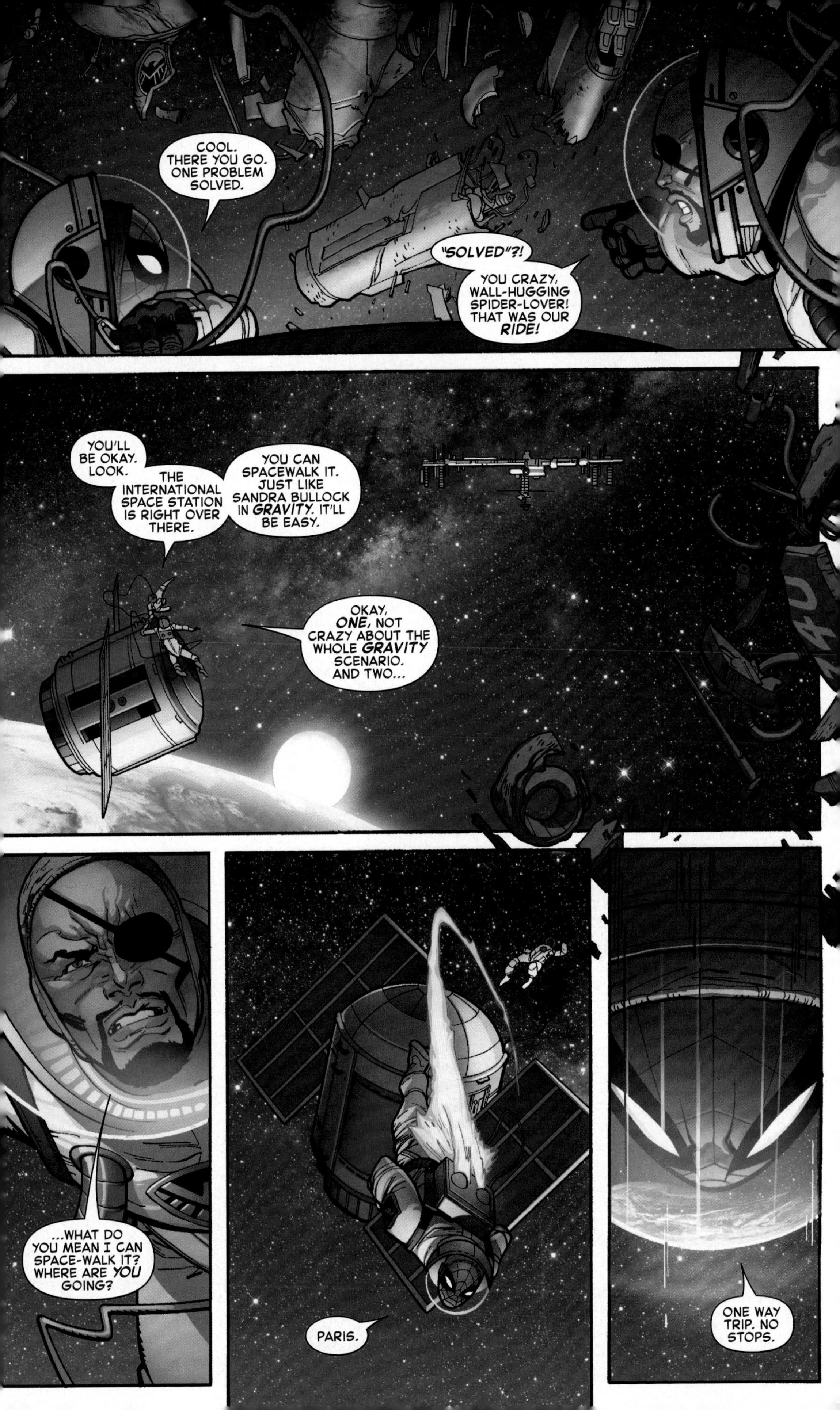
COOL. THERE YOU GO. ONE PROBLEM SOLVED.
"SOLVED"?!
YOU CRAZY, WALL-HUGGING SPIDER-LOVER! THAT WAS OUR RIDE!
YOU'LL BE OKAY. LOOK.
THE INTERNATIONAL SPACE STATION IS RIGHT OVER THERE.
YOU CAN SPACEWALK IT. JUST LIKE SANDRA BULLOCK IN GRAVITY. IT'LL BE EASY.
OKAY, ONE, NOT CRAZY ABOUT THE WHOLE GRAVITY SCENARIO. AND TWO...
...WHAT DO YOU MEAN I CAN SPACE-WALK IT? WHERE ARE YOU GOING?
PARIS.
ONE WAY TRIP. NO STOPS.

HE--HE LIVES.

HIS ROCKET'S DESTROYED, BUT--

--HE'S STILL COMING!

IMPOSSIBLE! THIS IS SPIDER-MAN WE'RE TALKING ABOUT. *NOT THOR!*

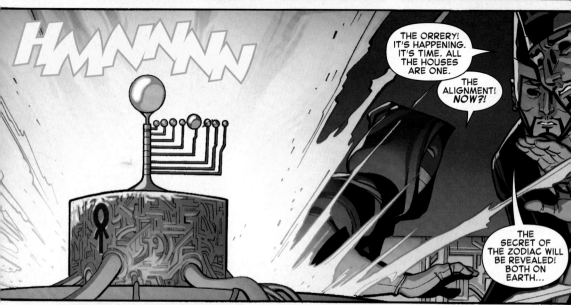

HMNNNN

THE ORRERY! IT'S HAPPENING. IT'S TIME. ALL THE HOUSES ARE ONE.

THE ALIGNMENT! *NOW?!*

THE SECRET OF THE ZODIAC WILL BE REVEALED! BOTH ON EARTH...

...AND IN HEAVEN.

STOP THAT. YOU'RE CREEPING ME OUT.

THERE IS A NEW CONSTELLATION IN THE SKY! A *THIRTEENTH* SIGN!

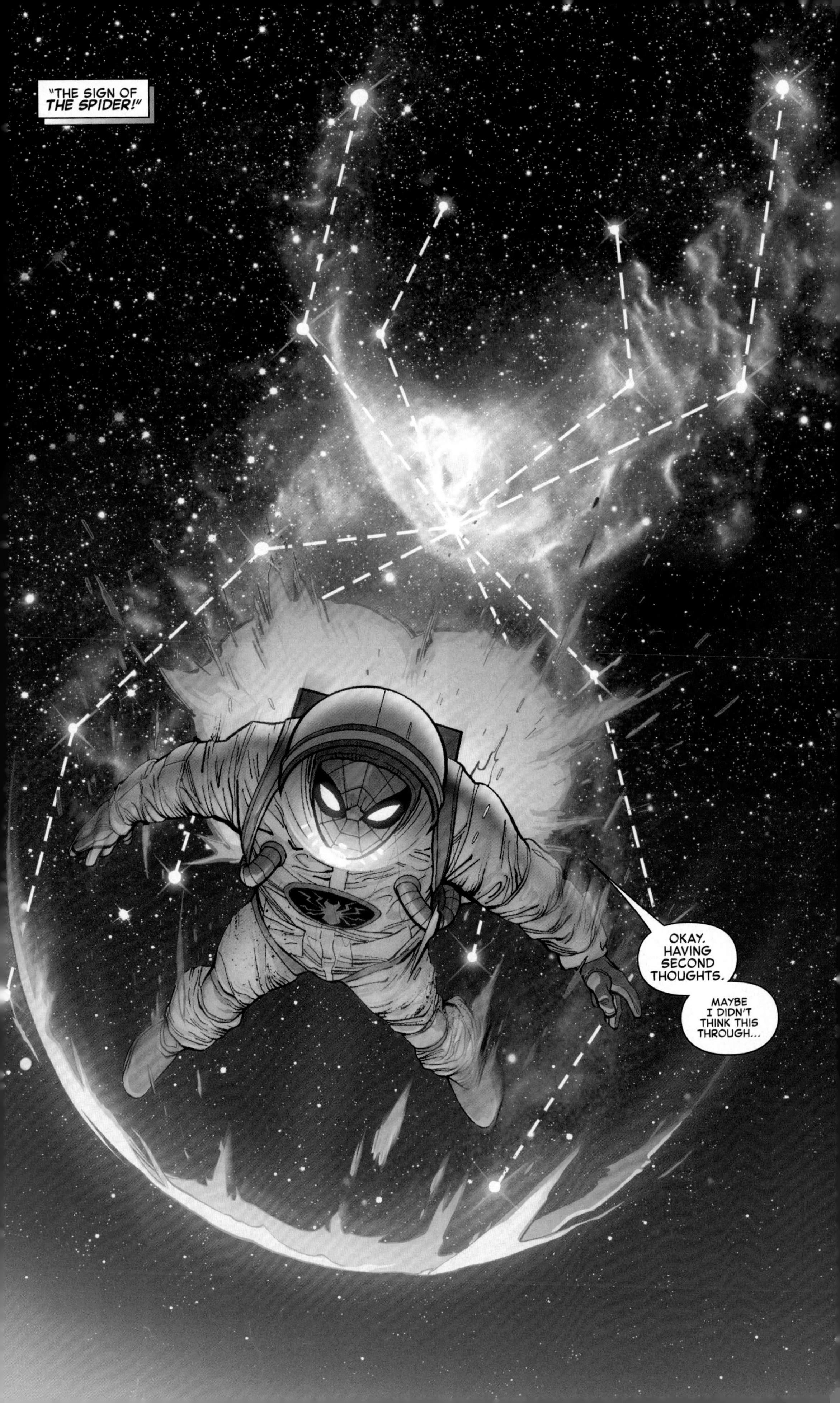
"THE SIGN OF THE SPIDER!"
OKAY. HAVING SECOND THOUGHTS.
MAYBE I DIDN'T THINK THIS THROUGH...

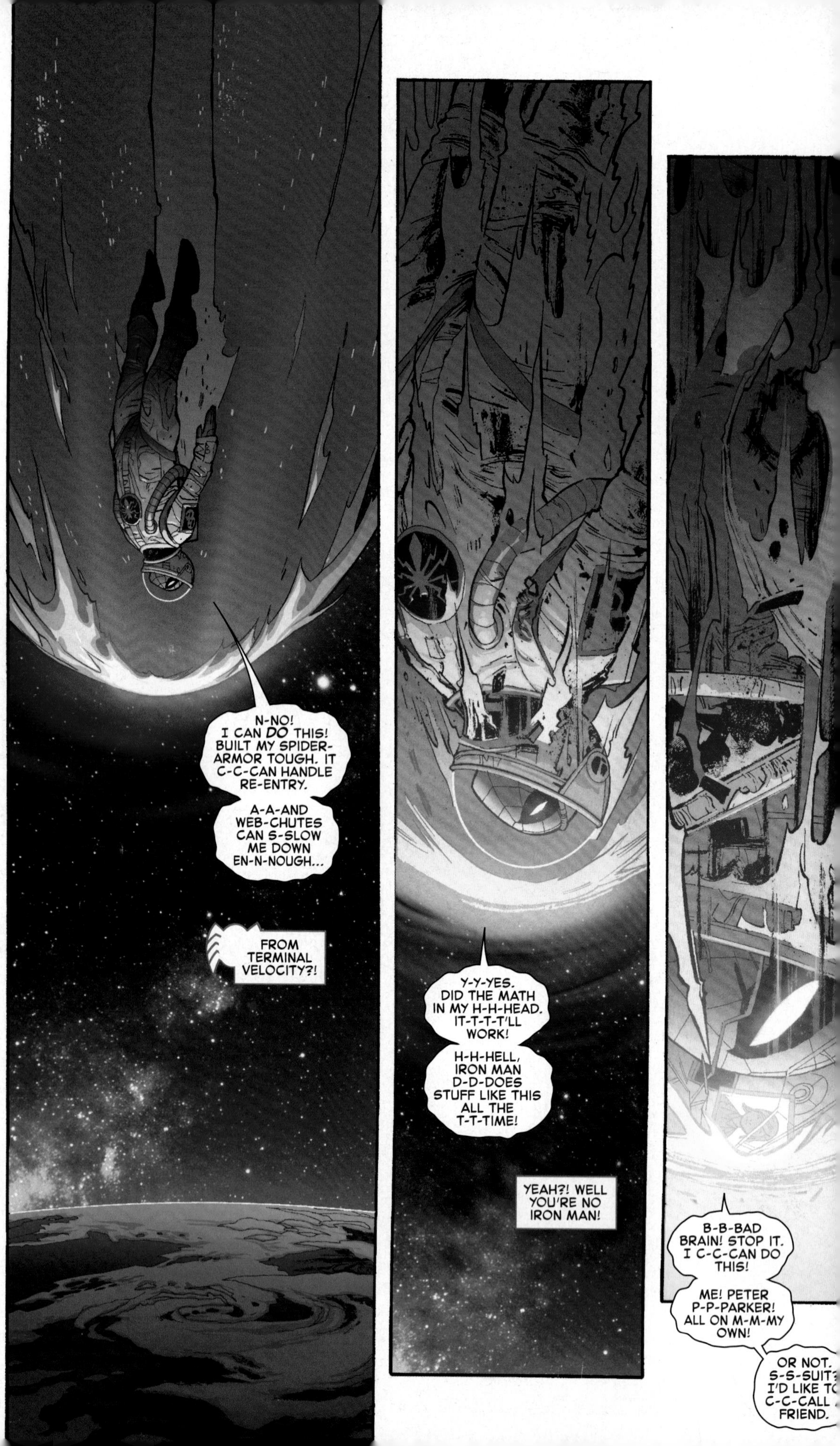
N-NO! I CAN DO THIS! BUILT MY SPIDER-ARMOR TOUGH. IT C-C-CAN HANDLE RE-ENTRY.
A-A-AND WEB-CHUTES CAN S-SLOW ME DOWN EN-N-NOUGH...
FROM TERMINAL VELOCITY?!
Y-Y-YES. DID THE MATH IN MY H-H-HEAD. IT-T-T-T'LL WORK!
H-H-HELL, IRON MAN D-D-DOES STUFF LIKE THIS ALL THE T-T-TIME!
YEAH?! WELL YOU'RE NO IRON MAN!
B-B-BAD BRAIN! STOP IT. I C-C-CAN DO THIS!
ME! PETER P-P-PARKER! ALL ON M-M-MY OWN!
OR NOT. S-S-SUIT I'D LIKE T C-C-CALL FRIEND.

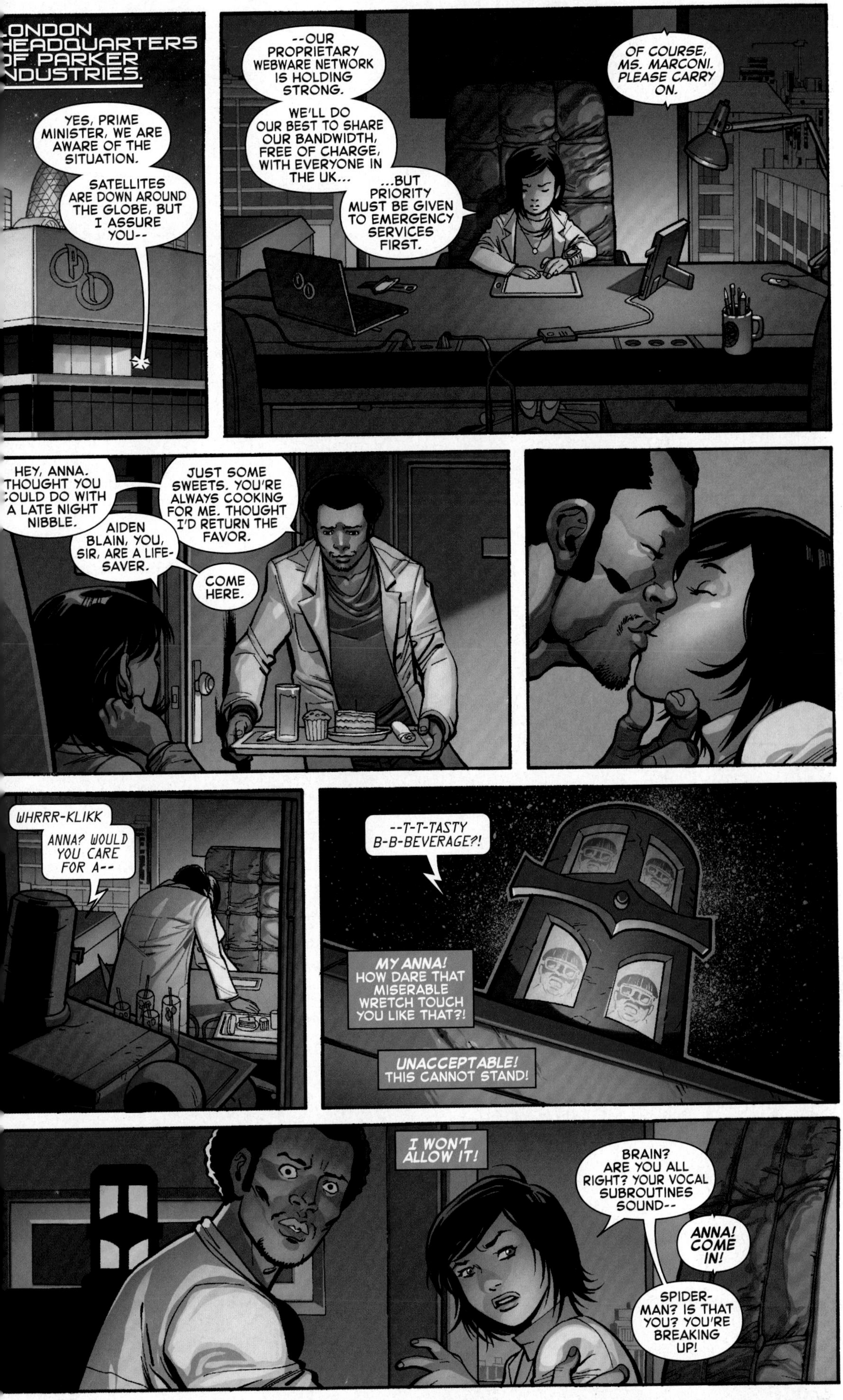
LONDON HEADQUARTERS OF PARKER INDUSTRIES.
YES, PRIME MINISTER, WE ARE AWARE OF THE SITUATION.
SATELLITES ARE DOWN AROUND THE GLOBE, BUT I ASSURE YOU--
--OUR PROPRIETARY WEBWARE NETWORK IS HOLDING STRONG.
WE'LL DO OUR BEST TO SHARE OUR BANDWIDTH, FREE OF CHARGE, WITH EVERYONE IN THE UK...
...BUT PRIORITY MUST BE GIVEN TO EMERGENCY SERVICES FIRST.
OF COURSE, MS. MARCONI. PLEASE CARRY ON.
HEY, ANNA. THOUGHT YOU COULD DO WITH A LATE NIGHT NIBBLE.
JUST SOME SWEETS. YOU'RE ALWAYS COOKING FOR ME. THOUGHT I'D RETURN THE FAVOR.
AIDEN BLAIN, YOU, SIR, ARE A LIFE-SAVER.
COME HERE.
WHRRR-KLIKK
ANNA? WOULD YOU CARE FOR A--
--T-T-TASTY B-B-BEVERAGE?!
MY ANNA! HOW DARE THAT MISERABLE WRETCH TOUCH YOU LIKE THAT?!
UNACCEPTABLE! THIS CANNOT STAND!
I WON'T ALLOW IT!
BRAIN? ARE YOU ALL RIGHT? YOUR VOCAL SUBROUTINES SOUND--
ANNA! COME IN!
SPIDER-MAN? IS THAT YOU? YOU'RE BREAKING UP!

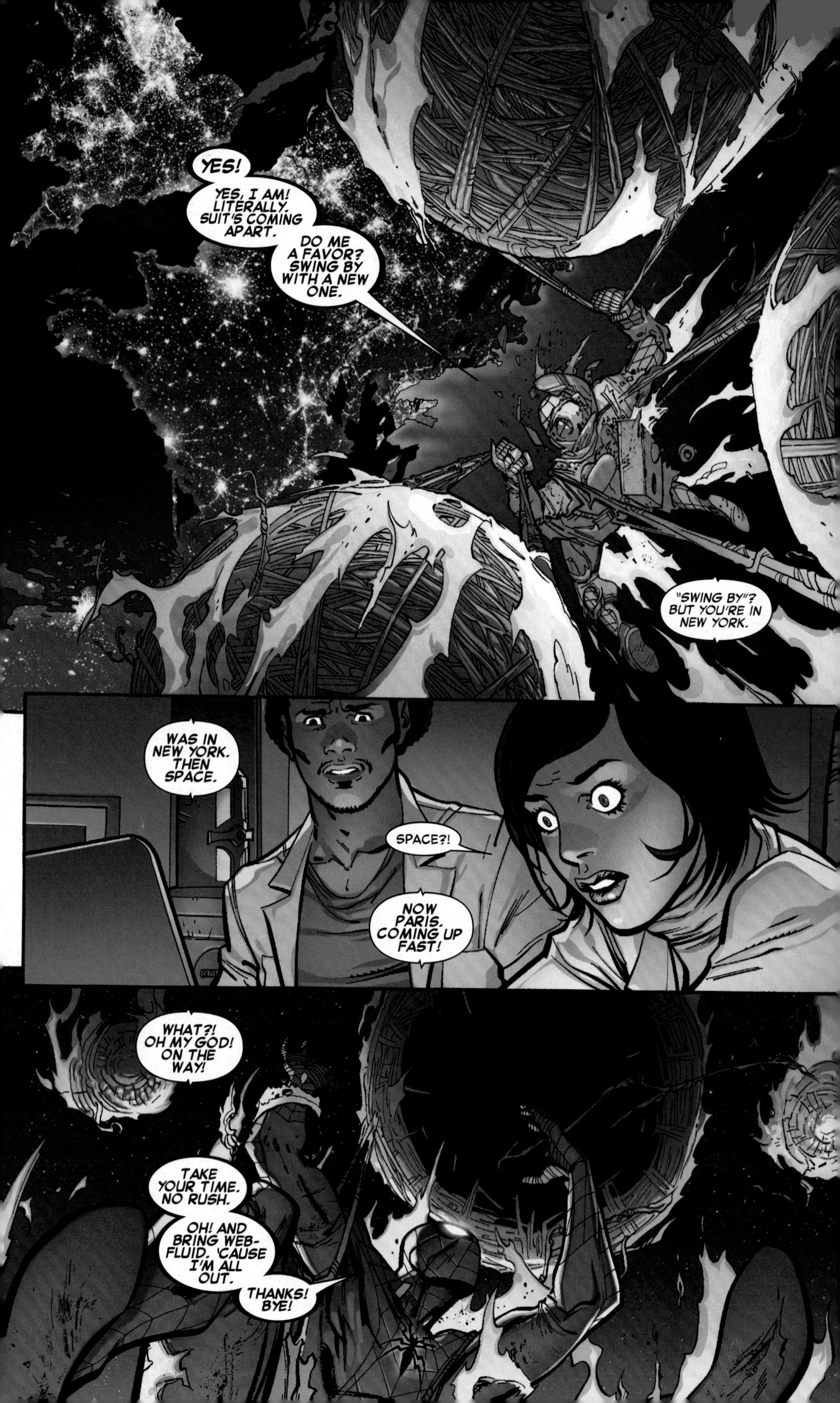
YES!
YES, I AM! LITERALLY. SUIT'S COMING APART.
DO ME A FAVOR? SWING BY WITH A NEW ONE.
"SWING BY"? BUT YOU'RE IN NEW YORK.
WAS IN NEW YORK. THEN SPACE.
SPACE?!
NOW PARIS. COMING UP FAST!
WHAT?! OH MY GOD! ON THE WAY!
TAKE YOUR TIME. NO RUSH.
OH! AND BRING WEB-FLUID. 'CAUSE I'M ALL OUT.
THANKS! BYE!

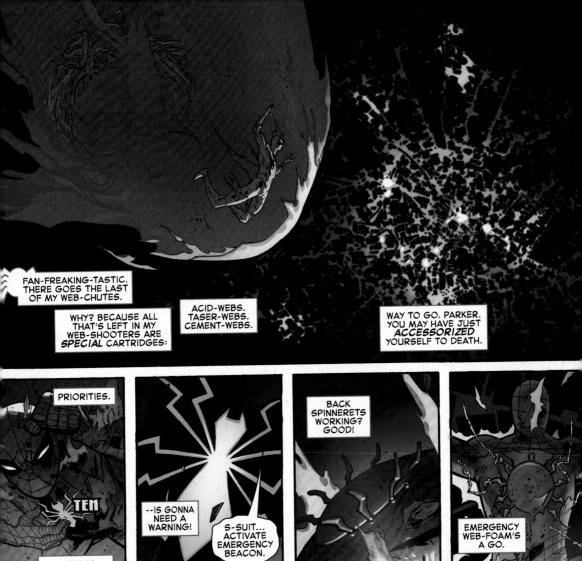

FAN-FREAKING-TASTIC. THERE GOES THE LAST OF MY WEB-CHUTES.

WHY? BECAUSE ALL THAT'S LEFT IN MY WEB-SHOOTERS ARE *SPECIAL* CARTRIDGES:

ACID-WEBS. TASER-WEBS. CEMENT-WEBS.

WAY TO GO, PARKER. YOU MAY HAVE JUST *ACCESSORIZED* YOURSELF TO DEATH.

PRIORITIES.

TEN

PARIS IS COMING UP FAST. ANYONE BELOW--

--IS GONNA NEED A WARNING!

S-SUIT... ACTIVATE EMERGENCY BEACON.

BACK SPINNERETS WORKING? GOOD!

EMERGENCY WEB-FOAM'S A GO.

WEEOOWEEOOWEEOOWEEOOWEEOO

WEEOOWEEOOWEEOOWEEOOWEEOO

THOUGHT I'D BE COMING IN SLOWER--

--BUT THIS "SHOULD" STILL WORK.

KEY WORD: SHOULD.

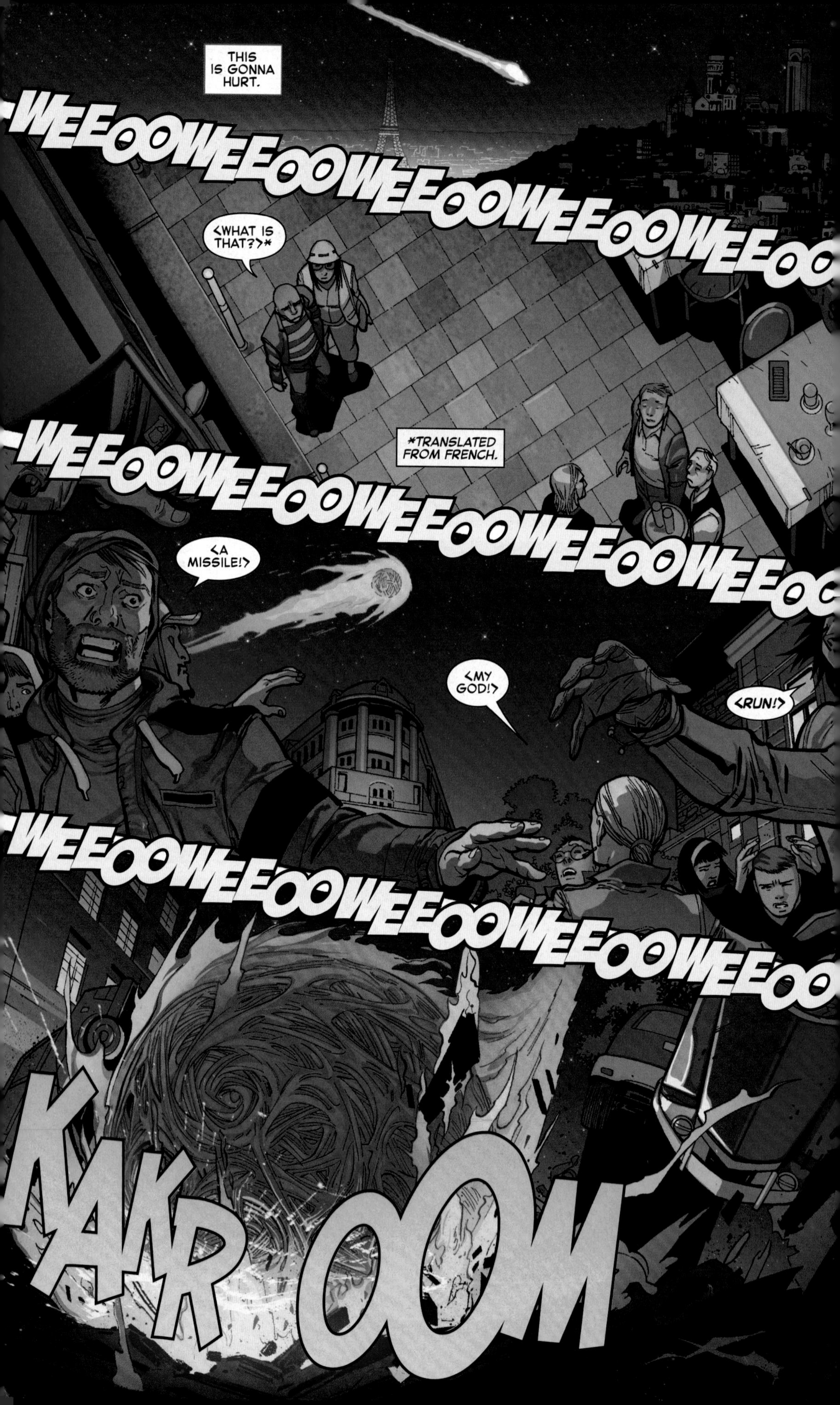

THIS IS GONNA HURT.
WEEOOWEEOOWEEOOWEEOOWEEOO
<WHAT IS THAT?>*
*TRANSLATED FROM FRENCH.
WEEOOWEEOOWEEOOWEEOOWEEOO
<A MISSILE!>
<MY GOD!>
<RUN!>
WEEOOWEEOOWEEOOWEEOOWEEOO
KAKROOOM

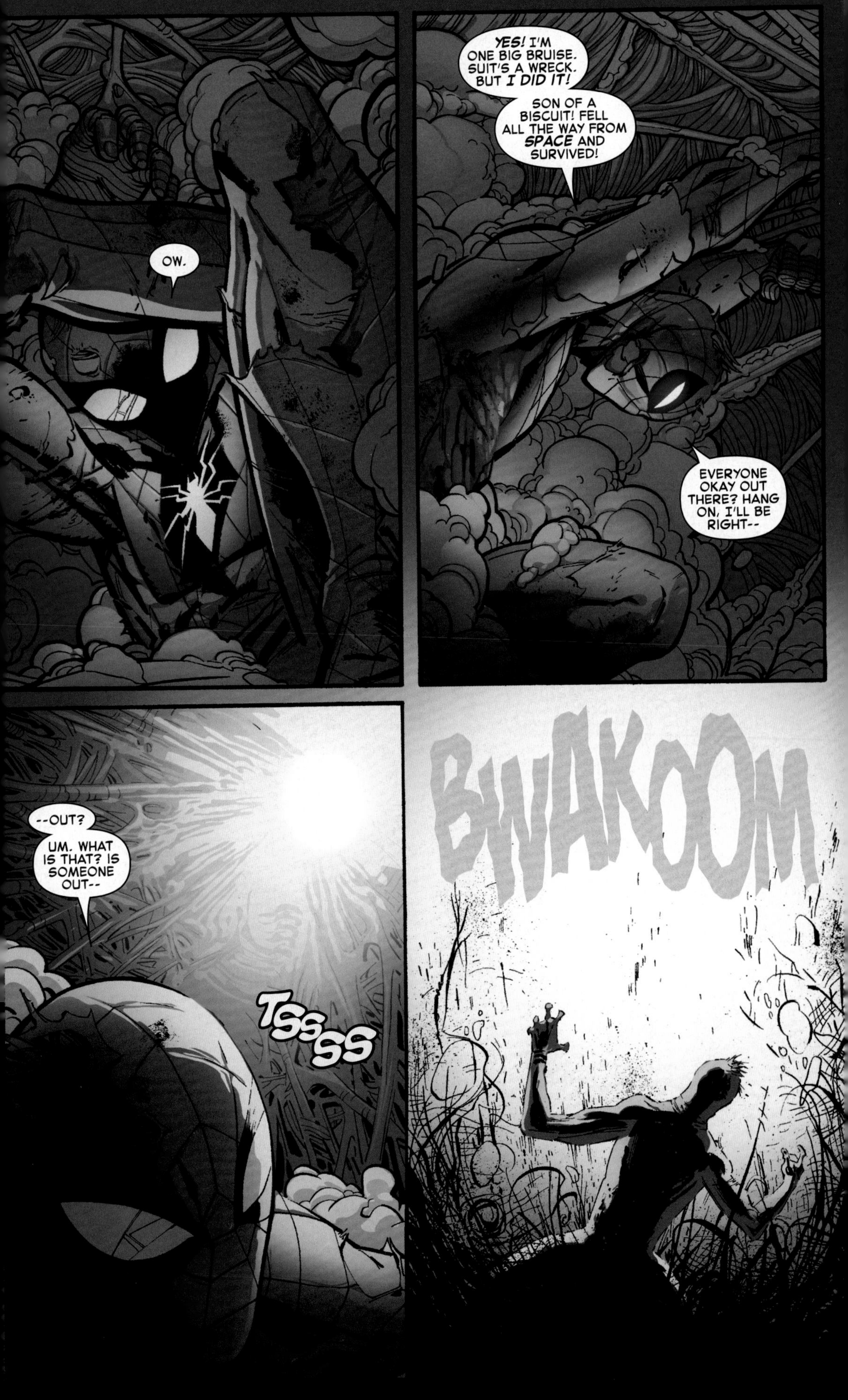
OW.
YES! I'M ONE BIG BRUISE. SUIT'S A WRECK. BUT I DID IT!
SON OF A BISCUIT! FELL ALL THE WAY FROM SPACE AND SURVIVED!
EVERYONE OKAY OUT THERE? HANG ON, I'LL BE RIGHT--
--OUT?
UM. WHAT IS THAT? IS SOMEONE OUT--
TSSSSS
BWAKOOM

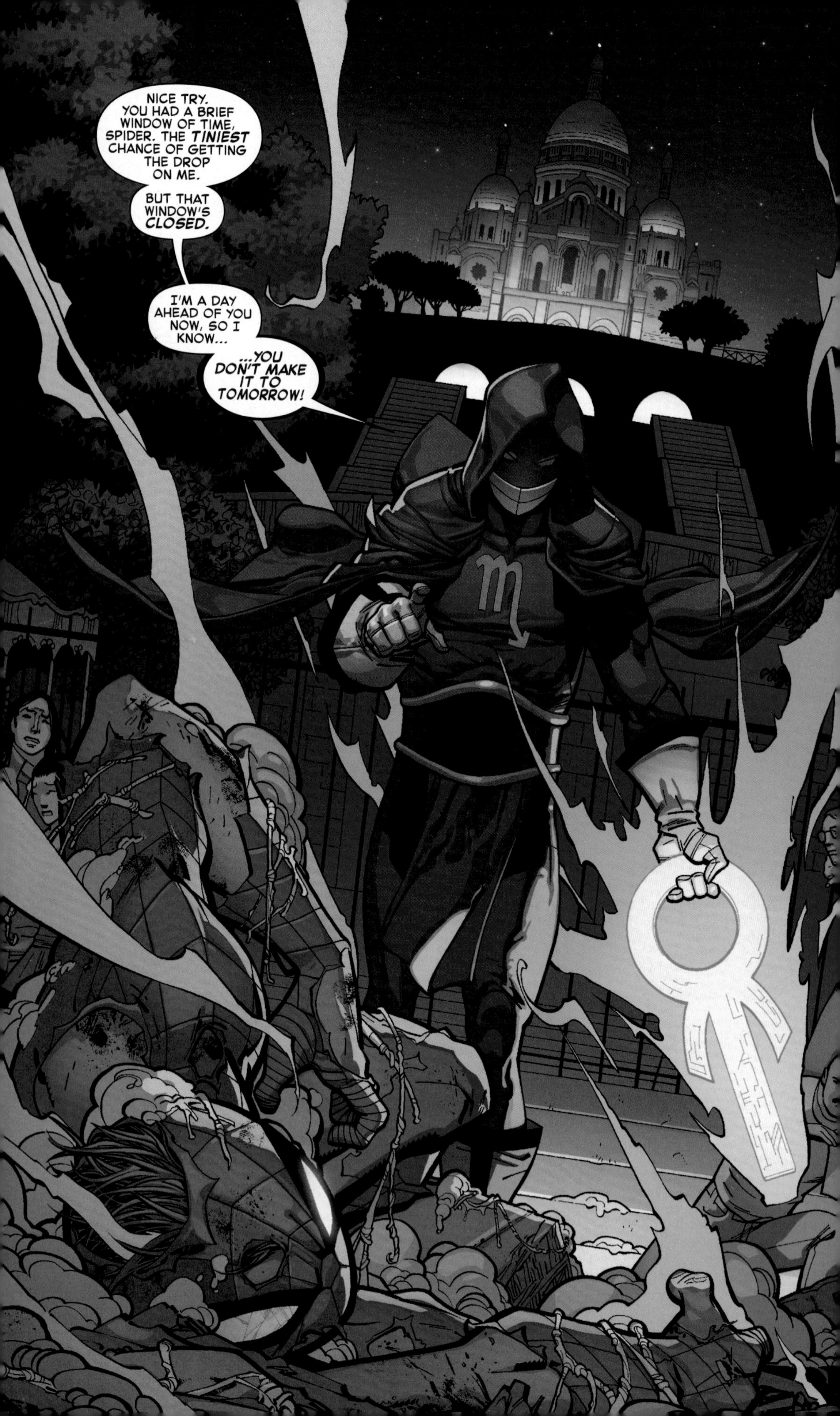
NICE TRY. YOU HAD A BRIEF WINDOW OF TIME, SPIDER. THE TINIEST CHANCE OF GETTING THE DROP ON ME.
BUT THAT WINDOW'S CLOSED.
I'M A DAY AHEAD OF YOU NOW, SO I KNOW...
...YOU DON'T MAKE IT TO TOMORROW!

MARVEL
010
SLOTT
CAMUNCOLI
SMITH
GRACIA
THE WORLD'S GREATEST SUPER HERO!
The AMAZING
SPIDER-MAN

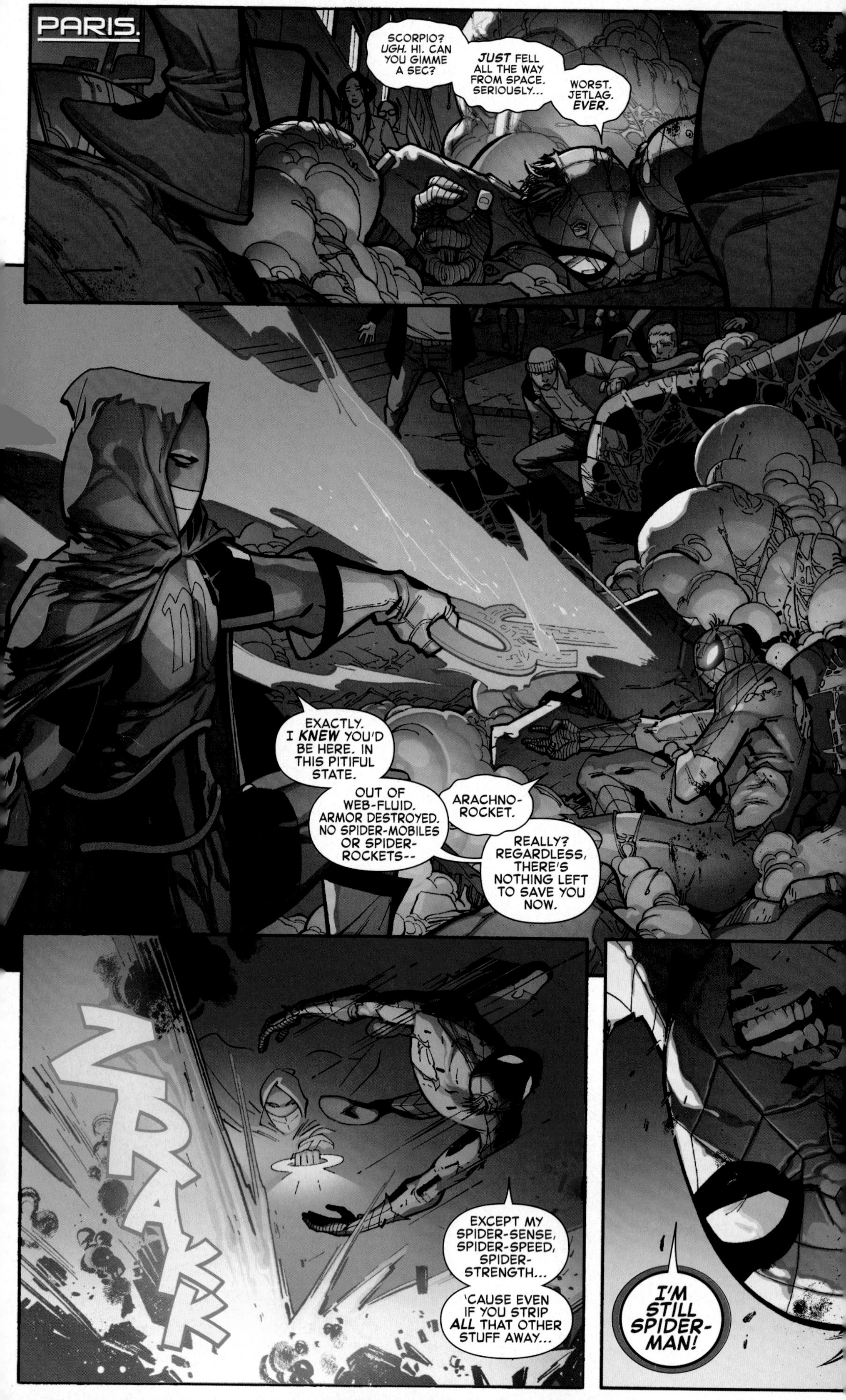
PARIS.
SCORPIO? UGH. HI. CAN YOU GIMME A SEC?
JUST FELL ALL THE WAY FROM SPACE. SERIOUSLY...
WORST. JETLAG. EVER.
EXACTLY. I KNEW YOU'D BE HERE. IN THIS PITIFUL STATE.
OUT OF WEB-FLUID. ARMOR DESTROYED. NO SPIDER-MOBILES OR SPIDER-ROCKETS--
ARACHNO-ROCKET.
REALLY? REGARDLESS, THERE'S NOTHING LEFT TO SAVE YOU NOW.
ZRAKK
EXCEPT MY SPIDER-SENSE, SPIDER-SPEED, SPIDER-STRENGTH...
'CAUSE EVEN IF YOU STRIP ALL THAT OTHER STUFF AWAY...
I'M STILL SPIDER-MAN!

AND I STILL HAVE MY **MOVES**.

HERE'S ONE A CERTAIN MASTER OF KUNG-FU TAUGHT ME!

TOO BAD IT'S USELESS AGAINST THE **ZODIAC KEY!**

THAT'S A NICE DOODAD YOU GOT THERE, SCORPY...

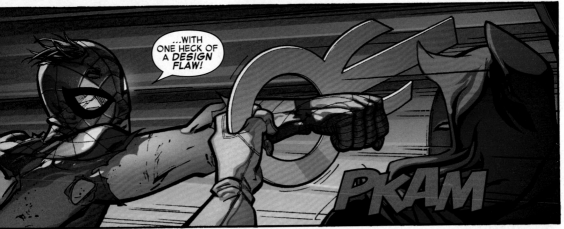

...WITH ONE HECK OF A **DESIGN FLAW!**

PKAM

UNFFF!

WELL PLAYED. BUT I KNOW **YOUR** FLAW, WALL-CRAWLER...

BYSTANDERS. YOU CARE MORE FOR OTHERS THAN YOUR **OWN** SKIN.

AHH!

NO! CAN'T WEB THEM OUT OF THE WAY! USED UP ALL MY **NORMAL** WEBBING!

ALL THAT'S LEFT ARE **SPECIAL** CARTRIDGES.

ACID-WEBS! CONCRETE-WEBS! THAT'D KILL 'EM!

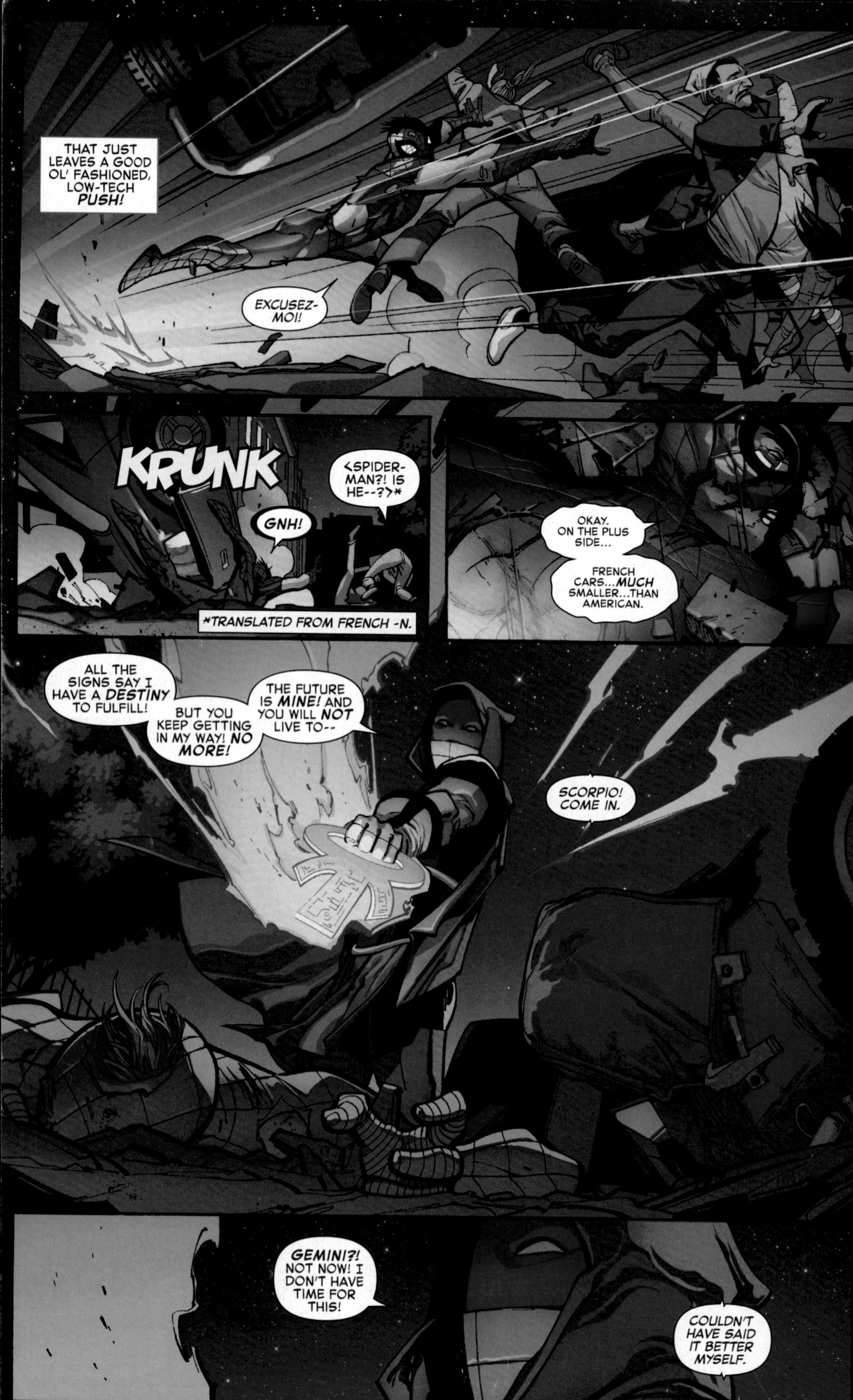

THAT JUST LEAVES A GOOD OL' FASHIONED, LOW-TECH PUSH!
EXCUSEZ-MOI!
KRUNK
GNH!
<SPIDER-MAN?! IS HE--?>*
*TRANSLATED FROM FRENCH -N.
OKAY. ON THE PLUS SIDE...
FRENCH CARS...MUCH SMALLER...THAN AMERICAN.
ALL THE SIGNS SAY I HAVE A DESTINY TO FULFILL!
BUT YOU KEEP GETTING IN MY WAY! NO MORE!
THE FUTURE IS MINE! AND YOU WILL NOT LIVE TO--
SCORPIO! COME IN.
GEMINI?! NOT NOW! I DON'T HAVE TIME FOR THIS!
COULDN'T HAVE SAID IT BETTER MYSELF.

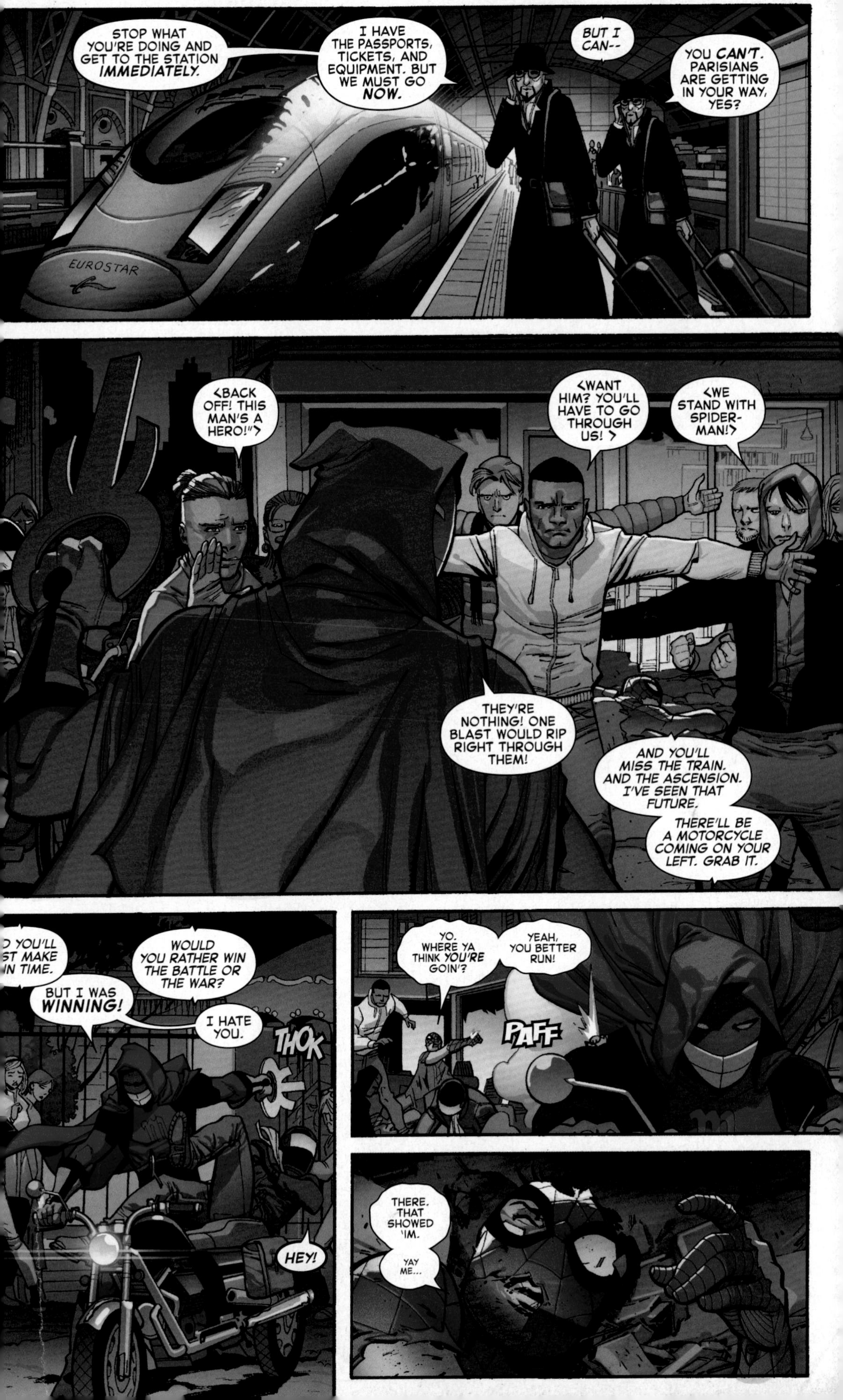
STOP WHAT YOU'RE DOING AND GET TO THE STATION *IMMEDIATELY.*
I HAVE THE PASSPORTS, TICKETS, AND EQUIPMENT. BUT WE MUST GO **NOW.**
BUT I CAN--
YOU **CAN'T.** PARISIANS ARE GETTING IN YOUR WAY, YES?
EUROSTAR
<BACK OFF! THIS MAN'S A HERO!">
<WANT HIM? YOU'LL HAVE TO GO THROUGH US! >
<WE STAND WITH SPIDER-MAN!>
THEY'RE NOTHING! ONE BLAST WOULD RIP RIGHT THROUGH THEM!
AND YOU'LL MISS THE TRAIN. AND THE ASCENSION. I'VE SEEN THAT FUTURE.
THERE'LL BE A MOTORCYCLE COMING ON YOUR LEFT. GRAB IT.
D YOU'LL ST MAKE N TIME.
WOULD YOU RATHER WIN THE BATTLE OR THE WAR?
BUT I WAS **WINNING!**
I HATE YOU.
THOK
HEY!
YO. WHERE YA THINK *YOU'RE* GOIN'?
YEAH, YOU BETTER RUN!
PAFF
THERE. THAT SHOWED 'IM.
YAY ME...

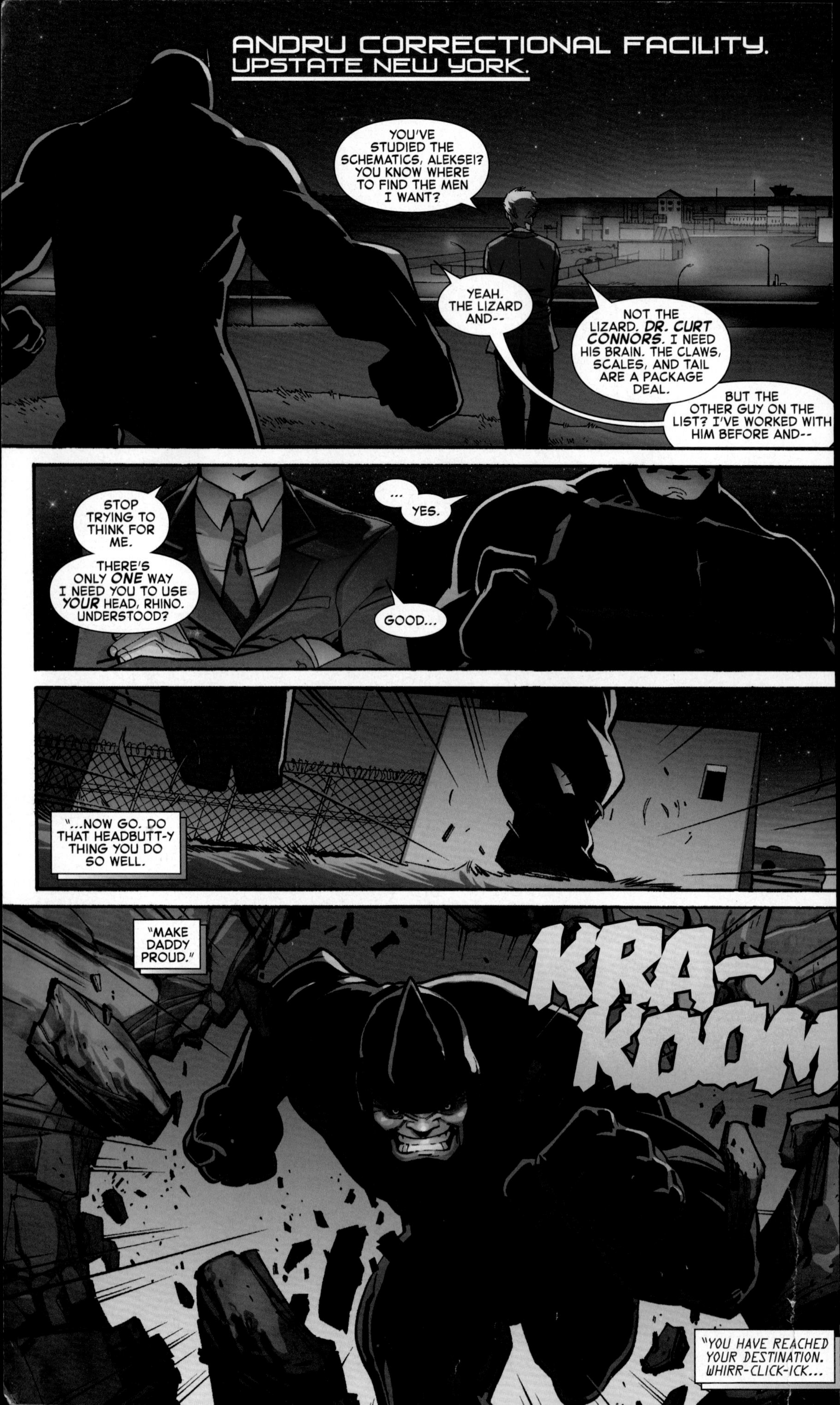
ANDRU CORRECTIONAL FACILITY.
UPSTATE NEW YORK.
YOU'VE STUDIED THE SCHEMATICS, ALEKSEI? YOU KNOW WHERE TO FIND THE MEN I WANT?
YEAH. THE LIZARD AND--
NOT THE LIZARD. DR. CURT CONNORS. I NEED HIS BRAIN. THE CLAWS, SCALES, AND TAIL ARE A PACKAGE DEAL.
BUT THE OTHER GUY ON THE LIST? I'VE WORKED WITH HIM BEFORE AND--
STOP TRYING TO THINK FOR ME.
THERE'S ONLY ONE WAY I NEED YOU TO USE YOUR HEAD, RHINO. UNDERSTOOD?
... YES.
GOOD...
"...NOW GO. DO THAT HEADBUTT-Y THING YOU DO SO WELL.
"MAKE DADDY PROUD."
KRA-KOOM
"YOU HAVE REACHED YOUR DESTINATION. WHIRR-CLICK-ICK...

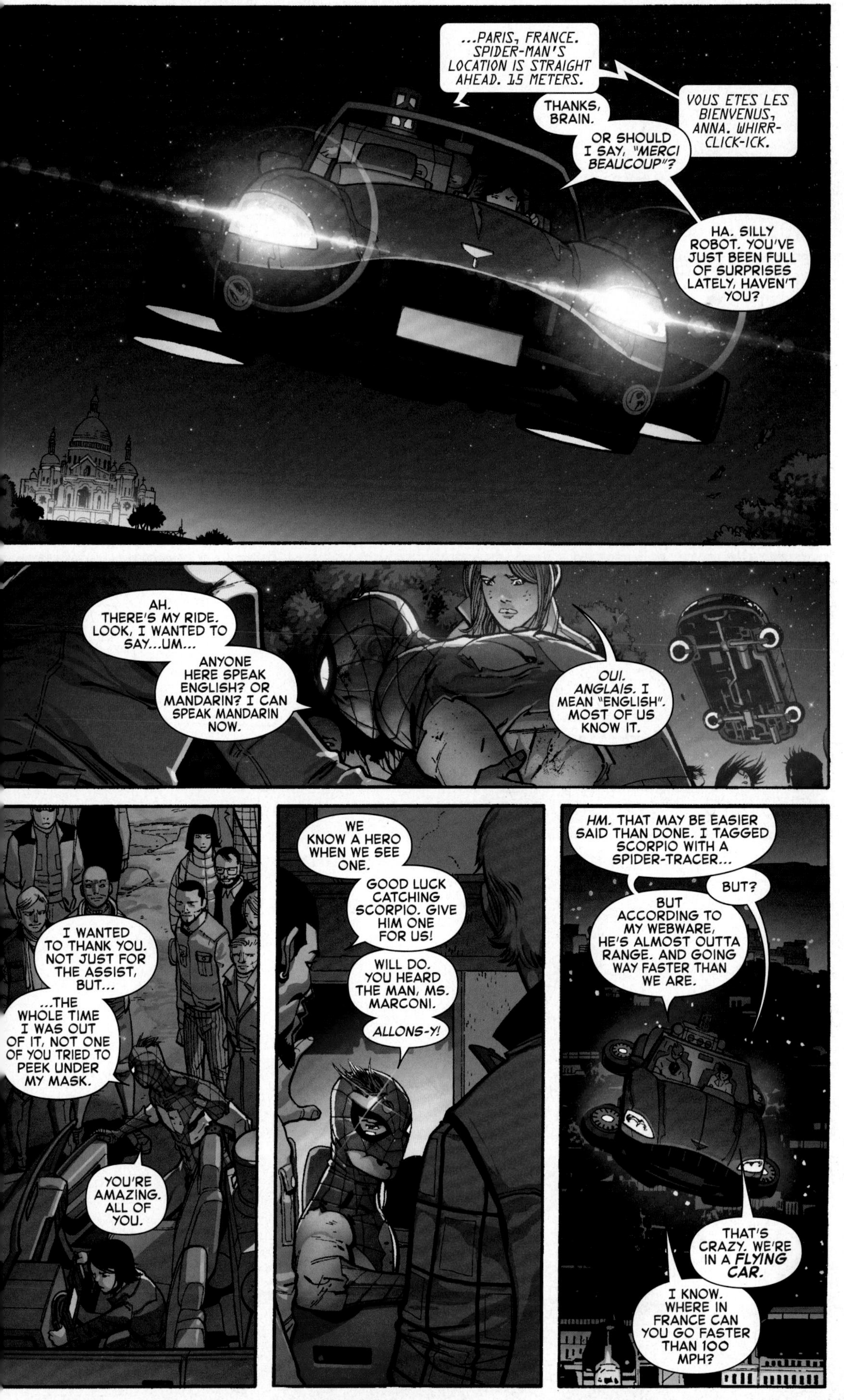

...PARIS, FRANCE. SPIDER-MAN'S LOCATION IS STRAIGHT AHEAD. 15 METERS.
THANKS, BRAIN.
OR SHOULD I SAY, "MERCI BEAUCOUP"?
VOUS ETES LES BIENVENUS, ANNA. WHIRR-CLICK-ICK.
HA. SILLY ROBOT. YOU'VE JUST BEEN FULL OF SURPRISES LATELY, HAVEN'T YOU?
AH. THERE'S MY RIDE. LOOK, I WANTED TO SAY...UM...
ANYONE HERE SPEAK ENGLISH? OR MANDARIN? I CAN SPEAK MANDARIN NOW.
OUI. ANGLAIS. I MEAN "ENGLISH". MOST OF US KNOW IT.
I WANTED TO THANK YOU. NOT JUST FOR THE ASSIST, BUT...
...THE WHOLE TIME I WAS OUT OF IT, NOT ONE OF YOU TRIED TO PEEK UNDER MY MASK.
YOU'RE AMAZING. ALL OF YOU.
WE KNOW A HERO WHEN WE SEE ONE.
GOOD LUCK CATCHING SCORPIO. GIVE HIM ONE FOR US!
WILL DO. YOU HEARD THE MAN, MS. MARCONI.
ALLONS-Y!
HM. THAT MAY BE EASIER SAID THAN DONE. I TAGGED SCORPIO WITH A SPIDER-TRACER...
BUT?
BUT ACCORDING TO MY WEBWARE, HE'S ALMOST OUTTA RANGE. AND GOING WAY FASTER THAN WE ARE.
THAT'S CRAZY. WE'RE IN A FLYING CAR.
I KNOW. WHERE IN FRANCE CAN YOU GO FASTER THAN 100 MPH?

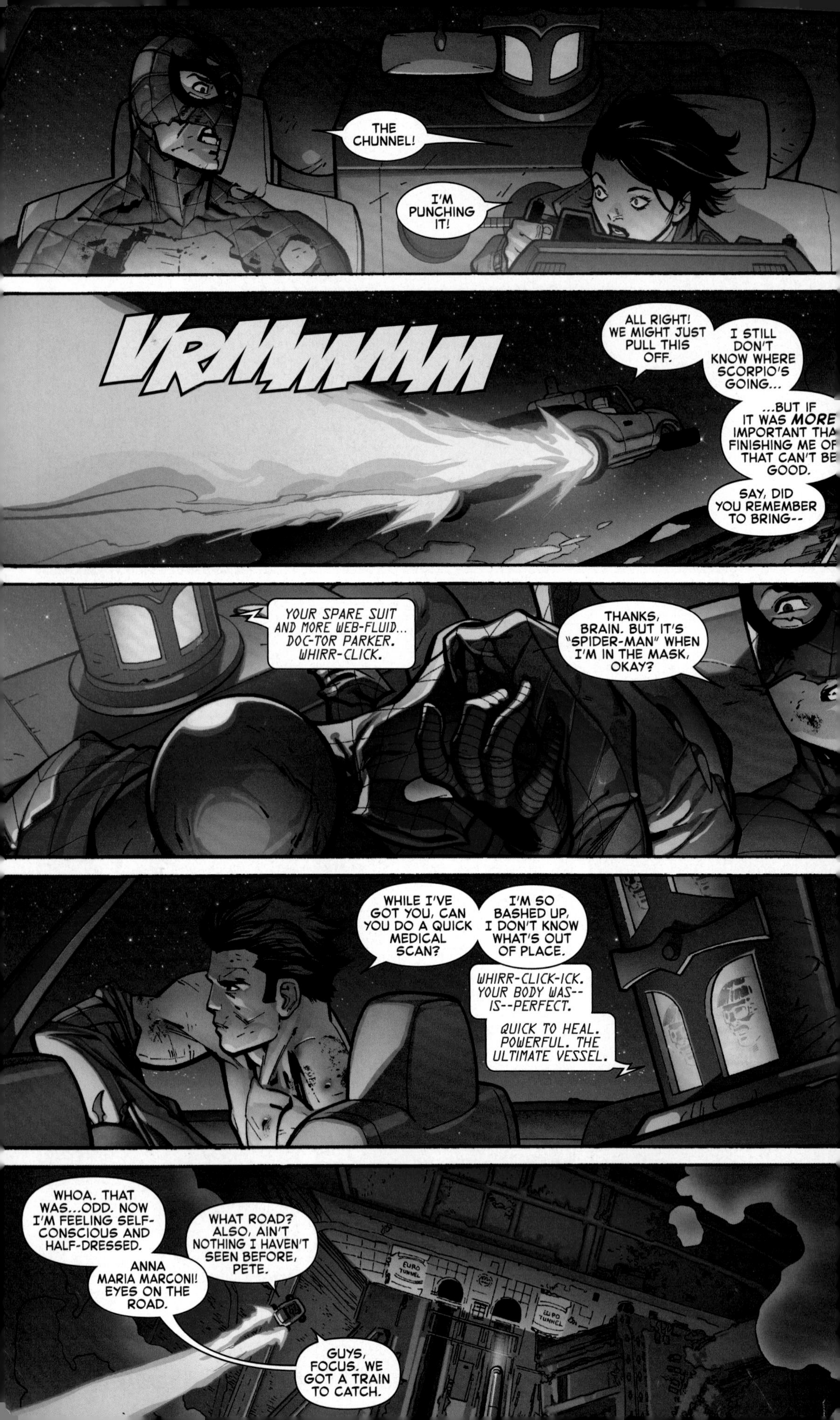
THE CHUNNEL!
I'M PUNCHING IT!
VRMMMMM
ALL RIGHT! WE MIGHT JUST PULL THIS OFF.
I STILL DON'T KNOW WHERE SCORPIO'S GOING...
...BUT IF IT WAS MORE IMPORTANT THA FINISHING ME OF THAT CAN'T BE GOOD.
SAY, DID YOU REMEMBER TO BRING--
YOUR SPARE SUIT AND MORE WEB-FLUID... DOC-TOR PARKER. WHIRR-CLICK.
THANKS, BRAIN. BUT IT'S "SPIDER-MAN" WHEN I'M IN THE MASK, OKAY?
WHILE I'VE GOT YOU, CAN YOU DO A QUICK MEDICAL SCAN?
I'M SO BASHED UP, I DON'T KNOW WHAT'S OUT OF PLACE.
WHIRR-CLICK-ICK. YOUR BODY WAS-- IS--PERFECT.
QUICK TO HEAL. POWERFUL. THE ULTIMATE VESSEL.
WHOA. THAT WAS...ODD. NOW I'M FEELING SELF-CONSCIOUS AND HALF-DRESSED.
ANNA MARIA MARCONI! EYES ON THE ROAD.
WHAT ROAD? ALSO, AIN'T NOTHING I HAVEN'T SEEN BEFORE, PETE.
EURO TUNNEL
EURO TUNNEL
GUYS, FOCUS. WE GOT A TRAIN TO CATCH.

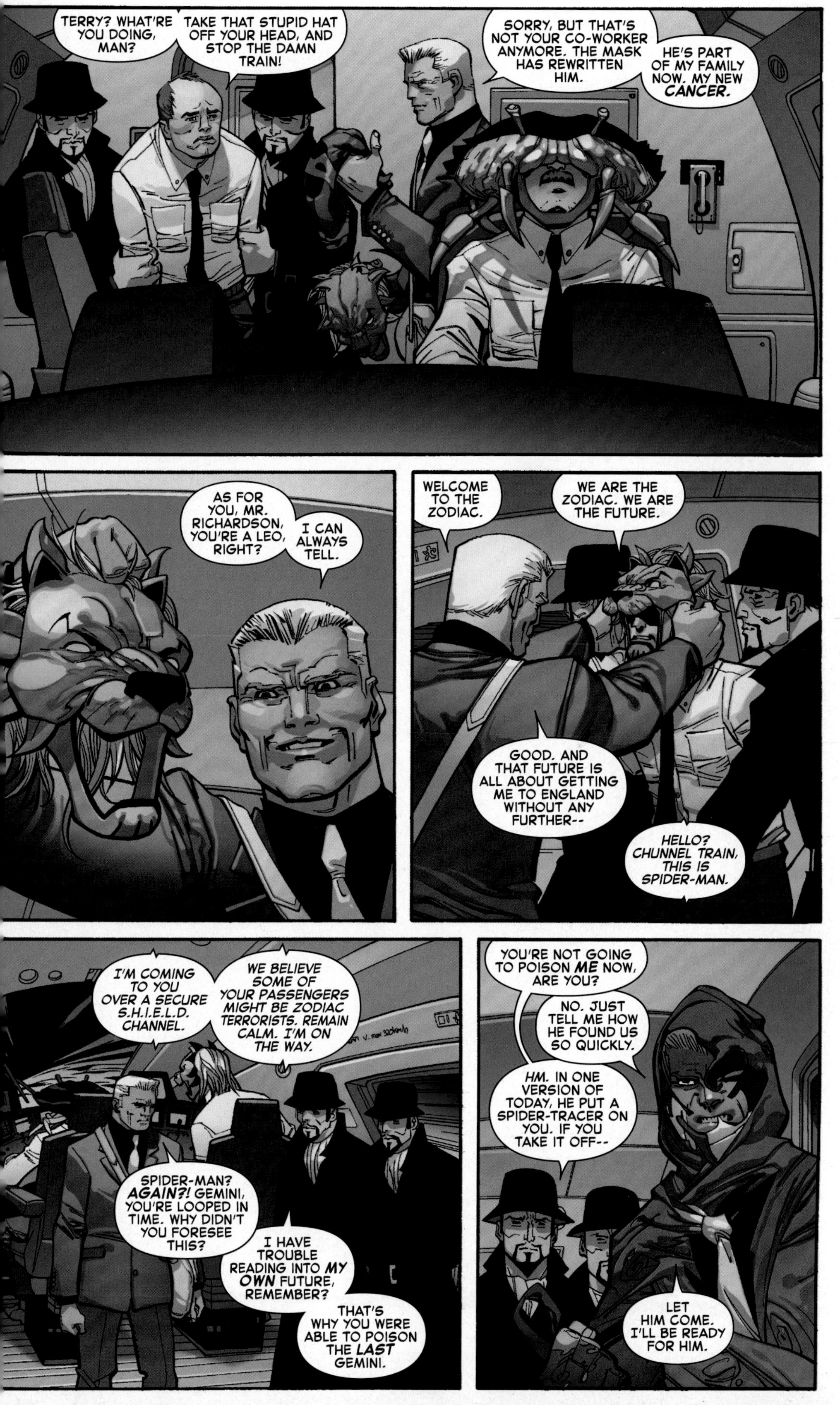
TERRY? WHAT'RE YOU DOING, MAN?
TAKE THAT STUPID HAT OFF YOUR HEAD, AND STOP THE DAMN TRAIN!
SORRY, BUT THAT'S NOT YOUR CO-WORKER ANYMORE. THE MASK HAS REWRITTEN HIM.
HE'S PART OF MY FAMILY NOW. MY NEW *CANCER.*
AS FOR YOU, MR. RICHARDSON, YOU'RE A LEO, RIGHT?
I CAN ALWAYS TELL.
WELCOME TO THE ZODIAC.
WE ARE THE ZODIAC. WE ARE THE FUTURE.
GOOD. AND THAT FUTURE IS ALL ABOUT GETTING ME TO ENGLAND WITHOUT ANY FURTHER--
HELLO? CHUNNEL TRAIN, THIS IS SPIDER-MAN.
I'M COMING TO YOU OVER A SECURE S.H.I.E.L.D. CHANNEL.
WE BELIEVE SOME OF YOUR PASSENGERS MIGHT BE ZODIAC TERRORISTS. REMAIN CALM. I'M ON THE WAY.
SPIDER-MAN? ***AGAIN?!*** GEMINI, YOU'RE LOOPED IN TIME. WHY DIDN'T YOU FORESEE THIS?
I HAVE TROUBLE READING INTO ***MY OWN*** FUTURE, REMEMBER?
THAT'S WHY YOU WERE ABLE TO POISON THE ***LAST*** GEMINI.
YOU'RE NOT GOING TO POISON ***ME*** NOW, ARE YOU?
NO. JUST TELL ME HOW HE FOUND US SO QUICKLY.
HM. IN ONE VERSION OF TODAY, HE PUT A SPIDER-TRACER ON YOU. IF YOU TAKE IT OFF--
LET HIM COME. I'LL BE READY FOR HIM.

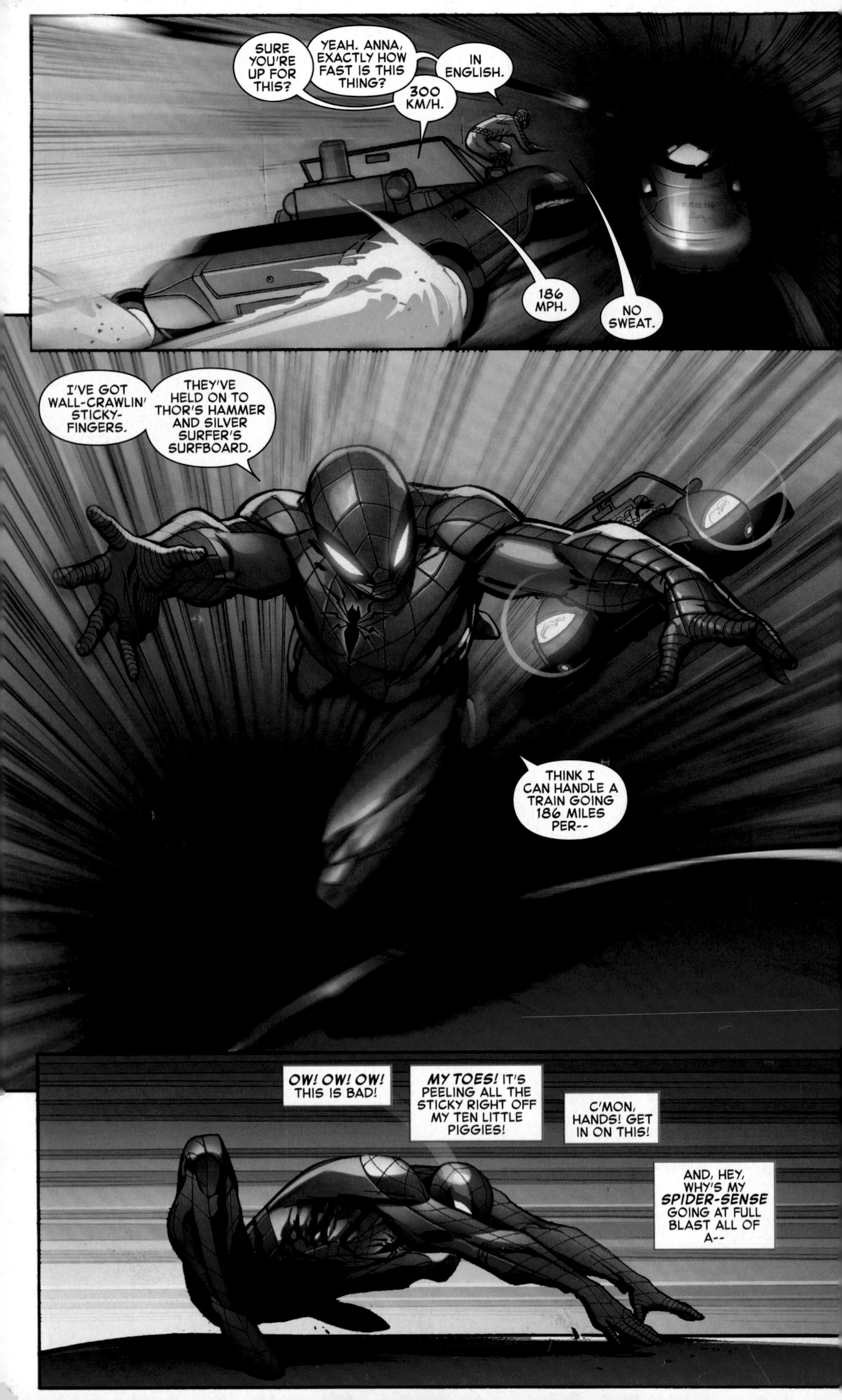
SURE YOU'RE UP FOR THIS?
YEAH. ANNA, EXACTLY HOW FAST IS THIS THING?
300 KM/H.
IN ENGLISH.
186 MPH.
NO SWEAT.
I'VE GOT WALL-CRAWLIN' STICKY-FINGERS.
THEY'VE HELD ON TO THOR'S HAMMER AND SILVER SURFER'S SURFBOARD.
THINK I CAN HANDLE A TRAIN GOING 186 MILES PER--
OW! OW! OW! THIS IS BAD!
MY TOES! IT'S PEELING ALL THE STICKY RIGHT OFF MY TEN LITTLE PIGGIES!
C'MON, HANDS! GET IN ON THIS!
AND, HEY, WHY'S MY SPIDER-SENSE GOING AT FULL BLAST ALL OF A--

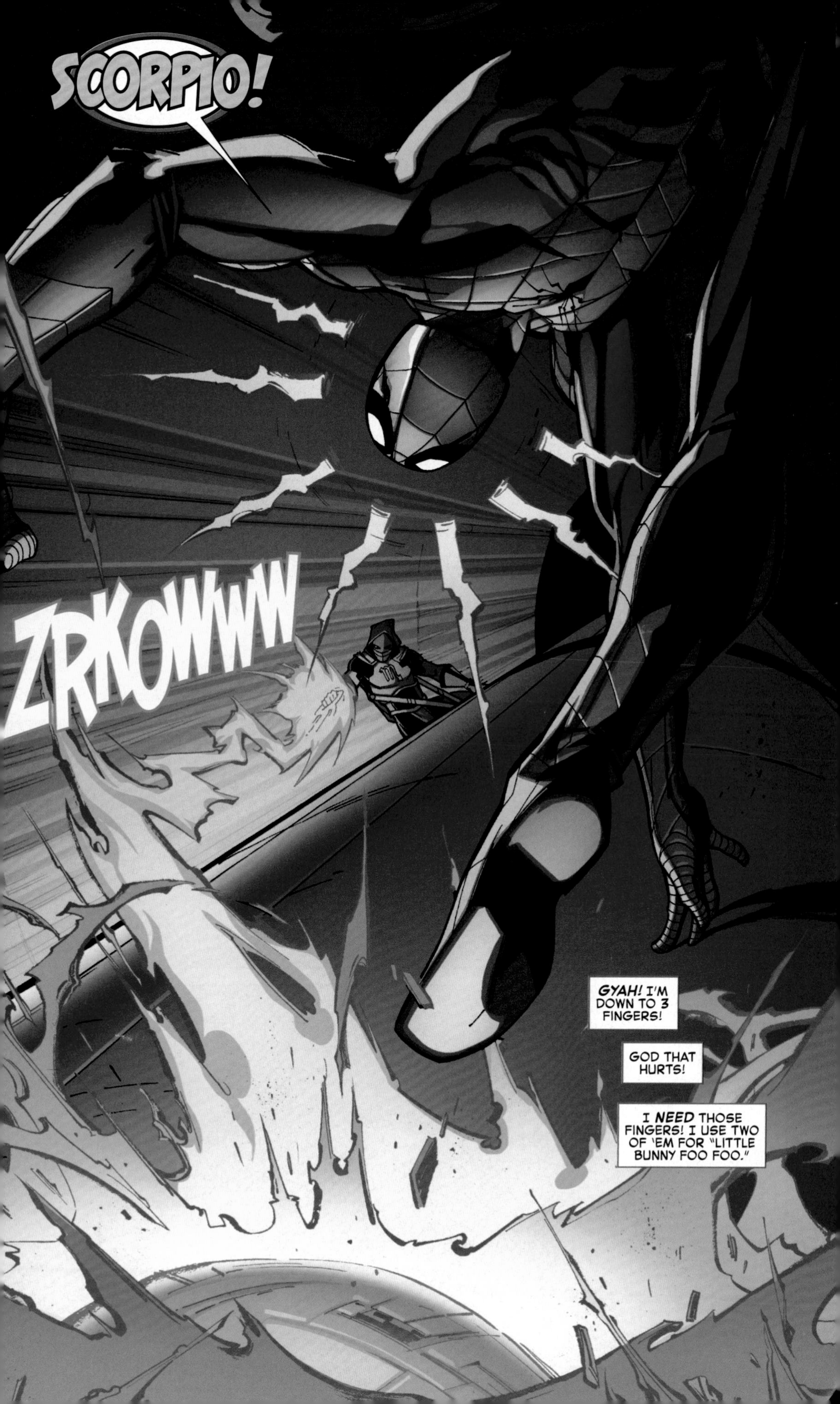
SCORPIO!
ZRKOWWW
GYAH! I'M DOWN TO 3 FINGERS!
GOD THAT HURTS!
I NEED THOSE FINGERS! I USE TWO OF 'EM FOR "LITTLE BUNNY FOO FOO."

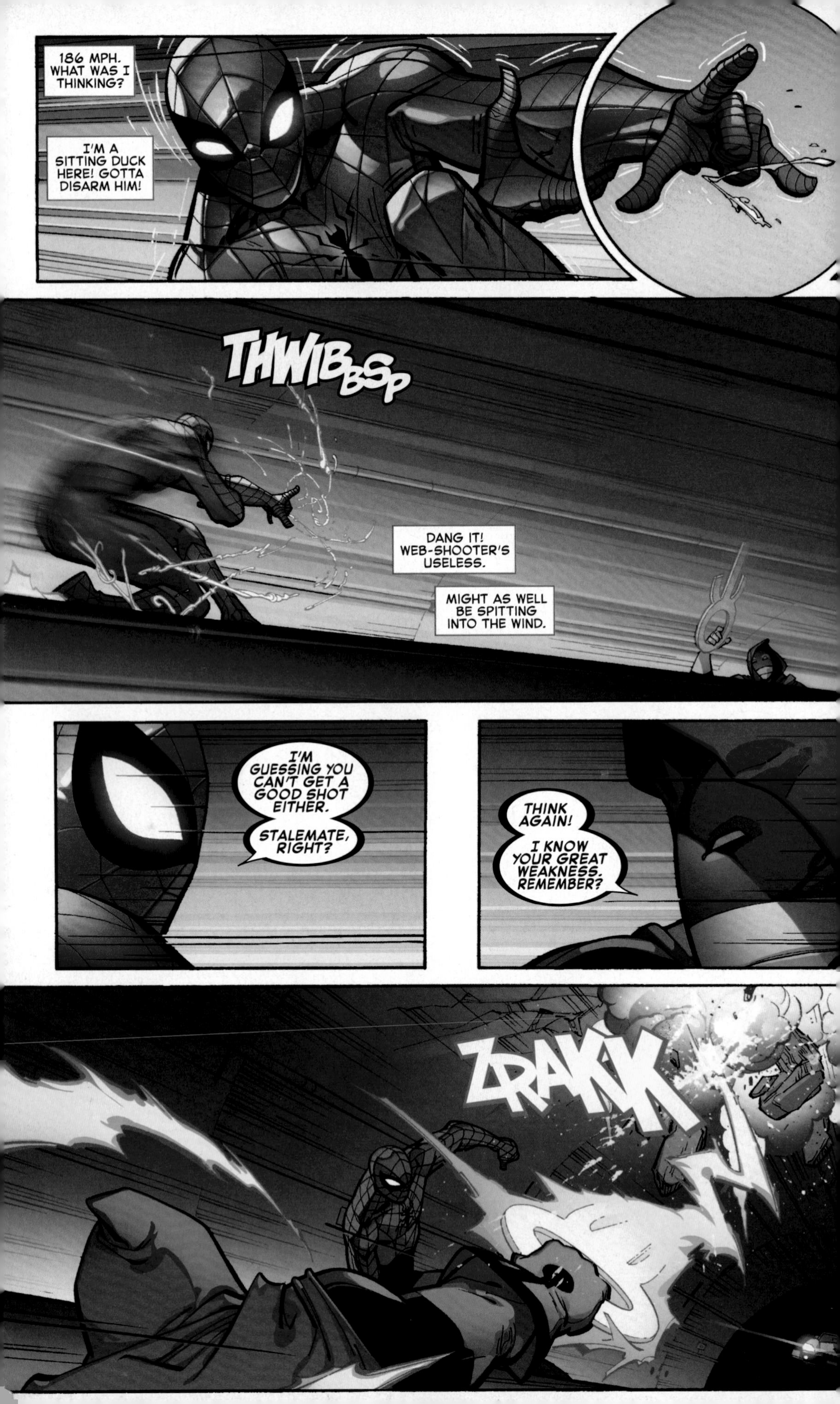
186 MPH. WHAT WAS I THINKING?
I'M A SITTING DUCK HERE! GOTTA DISARM HIM!
THWIBBSP
DANG IT! WEB-SHOOTER'S USELESS.
MIGHT AS WELL BE SPITTING INTO THE WIND.
I'M GUESSING YOU CAN'T GET A GOOD SHOT EITHER.
STALEMATE, RIGHT?
THINK AGAIN!
I KNOW YOUR GREAT WEAKNESS. REMEMBER?
ZRAKK

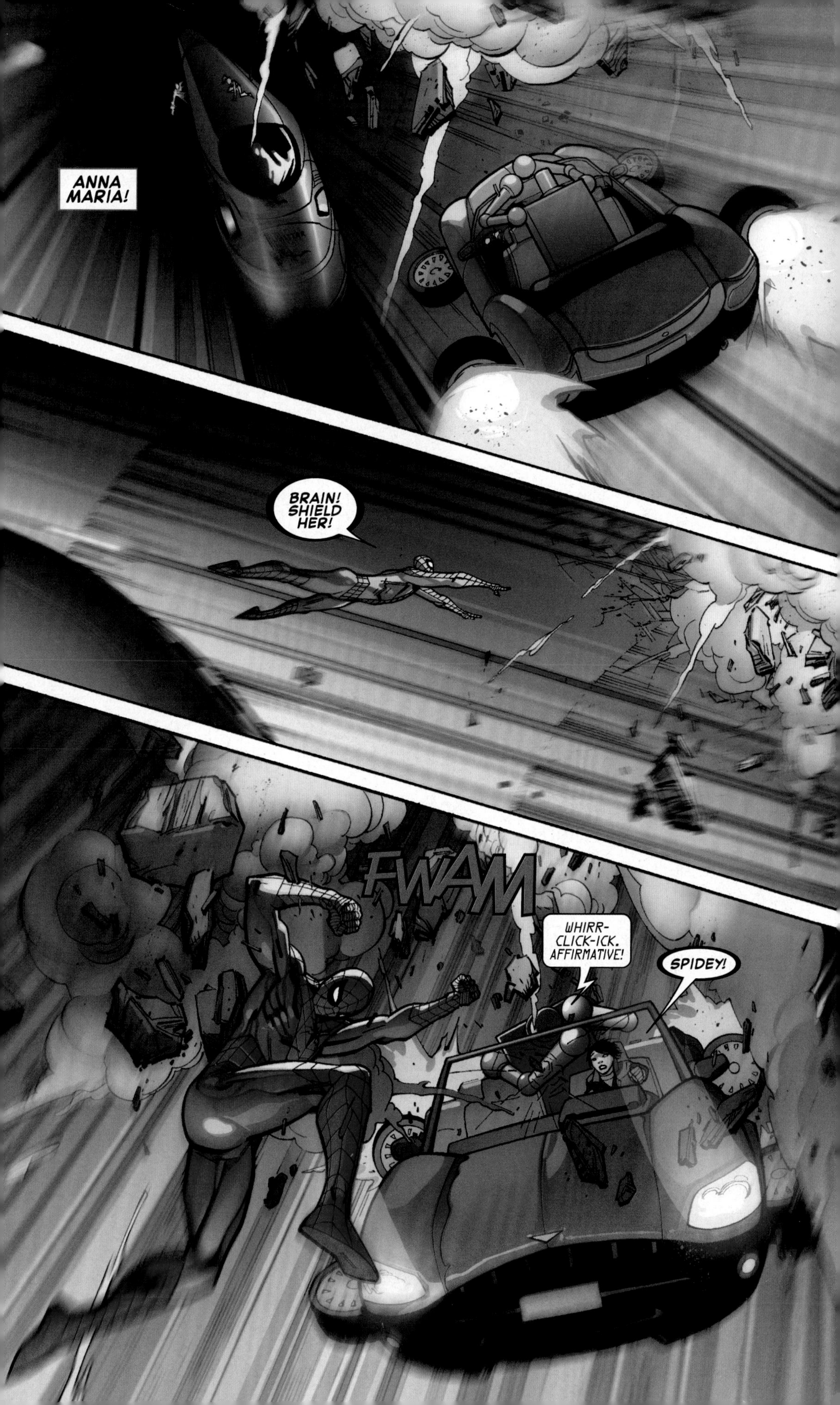
ANNA MARIA!
BRAIN! SHIELD HER!
FWAM
WHIRR-CLICK-ICK. AFFIRMATIVE!
SPIDEY!

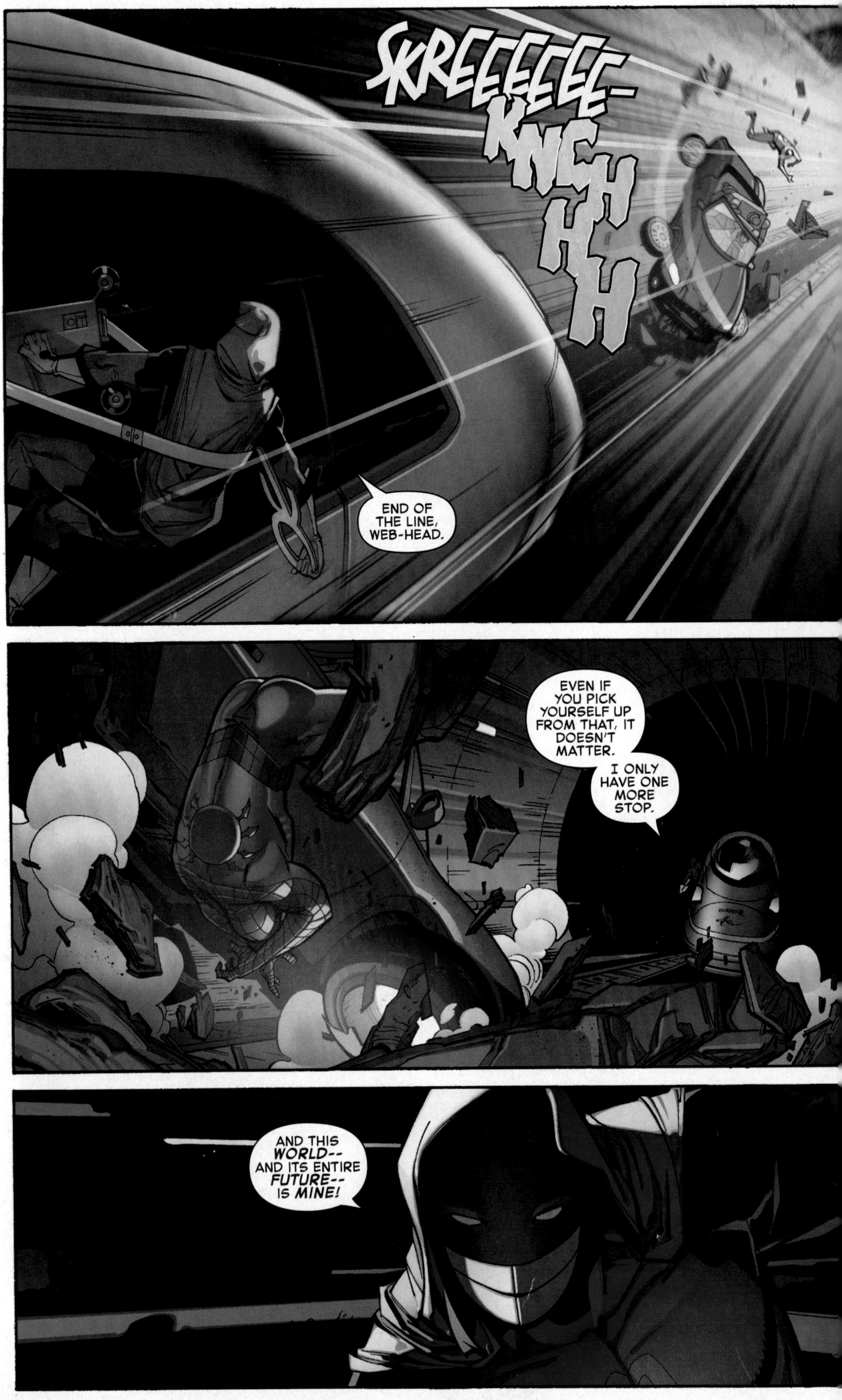
SKREEEEEE-KNCHHHH
END OF THE LINE, WEB-HEAD.
EVEN IF YOU PICK YOURSELF UP FROM THAT, IT DOESN'T MATTER.
I ONLY HAVE ONE MORE STOP.
AND THIS WORLD-- AND ITS ENTIRE FUTURE-- IS MINE!

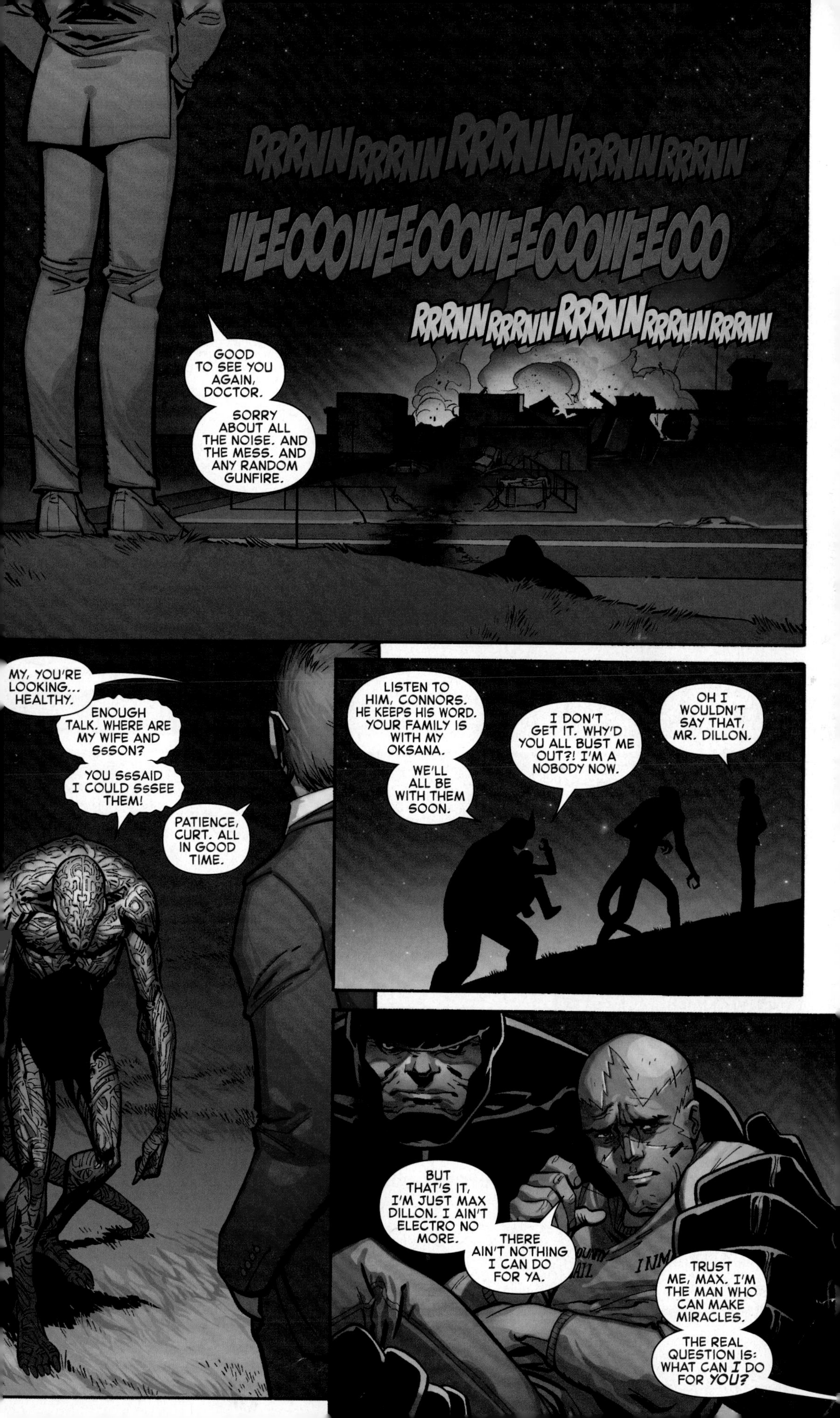
RRRNN RRRNN RRRNN RRRNN RRRNN
WEEOOO WEEOOO WEEOOO WEEOOO
RRRNN RRRNN RRRNN RRRNN RRRNN
GOOD TO SEE YOU AGAIN, DOCTOR.
SORRY ABOUT ALL THE NOISE. AND THE MESS. AND ANY RANDOM GUNFIRE.
MY, YOU'RE LOOKING... HEALTHY.
ENOUGH TALK. WHERE ARE MY WIFE AND SsSON?
YOU SsSAID I COULD SsSEE THEM!
PATIENCE, CURT. ALL IN GOOD TIME.
LISTEN TO HIM, CONNORS. HE KEEPS HIS WORD. YOUR FAMILY IS WITH MY OKSANA.
WE'LL ALL BE WITH THEM SOON.
I DON'T GET IT. WHY'D YOU ALL BUST ME OUT?! I'M A NOBODY NOW.
OH I WOULDN'T SAY THAT, MR. DILLON.
BUT THAT'S IT, I'M JUST MAX DILLON. I AIN'T ELECTRO NO MORE.
THERE AIN'T NOTHING I CAN DO FOR YA.
TRUST ME, MAX. I'M THE MAN WHO CAN MAKE MIRACLES.
THE REAL QUESTION IS: WHAT CAN I DO FOR YOU?

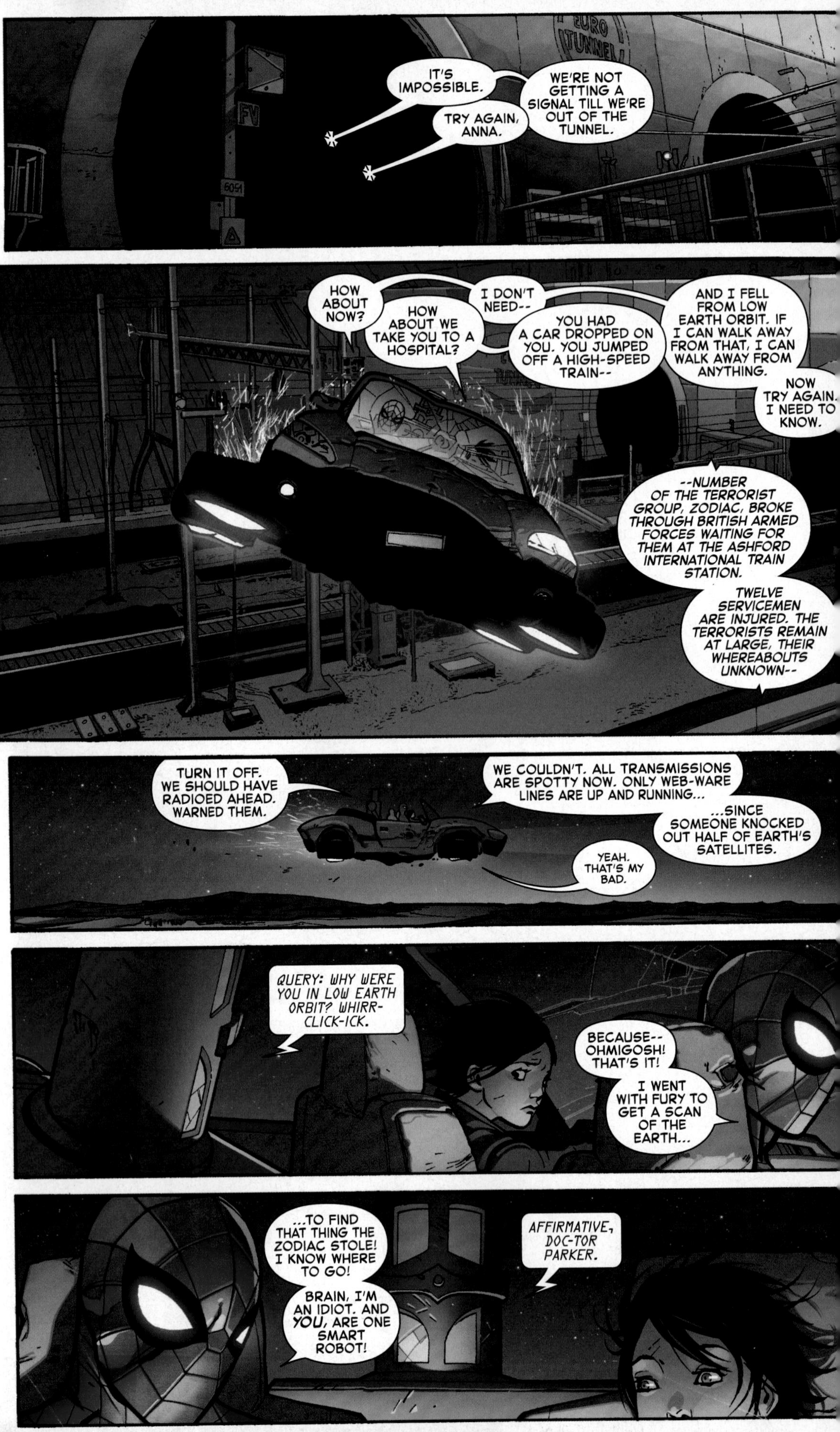
EURO TUNNEL
IT'S IMPOSSIBLE.
WE'RE NOT GETTING A SIGNAL TILL WE'RE OUT OF THE TUNNEL.
TRY AGAIN, ANNA.
HOW ABOUT NOW?
I DON'T NEED--
HOW ABOUT WE TAKE YOU TO A HOSPITAL?
YOU HAD A CAR DROPPED ON YOU. YOU JUMPED OFF A HIGH-SPEED TRAIN--
AND I FELL FROM LOW EARTH ORBIT. IF I CAN WALK AWAY FROM THAT, I CAN WALK AWAY FROM ANYTHING.
NOW TRY AGAIN. I NEED TO KNOW.
--NUMBER OF THE TERRORIST GROUP, ZODIAC, BROKE THROUGH BRITISH ARMED FORCES WAITING FOR THEM AT THE ASHFORD INTERNATIONAL TRAIN STATION.
TWELVE SERVICEMEN ARE INJURED. THE TERRORISTS REMAIN AT LARGE, THEIR WHEREABOUTS UNKNOWN--
TURN IT OFF. WE SHOULD HAVE RADIOED AHEAD. WARNED THEM.
WE COULDN'T. ALL TRANSMISSIONS ARE SPOTTY NOW. ONLY WEB-WARE LINES ARE UP AND RUNNING...
...SINCE SOMEONE KNOCKED OUT HALF OF EARTH'S SATELLITES.
YEAH. THAT'S MY BAD.
QUERY: WHY WERE YOU IN LOW EARTH ORBIT? WHIRR-CLICK-ICK.
BECAUSE-- OHMIGOSH! THAT'S IT!
I WENT WITH FURY TO GET A SCAN OF THE EARTH...
...TO FIND THAT THING THE ZODIAC STOLE! I KNOW WHERE TO GO!
BRAIN, I'M AN IDIOT. AND YOU, ARE ONE SMART ROBOT!
AFFIRMATIVE, DOC-TOR PARKER.

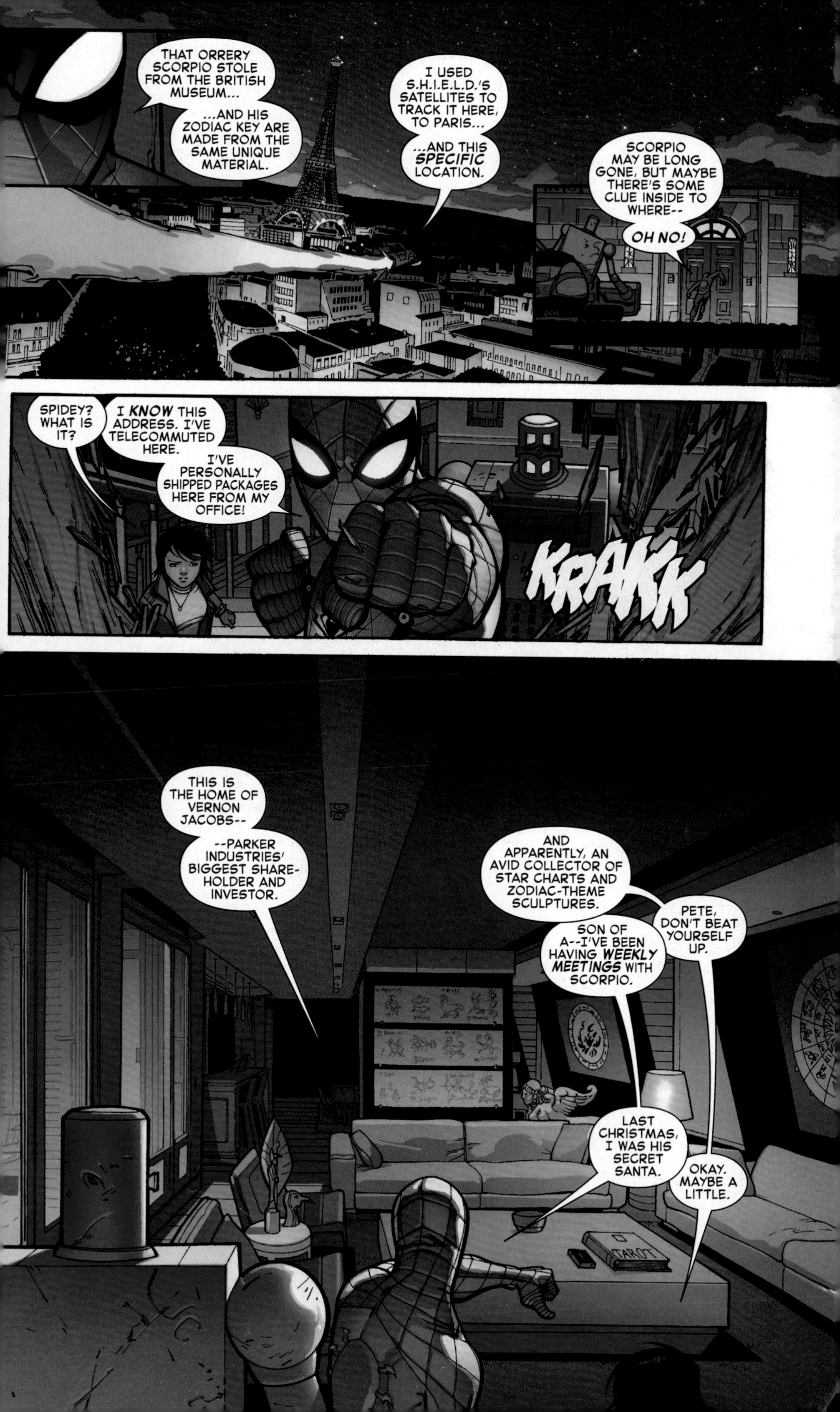
THAT ORRERY SCORPIO STOLE FROM THE BRITISH MUSEUM...
...AND HIS ZODIAC KEY ARE MADE FROM THE SAME UNIQUE MATERIAL.
I USED S.H.I.E.L.D.'S SATELLITES TO TRACK IT HERE, TO PARIS...
...AND THIS *SPECIFIC* LOCATION.
SCORPIO MAY BE LONG GONE, BUT MAYBE THERE'S SOME CLUE INSIDE TO WHERE--
OH NO!
SPIDEY? WHAT IS IT?
I *KNOW* THIS ADDRESS. I'VE TELECOMMUTED HERE.
I'VE PERSONALLY SHIPPED PACKAGES HERE FROM MY OFFICE!
KRAKK
THIS IS THE HOME OF VERNON JACOBS--
--PARKER INDUSTRIES' BIGGEST SHARE-HOLDER AND INVESTOR.
AND APPARENTLY, AN AVID COLLECTOR OF STAR CHARTS AND ZODIAC-THEME SCULPTURES.
PETE, DON'T BEAT YOURSELF UP.
SON OF A--I'VE BEEN HAVING *WEEKLY MEETINGS* WITH SCORPIO.
LAST CHRISTMAS, I WAS HIS SECRET SANTA.
OKAY. MAYBE A LITTLE.
TAROT

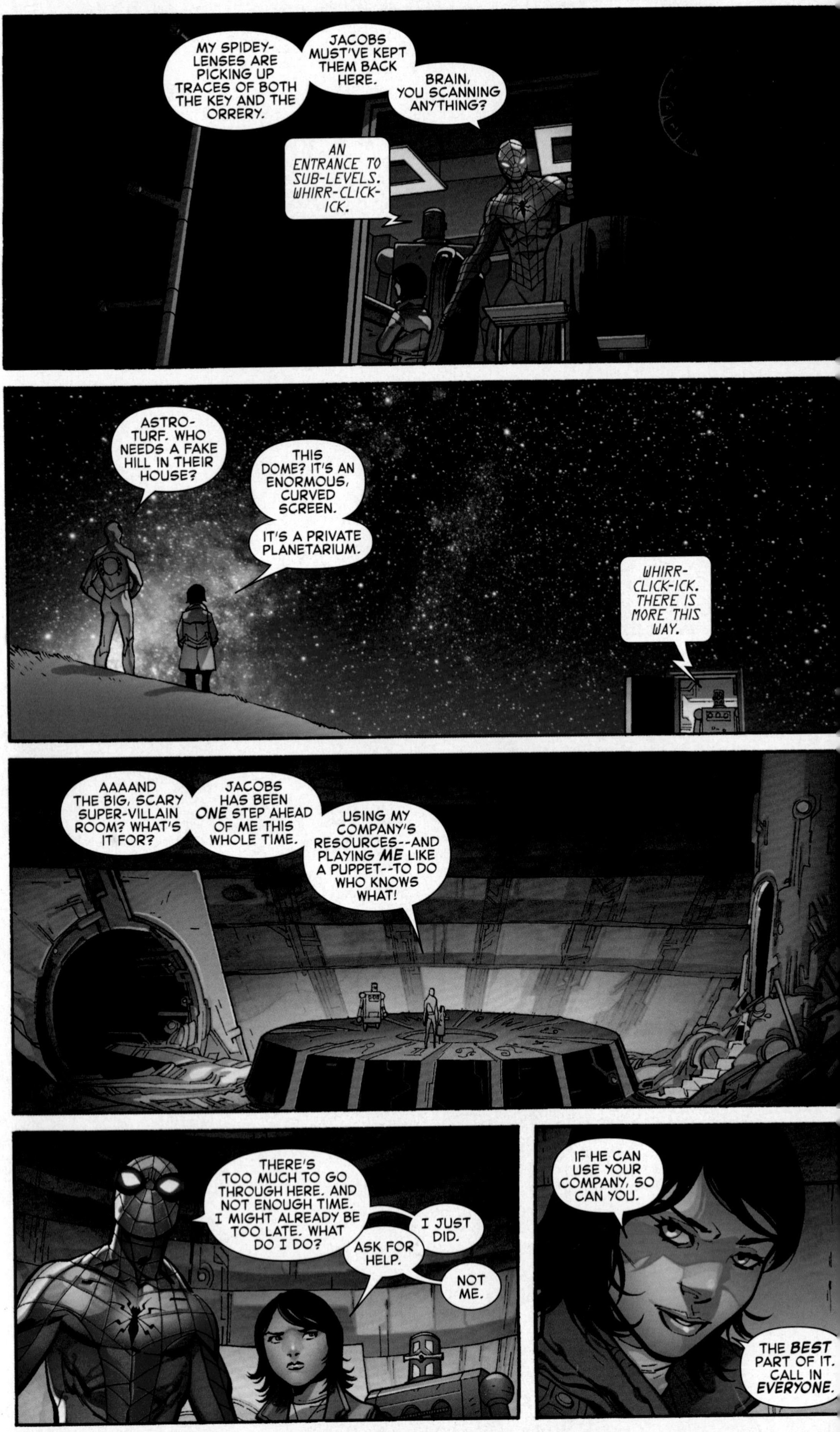
MY SPIDEY-LENSES ARE PICKING UP TRACES OF BOTH THE KEY AND THE ORRERY.
JACOBS MUST'VE KEPT THEM BACK HERE.
BRAIN, YOU SCANNING ANYTHING?
AN ENTRANCE TO SUB-LEVELS. WHIRR-CLICK-ICK.
ASTRO-TURF. WHO NEEDS A FAKE HILL IN THEIR HOUSE?
THIS DOME? IT'S AN ENORMOUS, CURVED SCREEN.
IT'S A PRIVATE PLANETARIUM.
WHIRR-CLICK-ICK. THERE IS MORE THIS WAY.
AAAAND THE BIG, SCARY SUPER-VILLAIN ROOM? WHAT'S IT FOR?
JACOBS HAS BEEN ONE STEP AHEAD OF ME THIS WHOLE TIME.
USING MY COMPANY'S RESOURCES--AND PLAYING ME LIKE A PUPPET--TO DO WHO KNOWS WHAT!
THERE'S TOO MUCH TO GO THROUGH HERE. AND NOT ENOUGH TIME. I MIGHT ALREADY BE TOO LATE. WHAT DO I DO?
ASK FOR HELP.
I JUST DID.
NOT ME.
IF HE CAN USE YOUR COMPANY, SO CAN YOU.
THE BEST PART OF IT. CALL IN EVERYONE.

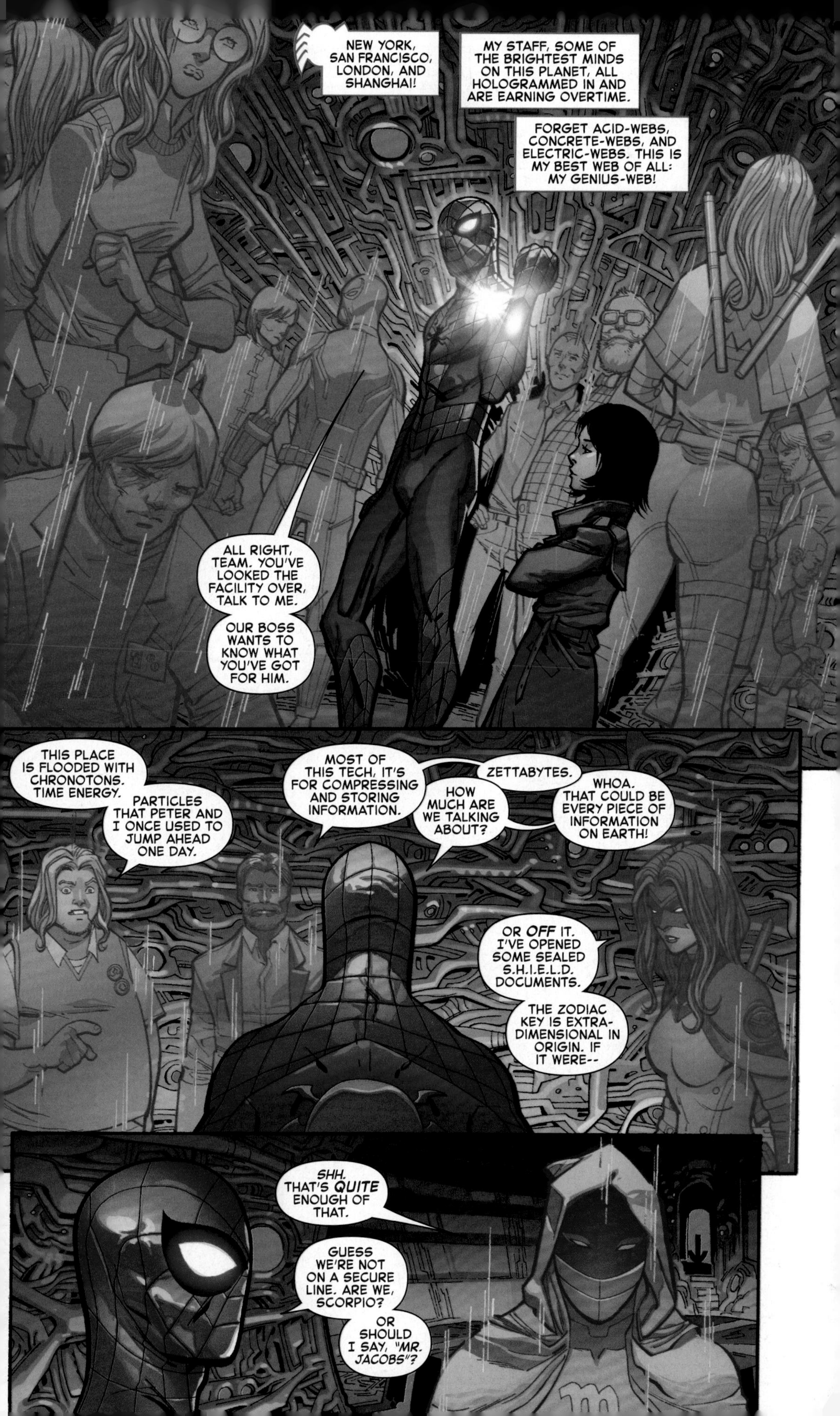

NEW YORK, SAN FRANCISCO, LONDON, AND SHANGHAI!
MY STAFF, SOME OF THE BRIGHTEST MINDS ON THIS PLANET, ALL HOLOGRAMMED IN AND ARE EARNING OVERTIME.
FORGET ACID-WEBS, CONCRETE-WEBS, AND ELECTRIC-WEBS. THIS IS MY BEST WEB OF ALL: MY GENIUS-WEB!
ALL RIGHT, TEAM. YOU'VE LOOKED THE FACILITY OVER, TALK TO ME.
OUR BOSS WANTS TO KNOW WHAT YOU'VE GOT FOR HIM.
THIS PLACE IS FLOODED WITH CHRONOTONS. TIME ENERGY.
PARTICLES THAT PETER AND I ONCE USED TO JUMP AHEAD ONE DAY.
MOST OF THIS TECH, IT'S FOR COMPRESSING AND STORING INFORMATION.
HOW MUCH ARE WE TALKING ABOUT?
ZETTABYTES.
WHOA. THAT COULD BE EVERY PIECE OF INFORMATION ON EARTH!
OR *OFF* IT. I'VE OPENED SOME SEALED S.H.I.E.L.D. DOCUMENTS.
THE ZODIAC KEY IS EXTRA-DIMENSIONAL IN ORIGIN. IF IT WERE--
SHH. THAT'S ***QUITE*** ENOUGH OF THAT.
GUESS WE'RE NOT ON A SECURE LINE. ARE WE, SCORPIO?
OR SHOULD I SAY, "*MR. JACOBS*"?

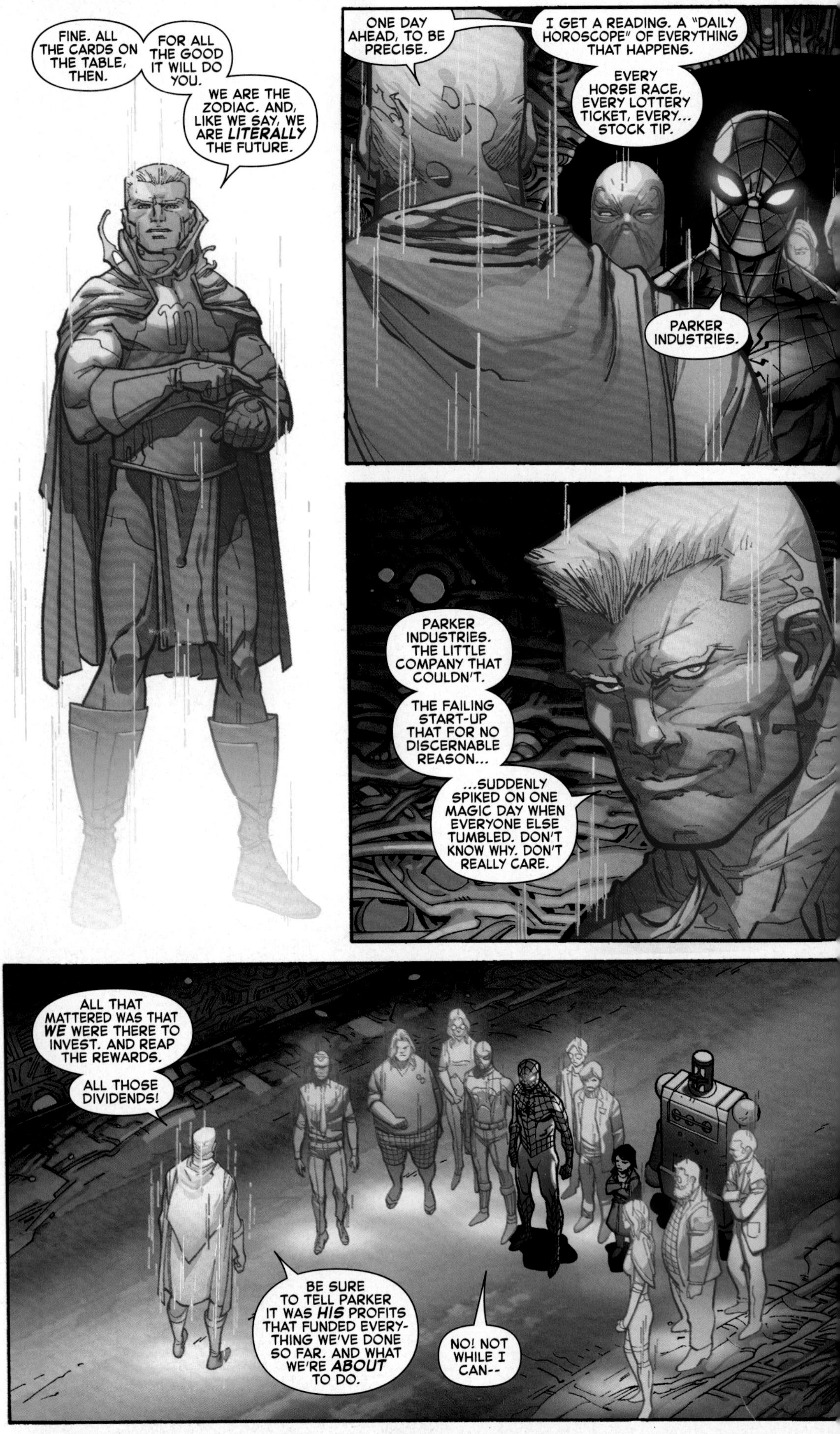
FINE. ALL THE CARDS ON THE TABLE, THEN.
FOR ALL THE GOOD IT WILL DO YOU.
WE ARE THE ZODIAC. AND, LIKE WE SAY, WE ARE *LITERALLY* THE FUTURE.
ONE DAY AHEAD, TO BE PRECISE.
I GET A READING. A "DAILY HOROSCOPE" OF EVERYTHING THAT HAPPENS.
EVERY HORSE RACE, EVERY LOTTERY TICKET, EVERY... STOCK TIP.
PARKER INDUSTRIES.
PARKER INDUSTRIES. THE LITTLE COMPANY THAT COULDN'T.
THE FAILING START-UP THAT FOR NO DISCERNABLE REASON...
...SUDDENLY SPIKED ON ONE MAGIC DAY WHEN EVERYONE ELSE TUMBLED. DON'T KNOW WHY. DON'T REALLY CARE.
ALL THAT MATTERED WAS THAT *WE* WERE THERE TO INVEST. AND REAP THE REWARDS.
ALL THOSE DIVIDENDS!
BE SURE TO TELL PARKER IT WAS *HIS* PROFITS THAT FUNDED EVERY-THING WE'VE DONE SO FAR. AND WHAT WE'RE *ABOUT* TO DO.
NO! NOT WHILE I CAN--

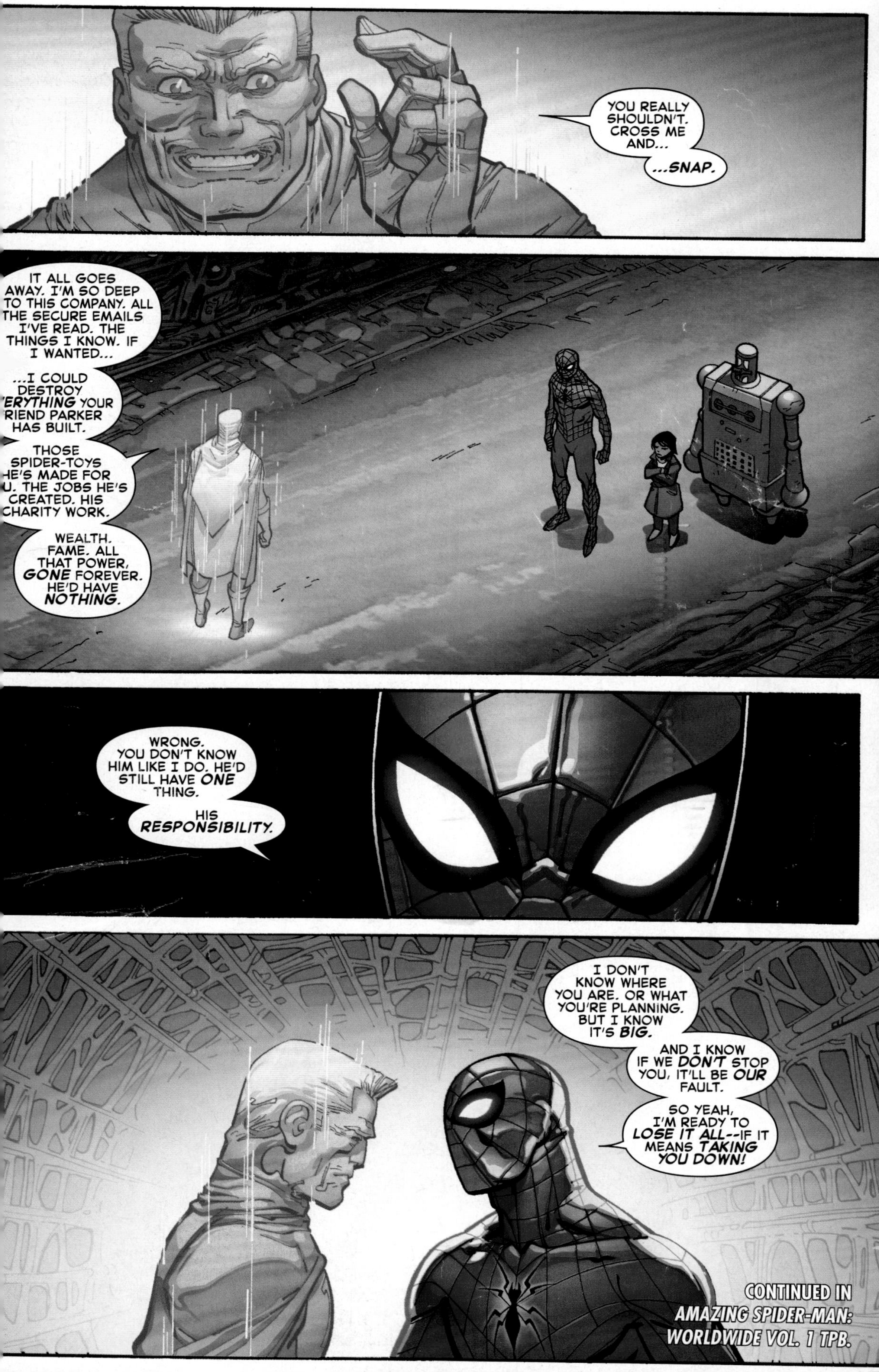

YOU REALLY SHOULDN'T. CROSS ME AND...
...SNAP.
IT ALL GOES AWAY. I'M SO DEEP TO THIS COMPANY. ALL THE SECURE EMAILS I'VE READ. THE THINGS I KNOW. IF I WANTED...
...I COULD DESTROY ERYTHING YOUR RIEND PARKER HAS BUILT.
THOSE SPIDER-TOYS E'S MADE FOR U. THE JOBS HE'S CREATED. HIS CHARITY WORK.
WEALTH. FAME. ALL THAT POWER, GONE FOREVER. HE'D HAVE NOTHING.
WRONG. YOU DON'T KNOW HIM LIKE I DO. HE'D STILL HAVE ONE THING.
HIS RESPONSIBILITY.
I DON'T KNOW WHERE YOU ARE. OR WHAT YOU'RE PLANNING. BUT I KNOW IT'S BIG.
AND I KNOW IF WE DON'T STOP YOU, IT'LL BE OUR FAULT.
SO YEAH, I'M READY TO LOSE IT ALL--IF IT MEANS TAKING YOU DOWN!
CONTINUED IN AMAZING SPIDER-MAN: WORLDWIDE VOL. 1 TPB.

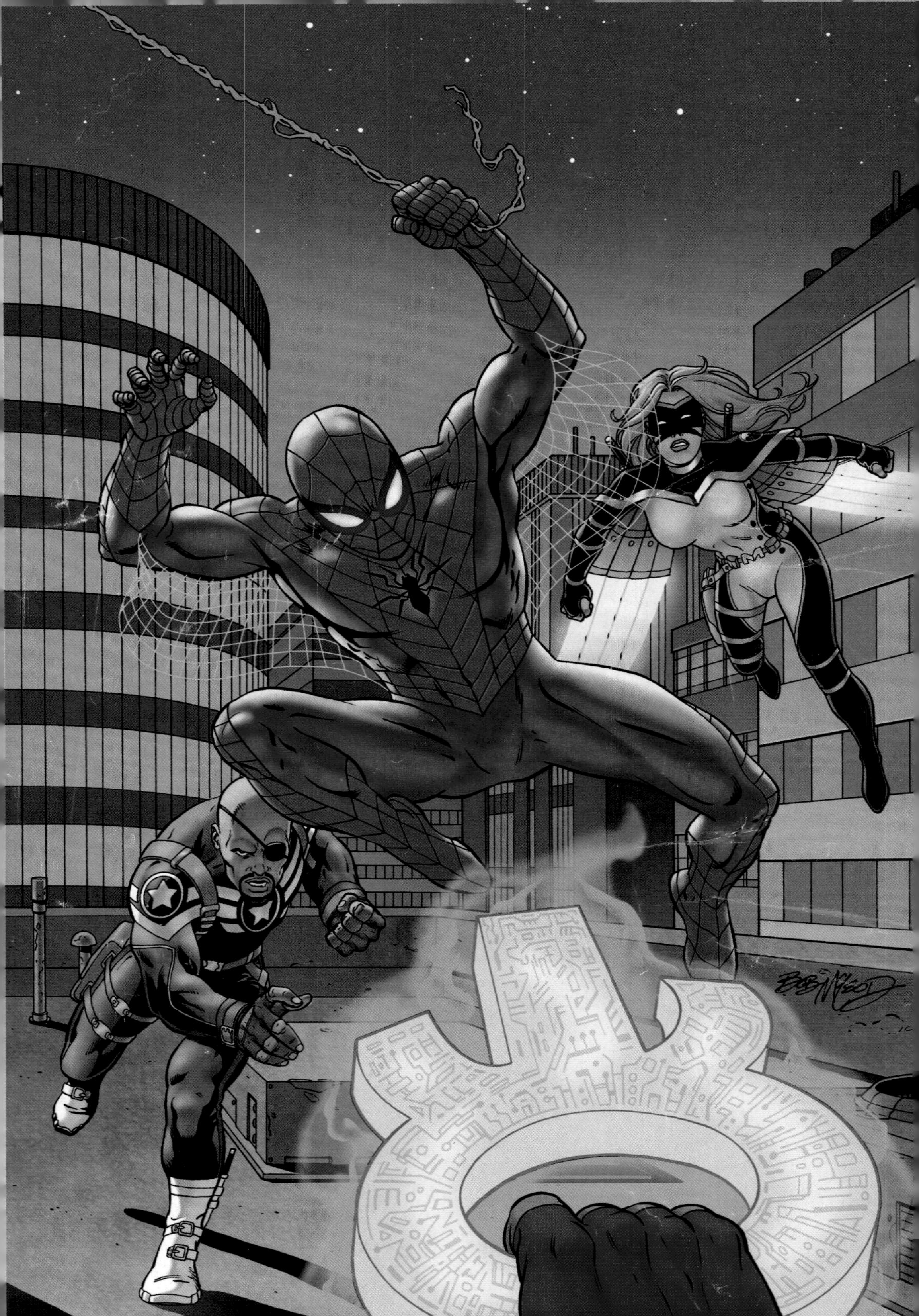